The State, Development and Politics in Ghana

THE STATE, DEVELOPMENT AND POLITICS IN GHANA

Emmanuel Hansen

and

Kwame A. Ninsin (Editors)

CODESRIA BOOK SERIES

The State, Development and Politics in Ghana

First published in 1989 by
CODESRIA BOOK SERIES
1 Ashdon Road, London NW10 4EH

CODESRIA is the Council for the Development of Economic and Social Research in Africa head-quartered in Senegal. It is an independent organisation whose principal objectives are facilitating research, promoting research-based publishing and creating multiple fora geared towards the exchange of views and information among African scholars. Its correspondence address is B.P. 3304, Dakar, Senegal.

ISBN 1 870784 04 9 (Paperback)
1 870784 05 7 (Hardback)

Cover designed by Simon Acquah
Production Consultants Foster & Phillips
Typeset by Emset, 1 Ashdon Road, London NW10 1EH
Printed by RyanPrint, 1 Ashdon Road, London NW10 1EH

DEDICATION

This book is dedicated to the memory of Emmanuel Hansen, Co-Editor, whose sudden and tragic death occurred in Arusha, Tanzania on November 13 1987.

CONTENTS

Abbreviations ix
Notes On Contributors xi
Acknowledgements xiii
Preface xv

Introduction: Thirty Seven Years of Development Experience 1
K.A. Ninsin

SECTION 1: POLITICAL AND ECONOMIC PROCESSES

Chapter 1. State, Capital and Labour Relations, 1961-198 15
K.A. Ninsin
2. From GTP to Assene: Aspects of Industrial Working Class Struggles 1982-1986 43
Yao Graham
3. Women's Political Organisations 1951-1987 .. 73
Edzodzinam Tsikata
4. Changing Relations Between the IMF and the Government of Ghana 1960-1987 94
Kwesi Jonah
5. Financial Intermediation and Economic Development 116
Nii Kwaku Sowa
6. Trends in Foreign Policy After Nkrumah 137
K. Boafo-Arthur

SECTION 2: AGRARIAN AND SOCIAL ISSUES

Chapter 7. The Land Question Since the 1950s 165
K.A. Ninsin

Chapter 8. The State and Food Agriculture 184
Emmanuel Hansen
9. Policies and Politics of Export Agriculture ... 222
E. Gyimah-Boadi
10. Problems of the Health Care
Delivery System 242
Kodjo Senah
Index 269

ABBREVIATIONS

ADB: Agriculture Development Bank
ADCL: Accra District Council of Labour
AFRC: Armed Forces Revolutionary Council
AGI: Association of Ghana Industries
ALU: Associations of Local Unions
ASOFIN: Association of Financial Institutions
AWAG: All Women's Association of Ghana
BHC: Bank for Housing and Construction
CDR: Committees for the Defence of the Revolution
CMB: Cocoa Marketing Board
CPC: Cocoa Purchasing Company
CPD: Cocoa Production Division
CPI: Consumer Price Index
CPP: Convention People's Party
CRP: Cocoa Rehabilitation Project
CSA: Civil Servants Association
DCL: District Council of Labour
DHMT: District Health Management Team
ERP: Economic Recovery Programme
FDC: Food Distribution Corporation
FEGAWO: Federation of Ghanaian Women
GCB: Ghana Commercial Bank
GEA: Ghana Employers' Association
GIHOC: Ghana Industrial Holding Corporation
GNAT: Ghana National Association of Teachers
GTP: Ghana Textile Printing Company Limited
GTP: Ghana Textiles Printing
ICC: Interim Co-ordinating Committee
ICU: Industrial and Commercial Workers Union
IDC: Industrial Development Corporation
IMC: Interim Management Committees
INCC: Interim National Corporation Committee
IRA: Industrial Relations Act
JFM: June Four Movement
KNRG: Kwame Nkrumah Revolutionary Guards

LBA:	Licensed Buying Agency
MDU:	Maritime and Dockworkers Union
MOA:	Ministry of Agriculture
NCGW:	National Council of Ghana Women
NCWD:	National Council on Women and Development
NDC:	National Defence Committee
NDM:	New Democratic Movement
NIB:	National Investment Bank
NLC:	National Liberation Council
NRC:	National Redemption Council
NUHS:	National Union of Ghana Students
OFY:	Operation Feed Yourself
PBA:	Produce Buying Agency
PDC:	People's Defence Committees
PFC:	Pioneer Food Cannary
PHC:	Primary Health Care
PMFJ:	People's Movement for Freedom and Justice
PNDC:	Provisional Defence Council
PNP:	People's National Party
PP:	Progress Party
SADL:	Ghana Association of Democratic Lawyers
SFC:	State Fishing Corporation
SJNC:	Standing Joint Negotiating Committee
SMC:	Supreme Military Council
SSB:	Social Security Bank
SSNIT:	Social Security and National Insurance Trust
TBA:	Traditional Birth Attendants
TUC:	Trade Union Congress
UAC:	United African Company
UGFCC:	United Ghana Farmers' Co-operative Council
URADEP:	Upper Regional Agricultural Development Project
VALCO:	Volta Aluminium Company
WB:	Workers' Brigade
WDC:	Workers Defence Committees

NOTES ON CONTRIBUTORS

Kwame Boafo-Arthur: Lecturer in International Politics at the Department of Politicial Science, University of Ghana, Legon. His research interest lies in foreign aid and development and international economic relations.

Yao Graham: Private legal practitioner. His research and publications deal with labour in Ghanaian politics and with foreign investment in Ghana's agricultural sector.

E. Gyimah-Boadi: Lecturer at the Department of Political Science, University of Ghana. He has published work on Ghanaian politics, public administration and rural development.

Emmanuel Hansen: He was Senior Lecturer at the Department of Political Science, University of Ghana until 1979 and later Fellow at the Institute of Commonwealth Studies, University of London until his untimely death.

Kwesi Jonah: Has published widely on political theory, the problems of food and military intervention in African politics, and on the problem of peace on the continent. Is a Lecturer at the Department of Political Science, University of Ghana. His research and publications have dealt with aspects of Ghanaian politics and development.

Kwame A. Ninsin: Senior Lecturer in African Politics and Comparative Politics at the Department of Political Science, University of Ghana, Legon. He has researched and published on various aspects of Ghanaian politics and development issues.

Kodjo A. Senah: Lecturer at the Department of Sociology, University of Ghana. His research and publications deal mainly with medical sociology. His current interest is in pharmaceutical anthropology.

Nii Kwaku Sowa: Acting Head, Department of Economics, University of Ghana. His research and publications are centred on monetary and financial policy in Ghana.

Edzodzinam Tsikata: Private legal practitioner, Accra. Her research has centred on women and development, and women in Ghanaian politics.

ACKNOWLEDGEMENTS

We wish to record our deepest appreciation to CODESRIA for their intellectual, moral, and financial support. But for them this collection would be unthinkable. We also thank Mrs. Esi Mensah of the Department of Economics at Legon for the tremendous labour she put into typing the papers in their various stages of revision. Without her enormous patience and diligence we could not have made the final deadline. Nonetheless, the contributors are individually responsible for the views expressed in their respective papers.

The Editors

This book is the outcome of CODESRIA's project on National Working Groups. CODESRIA would like to express its gratitude to the Swedish Agency for Research Co-operation (SAREC), the Danish Agency for International Development (DANIDA) and the International Development Research Centre (IDRC) for support of research activities and publication on the research results.

PREFACE

The current crisis has forced every one to re-examine the development experience of Africa to find out 'what exactly went wrong'. In this re-examination, Ghana has attracted a lot of attention. This is not surprising. Ghana occupies a privileged position in both the historical and political consciousness of Africa. Its political and economic vicissitudes, since its path-breaking attainment of national sovereignty in 1957, encapsulate in a highly condensed form the wide range of African experiences.

Its political rule has encompassed virtually the whole gamut of African political rule — highly personalized political rule, populism, parliamentary democracy, military dictatorships, kleptocratic militiary rule etc. Its foreign policy postures have ranged from exemplary anti-imperialist pan-Africanism to a neocolonial subservience. At times, the most indefatigable champion of the liberation movement, the same Ghana has appeared at least on one occasion as a bane to the liberation movements which were most humiliatingly forced to close their bases after the fall of the illustrious Nkrumah. Its experience in economic policy making has ranged from statist-nationalist policies, to classical neocolonial policies — from more or less serious 'planning' to laissez-faire-ism. Once the *bête noire* of foreign financial institutions, Ghana is now paraded as the exemplary pupil of economic management under structural adjustment programme. Over the years, the leadership has been most articulate in explaining its rather dramatic change of course in economic management and policy thrusts.

It is this wide ranging experience and the country's privileged position in Africa's political history that has made Ghana singularly fascinating among Africans and non-Africans. There are times when one has the unsettling feeling that Ghana still occupies a leading role in Africa and that it is a 'pioneer' of not only independence but a number of unsavoury experiences of the continent. This prospect makes Ghana such an important concern for those interested in the future of the continent. Its lessons need to be widely shared in the continent.

Although many observers have analysed the complex and fascinating case of Ghana, the analysis has tended to be dispersed, and unfocussed. The baffling range of Ghana's economic, political and diplomatic experiences has been used in some circles to abandon serious analyses of its experience and to resort to anecdotal and piquantly garnered accounts of its debacle. Fascinated by the resilience of its people and their ingenious 'survival strategies' under severe economic dislocation, these studies have tended to treat the state as an essentially irrelevant incumberance on Ghanaian civil society. The people's strategies of survival have been portrayed in idyllic terms that downplay the social struggles that are taking place outside the domicile within which the 'survival strategies' are played out. While these studies make fascinating reading, especially for the non-African reader, they have merely added to the obfuscation of the Ghanaian reality, concentrating as they do on the exotic and ephemeral, the domiciliary in isolation from the social.

The collection of essays in this volume brings together a number of Ghanaian scholars to reflect on their country's experience from different perspectives. Whatever one says about these essays, they are a serious attempt by Ghanaian scholars to come to grips with the reality of their society. The studies clearly point out that as long as social struggles are a main feature of society, the question of the state will remain central, no matter how distant the state might seem in the day to day lives of people. Our hope is that it will not merely add a Ghanaian voice to the many analyses of Ghana, enrich the debates in Ghana and contribute to the search for viable paths of development. We also hope that it will contribute to our understanding of the 'Black Star' of Africa.

The working group chose to dedicate the collection to the late Emmanual Hansen, one of the co-editors. I would like to end this preface by joining the Ghanaian colleagues in paying tribute to him for his many activities in the promotion of social sciences in Africa. Emmanual Hansen was deeply involved in this project and his infectious enthusiasm played no insignificant role in getting the group together. Hansen was very much occupied with the many constraints on distribution of books in Africa — especially the foreign exchange constraint to book imports and the ubiquitous censorship. It was his deep wish that this book would be readily available, if not in all African countries, at least in Ghana. CODESRIA will do everything to make his wish come true.

Thandika Mkandawire
Executive Secretary
Dakar, June, 1989

INTRODUCTION: THIRTY-SEVEN YEARS OF DEVELOPMENT EXPERIENCE

Kwame A. Ninsin

THE BETRAYAL

Shortly after independence, Kwame Nkrumah, who was then Prime Minister, challenged the National Assembly in these words: 'The welfare of our people is our chief pride and it is by this that my Government will ask to be judged'. By the time the Nkrumah government was overthrown in 1966, much improvement in the living conditions of the people had been realised, especially through the expansion of, and improved access to education, water supply, employment and health services. And yet a lot more remained to be done.

Twenty three years later, it is becoming increasingly evident that we may have to start afresh to create the social conditions necessary for improving our welfare. On the one hand, it would appear that the country's successive political leaders have not heeded the supreme aspirations of the people as they joined forces with them in the struggle for independence: namely, 'to win material benefits, to live better and in peace, to see their lives go forward, (and) to guarantee the future of their children' (Amilcar Cabral).

On the other hand, these tragic results of our nationhood would seem to be a vindication of Franz Fanon's lamentation that our country had won a mere flag independence which left the colonial political, economic and social structures and processes intact. But, in fact, the explanation for our dismal performance lies in both; for if our independence had transcended flag independence to transform the prevailing economic, political and social structures, the material and spiritual advancement of the people would not have been so remorselessly compromised, and then betrayed.

The roots of this betrayal lie in the character of the social forces that dominated the nationalist movement and successive governing coalitions. The petty bourgeoisie that led the independence struggle into victory did not have the necessary economic base to ensure their own political autonomy as a class as well as the autonomy of the state from external political and economic forces.

As a result of this weakness the petty-bourgeoisie manifested two tendencies: (a) it depended heavily on external economic interests which implied a *de facto* sharing of political power with such interests; and (b) it indulged itself freely and remorselessly in amassing wealth at the expense of the masses of the people whose sacrifices assured the success of the independence struggle and who have continued to labour relentlessly to produce the nation's wealth.

They were determined to become bourgeois. They have achieved considerable success in this class project with the active connivance of external economic and political interests, the bureaucrats in the leading institutions of state, and their counterparts in commerce. This tendency was perceived by Cabral. Hence he had forewarned that the petty-bourgeoisie would not 'strengthen its revolutionary consciousness, (it would not)... repudiate the temptation to become 'bourgeois', and the natural pretentions of its class mentality; (it would not)... identify with the class of workers, not to oppose the normal development of the revolution'. It would not commit 'suicide as a class'. In pursuit of their class objectives this class systematically fashioned state policy in a manner that would uphold and enhance their interests. The interest of the underclass was subordinated to theirs. Hence, the material conditions of the masses of the people have not improved significantly since the 1950s; and especially during the last decade the mood of the country has been dominated by anguish and dismay.

It is because of this failure that the people have developed neither a strong sense of legitimacy for the state nor faith in the capacity of successive governments to change their appalling living conditions and the tragic sense of social insecurity which now seems to pervade the entire society.

DEVELOPMENT PROBLEMS

What then have been the problems confronting our country since we embarked on the road to independent nationhood and how have they been tackled? We shall discuss first the development problems and then the strategies that have been employed to deal with these problems.

At independence, the country was, to all intents and purposes backward politically, economically and socially. Politically, only the repressive institutions of state had been reasonably well developed for the obvious goal of ensuring the realisation of the colonial purposes of domination and exploitation. The more fundamental organs necessary for institutionalising a democratic life had not been allowed to grow until the mass political agitations of the 1948-51 period. After these events fragments of democratic institutions and practices were hurriedly pieced together. The economy had been nurtured as a monocrop trading system: it became alive only with growth in the cocoa industry and sank into stagnation when this industry went into a slumber.

The development of industry had been totally neglected. As such the country depended heavily on imports for the basic needs of the people — including food, and also for the most trivial industrial goods. By 1950 the economy still lacked even the slightest technical capacity to generate employment, new consumer products and additional income. In the social sector, the educational, health, water and transport services were at a very backward stage of development — in spite of the glamorous 'revolution' initiated by Guggisberg in these areas. Furthermore, there had been a deliberate policy of sustaining not just the communal basis of government but also the primordial basis of social solidarity and territorial organisation. Lugard's carefully-forged system of indirect rule was aimed at achieving these goals. The level of national and territorial integration was therefore extremely low.

As a result of these grave lapses in colonial development policy the government of the newly independent country was not only confronted with the ugly problems of widespread poverty, ignorance, disease, squalor and mounting unemployment; but also a superficial sense of territorial and national community; and a precarious basis of legitimacy for state institutions. All of these added up to a colossal monument of social backwardness erected by colonialism to its own glory. This was the heritage of Ghana-the model colony, that attained independence on March 6 1957.

THE SOLUTIONS

The solutions to this mosaic of development problems have been embodied in the various development strategies that have been formulated and implemented by successive regimes. The development strategies may be distinguished as follows:

(a) industrialisation-by-invitation (1952-59);

(b) the statist (1960-65);
(c) the liberal (1966-71);
(d) the indigenisation (1972-79) and
(e) the ultra-liberal (since 1982) development strategies.

These various development strategies do reflect the way in which the faction of the political class that assumed power at any particular time has understood the development problems confronting the country.

The government of the Convention People's Party (CPP) which assumed power in the internal self-government arrangement of 1951 was led by the lower stratum of the petty-bourgeoisie. They represented people of small property — and who engaged mainly in commerce, agriculture and the professions. They were the ones who had been in revolt against chiefs, the older generation of the intelligentsia, and merchants and who eventually placed themselves at the helm of the independence struggle as it entered its final phase.

As the political events of the 1951-57 period showed, their claim to exercise state power was challenged not only by the powerful chiefs and wealthy cocoa farmers acting in alliance with the established men of commerce and the professions. Even the colonial administration had to be compelled by the logic of the party's electoral support to concede, rather reluctantly, that the CPP was the true expression of the legitimate aspirations of the Ghanaian people in their struggle for independence. The regionalisation of power and other entrenched clauses of the Independence Constitution were therefore not an accidental compromise.

The purpose of those arrangements was not simply to limit the so-called creeping dictatorship of the CPP leadership. There was the more important objective of constraining the political power of the 'Varandah Boys' against the quasi-feudal and bourgeois interests of chiefs and their allies in commerce and the professions.

The response of the CPP leadership to this threat was to appease the colonialists by deradicalising the nationalist movement and resorting to closer collaboration with them. Of course, that betrayal of the movement was also dictated in part by the dominant petty bourgeois character of the CPP leadership. This group was keen on using state power to overcome its own economic weakness. The Party's acceptance of the Arthur-Lewis model of industrialisation-by-invitation, despite the fact that on the eve of independence the country had the necessary capital for initiating modest industrialisation on its own, was the result of these compromises.

The moment of truth dawned when the inherently fragile and unstable character of the mono-crop trading economy increasingly manifested itself in the decline of export earnings as the world price of cocoa fell vis-a-vis the rising levels of imports to meet expanding private and public consumption.

To compound the regime's problems the expected volume of investments did not materialise. The government was therefore confronted with the only option of having to rely heavily on the country's depleted external reserves to finance both imports and development programmes.

Furthermore, an old problem of the colonial economy was beginning to engage the government's attention; namely, foreign domination. Foreign economic interests had been in total control of industries such as commerce, mining, timber, shipping and banking. In fact, they had once monopolised even the internal marketing of cocoa. What this meant during the 1950s is that they compounded the government's creeping problem of shortage of capital for internal development by externalising a substantial proportion of the nation's wealth in the form of profits, dividends and so on.

The cumulative effect was the growing realisation that the colonial economy the government had inherited was more than an open economy. It was above all a perforated economy through which the country lost enormous capital to a wide range of foreign economic interests. In those conditions, the crisis of accumulation overshadowed the political and social crises. In particular the question of democracy was relegated to the periphery of official concerns.

It was to overcome this crisis of accumulation, or at least contain it, that the CPP government abandoned the Lewis model of development and opted for an interventionist policy during the 1960-65 period. In doing so, the CPP did not attempt to build socialism as is generally assumed. It used the power of the state to compete with foreign economic interests operating in various sectors of the economy for hegemony. In other words, it sought to build state capitalism which it regarded as a necessary preparation towards socialism. And to this end, it sought to control the economy both at the level of production and distribution through the mechanism of the state enterprise which was effectively employed to penetrate various sectors of the economy except the cocoa industry.

The reason for this exception is that cocoa, the main stay of the economy, is controlled by the peasantry. However, intervention at the level of production was substituted with intervention and control at the marketing level to ensure the appropriation of surplus cocoa income from the industry. The purpose of that appropriation was to generate the necessary revenue to finance the industrialisation and social investment programmes of the Party. The Cocoa Marketing Board was the instrument of appropriation.

Similar interventions were made in the financial and banking sectors. As with the other state and parastatal institutions which were created by the CPP government, the goal in the latter instance was not simply to break the foreign control of the economy but also to create instruments of capital mobilisation and accumulation for internal development.

By the beginning of this second phase the political opposition had intensified the use of extra-constitutional methods. The threat of disorder became increasingly evident. The government's resort to state capitalism was therefore as much an economic strategy as a political one. As the Seven Year Development Plan and the Party's Programme for Work and Happiness aptly summarised, the birth of an independent Ghanaian private capitalist class was for the government a wishful proposition; for it would negate its egalitarian objectives. Eventually therefore, state control of the economy was translated into collectivism in the political sphere. The single party — the CPP, became the organisational weapon by which the militant fraction of the petty-bourgeoisie sought to dominate the politics and eventually the economy of the country.

In spite of these gallant efforts the economy could not be liberated from its inherent tendency towards crisis. By 1965 the economic crisis was becoming severe; and the material conditions of the majority of Ghanaians were showing serious signs of deterioration once more. Economic and social decline was paralleled by political decline as the CPP degenerated into a den for opportunists and petty political tyrants, and the national leadership inclined more toward authoritarianism than democracy. The disenchantement that followed nurtured the political conditions that facilitated the coup d'etat of February 28 1966.

The overthrow of the CPP government ushered into power the moderate wing of the petty-bourgeoisie. This fraction comprised chiefs, wealthy cocoa farmers, merchants, professionals and their counterparts in the armed and police forces. The political orientation of this group differed from that of the militant fraction which dominated the CPP. Their perception of the development problems of the country was therefore also different.

For them the problem of the Ghanaian economy stemmed from the excessive involvement of the state in its operations; the attempt to restrain the further growth of foreign domination of the economy; and the constraints imposed on the growth of Ghanaian private enterprise. They professed unqualified faith in the prevailing international economic order and wanted the country to re-establish its credibility as a diligent participant; because the country could not develop without the active patronage of foreign capital from the Western countries.

Between 1966 and 1971 the package of economic policies that was pursued summed up this new perspective on development. The National Liberation Council (1966-1969) and the Progress Party (1969-1971) governments sought actively to win the confidence of foreign investors. They did so by trying to contain the inflationary pressures and realigning internal prices to those prevailing in the world economy — through devaluation of the currency, deregulation of prices, liberalization of external trade, and other monetary measures. The drive to restore the primacy of private enterprise as the engine of development proceeded hand in hand with a systematic assault on public sector enterprise and employment; on wages and salaries; and on state subsidies for a number of consumer goods and social services.

On the whole the standard of living of Ghanaians deteriorated further as a result of these measures. These negative social effects provoked some of the fiercest battles the state has had to fight with workers. By 1970 workers had been joined by the country's university students and sections of the petty-bourgeoisie who also could not cope with the impact of the monetary policies. Meanwhile, the incipient capitalist class was actively taking advantage of the situation to secure for themselves little empires in commerce and manufacturing.

Because of the low level of political organization and consciousness among the general population, the expression of political and economic discontent has usually become the moral responsibility of the petty-bourgeoisie, workers and students. These groups have the unique advantage of being simultaneously close to the top and the bottom of the social structure in terms of economic as well as political benefits, aspirations and frustrations. Accordingly their political agitations tend to express the level of discontent of the majority of Ghanaians.

However, it was not until the PP government directly attacked the privileges of the country's strategically placed middle class groups who were based in industry, the army and the state bureaucracy that the military leadership found it opportune to break another political-economic myth. On February 28, 1966 it was the myth of statism as advocated by the CPP government that was broken, but on January 21, 1972 it was the myth of liberalism that was smashed. Both of them had proved economically inefficacious and politically repressive.

The dilemma that confronted the National Redemption Council (NRC) — which later renamed itself as the Supreme Military Council (SMC), when it assumed power on January 21, 1972 is that both the statist and liberal options seemed foreclosed. But the dilemma was not just an economic one. It was, above all, political. Whereas the limitations of the statist strategy had provoked the utmost fury and hostility of the political right and capitalist interests, the effect of the liberal development strategy was the alienation of both capitalists and workers without making them either allies or sworn enemies of the state. These two major social classes as well as the intermediary social classes appeared just in need of relief from the effects of the economic crisis and political repression. The currency devaluation of December 1971, against the background of soaring debt and deteriorating terms of external trade, provided a convenient external enemy — foreign donors and trading partners.

The prevailing political situation therefore recommended appropriate solutions to the dilemma which confronted the new regime. The first solution took the form of mobilising all the key social forces for implementing a programme of economic nationalism. The second sought to exploit the surging economic nationalism for development purposes. 'Repudiate Bad debt!' 'Unilaterally Reschedule Good Debt!' 'Operation Feed Yourself!' And 'Let Us Capture the Commanding Heights of the Economy for Ghanaians!' These became emotive slogans by which the nation was rallied behind the new government in its crusade to 'Redeem' the country's economy from foreign control and manipulation.

Within two years both the regime and the entire nation had reason to celebrate the 'Festival of Food Self-sufficiency'. There was also considerable relief from the crushing and humiliating weight of foreign debt as donor governments and agencies accomodated the resurgent economic nationalism of the country and rescheduled the repayment of the external debt on very liberal terms. Then followed the indigenisation measures which were pursued through either exclusive state participation in key foreign-owned enterprises; participation by both state and private Ghanaian capital in another group of foreign enterprises; and the outright take-over of a third group of foreign-owned enterprises by Ghanaian capital.

Even workers in certain foreign owned enterprises were encouraged to purchase shares in such enterprises so that they could also become small capitalists. For both the Ghanaian capitalist class and workers therefore, these measures must have brought a feeling that the promised economic kingdom had at last dawned. This was the illusion of the 1975-77 period.

In a fundamental way the miracle of the indigenisation strategy was bound to prove illusory because it was a poor attempt at tinkering with the iron shell of the neo-colonial economy. It merely gave the nascent capitalist class a greater stake than before, in the neo-colonial economy: it did not, and could not, change it. In a less fundamental, but politically significant way, indigenisation succeeded more than its liberal counterpart to advance the growth of the Ghanaian 'capitalist class'. But even before the set of indigenisation policies could be fully implemented both the capitalist class and workers had returned to the political arena to fight against the regime for mismanaging the economy. Thus, by 1978 the regime, that had once symbolised the unity of the nation's contending classes, was under siege from the most important social groups.

In a way, one could argue that indigenisation had exposed the grave inequalities inherent in the neo-colonial economy and driven a firm wedge between capitalists and the state, on the one hand and the rest of society, on the other. The reason is that indigenisation as a strategy of development simply bolstered the political and economic position of the capitalist class — big, medium and small. In the process it left the economy in shambles with devastating consequences for the living conditions of workers and other members of the lower classes.

The political representatives of both the lower classes and capitalist class revolted against the SMC government because it had not only destroyed the economy but it had also created a social crisis of considerable magnitude. For instance, during this period the level of prostitution, divorce, juvenile diliquency and unemployment increased sharply; and so did the lust for wealth through the most unfair and corrupt means reach epidemic proportions. It is this highly decadent economic and social situation that produced the military uprising of June 4, 1979 and gave birth to the Armed Forces Revolutionary Council (AFRC).

Between September 1979, when the AFRC abdicated political power, and December 1981, the constitutionally elected government of the People's National Party (PNP) tried in vain to grapple with these multiple crises. Meanwhile there had been a resurgence of the demands that had been pressed especially during the last decade; namely, the demand for a living wage, for employment, housing, education, health services — in general, for improvements in the living conditions of the broad sections of the people. These deepened the political crisis and compounded the economic and social crises.

What did these developments mean? They meant that a crisis of confidence had finally burst into the open: the broad sections of the people had lost confidence in the capacity of the 'political class' to take measures to protect and advance their democratic rights. It should be recalled that during the 1970s the organised and articulate sections of the under-class persistently demanded that these rights be placed on the political agenda of the ruling classes. They regarded these as fundamental rights which should therefore be cherished and safeguarded. But up to the time of its overthrow by the PNDC in 1981, the PNP government was still gropping about for appropriate solutions to these multiple crises.

From its inception on December 31 1981 to the latter part of 1984, the political representatives of the under-class were convinced that the PNDC embodied a popular response to these crises, and would eventually pave the way for their resolution in a democratic way. This conviction was at least strengthened by the fact that the new government had created new political institutions which, it was envisaged, would be instruments for intervening in the existing state institutions and thereby create a democratic opening whereby the broad masses of the people could assert their collective power and initiative in the development of the country.

By the close of 1984 however, these convictions had been confounded. The main preoccupations of the new regime had shifted to finding solutions to the fiscal and accumulation crises of the state and bourgeoisie, respectively. Thus once again what we have generally referred to as the accumulation crisis of the state had preempted the popular drive for democracy.

The abandonment of this democratic agenda bears the seeds of authoritarianism. Especially, for the broad masses of the people, its implications are bound to be most deleterious. It means that they will have to bear many more years of deprivation to ensure that the ruling class have achieved a certain minimum level of accumulation; that they have at least contained the recurring fiscal crisis of the state; that they have secured to some extent the creditworthiness of the state on the international capital market — all this and many more, before their democratic rights would be addressed. This is the fatal catch: to get the masses of the people to succumb to such an indefinite period of deprivation would require considerable amount of state repression.

In a nutshell, this chequered history raises the question: Development for whom? The collection of papers in this volume deal with various aspects of this very pertinent question. Some deal with it directly; and others indirectly. This is due to the fact that the problematic of the state and development in our country since independence was not formally articulated either before the contributors prepared their manuscripts, or during the seminar that was called to discuss the various papers. This was a deliberate omission, which was meant to give the contributors the freedom to address the issues as they understood them as Ghanaians.

Despite this latitude, it will be noted that, without exception, all the papers deal with some aspects of the problem of development; the struggle of various social groups in relation to the issues raised by the development policies of regimes; the extent to which state power has been employed by various governments to settle such struggles; and the results of such endeavours.

Furthermore, one can extrapolate a meaning of development that underpins the contributions; namely, that development implies equity in the sharing of the resources for achieving improvements in ones life situation as well as equity in distributing the aggregate national output. This is what binds the collection into a formidable entity: for this is what development of any human society is about.

The papers are presented in two sections. Section 1 deals with political and economic structures, issues and practices. The contributions by Ninsin and Graham should be read together. They deal with the changing relations of the state with key social groups like the bourgeoisie and labour, as well as the role of foreign and domestic capitals in the whole drama of development since the 1960s. While Ninsin's paper addresses these problems at a macro-level, Graham's provides a micro-study of two recent instances to complete the picture. Tsikata, on the other hand, addresses the problems associated with women and their attempts to construct political organisations to deal with their existential problems. She shows how the ruling class has appropriated and distorted the urgent problems facing women simply to serve their own class objectives; and also how successive regimes, acting in response to the same class impulse, have co-opted such women's organisations to serve the task of consolidating their rule and the hegemony of the ruling class. The subject of intervention in the Ghanaian economy by foreign capital is taken up again in Jonah's paper.

Again, in contrast with the general treatment of the subject in Ninsin's paper, Jonah's paper poignantly illustrates the point using the recurring intervention of the World Bank and International Monetary Fund since the 1960s as a specific case. This paper draws attention to the consequences of such interventions for the conduct of successive governments during the period under consideration.

In the paper by Sowah, it is argued that the financial institutions which are expected to offer leadership in the mobilization of capital and its investment in the most productive sectors of the economy have behaved exactly like their colonial predecessors. They have been almost passive regarding capital mobilization, and have invested where it is safest — that is, in commerce. Of course commerce has been the traditional grazing ground of the ruling classes. The banks must therefore be seen as responding to specific investment priorities of the ruling classes.

The results of skewed investment practices and other policies are now evident for everybody to see — whether it is the result of poor intermediation by the financial institutions, the misapplication of national resources by successive regimes or the bankruptcy of class policies. Over the past 20 years Ghana's prestige, honour and independence among the community of sovereign nations have diminished; and Ghanaians have had to bear the cross of this national failure around the world. Furthermore, the development crisis has compromised the sovereignty and independence of successive regimes in global politics. Indeed it has enfeebled them, made them vacillate and often submit to external dictation. This is the message of Boafo-Arthur's paper.

In Section II, Hansen and Gyimah-Boadi's papers deal with agricultural policy. Both contributions agree that public policy in this sector has failed to transform agricultural practices and thereby raise productivity. Hansen's paper, which is on food agriculture, blames the failure on the subordination of the interest of the peasantry — the producers of the bulk of the country's food needs — to that of the ruling classes despite the incontrovertible evidence that the ruling classes are not making the expected impact on food production in the country. On the other hand, the Gyimah-Boadi paper argues that the appropriation of the agricultural surplus to promote the political interest of the ruling class accounts for the failure of public policy in this sector. This is another way of saying that the pursuit of ruling class interest in agriculture has undermined growth.

The Ninsin paper on the land question provides a broader context for examining the problem of agriculture in the country. It argues that the determination and resolution of the land question have, over the years, favoured the ruling class. Hence the rush to invest in food and cash crop production during the last decade. This explanation must be regarded as a useful backdrop to the analysis and conclusions of the two papers by Hansen and Gyimah-Boadi.

Finally, Senah's paper deals with the health question. He shows how the right of the broad sections of the population to quality and inexpensive medical care is being gradually circumscribed in the name of free enterprise as the ruling class struggles to solve its accumulation crisis.

The conclusions of these collections should give us hard food for deep thought. The ever widening circle of poverty and destitution; the declining international image of our country and peoples; the institutionalisation of economic crisis which has resulted in a unique Ghanaian diaspora with all its fatalities; political and social divisions which seem to be breeding endemic political instability — these unfathomable and sombre depths of economic, social and political crises seem to be the only visible heritagle of thirty-seven years of self-government. They offer us nothing for celebration as an independent nation. Rather they suggest the urgent need for a radical reappraisal of our national goals, and how to attain them.

SECTION 1

POLITICAL AND ECONOMIC PROCESSES

1. STATE, CAPITAL AND LABOUR RELATIONS, 1961-1987

Kwame A. Ninsin

INTRODUCTION

In this chapter we examine capital-labour relations since 1961. Our starting point is 1961 because Ghana had not only become a republic a year earlier, and a *defacto* one-party state with the CPP as the sole political party; but more especially, the mechanisms for a centralized control over society, economy and politics were put in place from this date. These, we believe, should make the subject of this chapter quite revealing.

The analysis shows how the state has responded to, and resolved, the contradictions between these two social forces of production, viz, capital and labour. It is argued that in a dependent capitalist economy such as Ghana's the national bourgeoisie is unable to lay the basis for a self-sustaining capitalist development because of the scarcity of capital. State power has therefore to be employed more agressively and repeatedly in the economy and society to promote capital accumulation and also create the social conditions necessary for this accumulation to take place. In the process, the state tends to act more visibly on the side of capital, in both the economy and politics, and against labour as well as other non-capitalist elements in society.

In effect, the changing character of capital-labour relations can be understood in the context of the accumulation crisis and the imperative to transcend it. Also capital-labour relations tend to be expressed more in the form of direct confrontations between the state and labour because of the capitalist character of the latter.

There are two principal parts to this chapter followed by a concluding section. The first part, which has four main components, examines the structural basis of the ruling and working classes as well as those changes since 1961 which have determined the relative strength of these classes. In particular, attention is drawn to the persistence of foreign domination of the economy despite the growth of state and private Ghanaian capitalism during the period under consideration. The implications of these developments are discussed.

The second part has three components and analyses the growing contradictions between capital and labour. It relates the intensity of these contradictions to the escalating crisis of the economy as well as the changes in state power as determined by the intensity of the economic crisis. The period 1982-1987 is considered as a critical period in state-capital-labour relations, next only to the 1966-71 period. It is marked by the rise of the populist authoritarian state.

THE WEAK RULING CLASSES

The Ghanaian ruling classes have not emerged on the strength of their own industry and creativity in the economic and political sectors of society. They are the product of British merchant capital[1]. It is noteworthy also that British imperial domination of Ghanaian society involved the export to the colony not just of British capital but also of the dominant social values, ideas and institutions of English society, including political and legal ones[2].

Since independence, the leading political institutions inherited from British colonial rule have been maintained. As the report of the 1968 Constitutional Commission[3] shows, the corresponding norms and ideas have been affirmed; and they are still cherished.

The implications of colonial domination for the Ghanaian ruling classes is that they were unable to assert themselves to a position of effective political and economic dominance. The representatives of British capitalist interests occupied this role until independence. The outcome of that process was a structurally disequilibrated economy which favoured accumulation in the agrarian sector[4] and undermined indigenous industrialization[5].

As such the Ghanaian bourgeois class, although it has been growing since independence, lacks adequate capital for initiating an independent process of social transformation. It is this same limitation that has affected its ability to evolve independently appropriate political and ideological infrastructure to support its own rule.

FOREIGN ECONOMIC DOMINATION AND ITS IMPLICATIONS

By independence in 1957, the economy was entirely in the hands of foreign investors. The mining sector was wholly owned and managed by British investors; and 50% of wholesale and retail trading was controlled by foreign monopolies. The same foreign monopolies controlled almost the whole of the other sectors as well; namely 74.4% of import trade, 77.0% of timber and saw-milling and 90.0% of manufacturing. They enjoyed an additional monopoly in the banking, insurance and shipping industries[6].

Between 1960 and 1965, the CPP government pursued a vigorous statist economic development programme. But even that could not break the monopoly being exercised over the economy by international capital. It merely reduced it. By 1970, the free enterprise economic policies of the National Liberation Council (NLC) and Progress Party (PP) governments had helped immensely to restore the grounds that international capital had lost under the CPP regime[7]. What was essentially a pro-imperialist policy thrust was accelerated through the indigenisation policies of the National Redemption Council (NRC) — Supreme Military Council (SMC) government of I.K. Acheampong[8].

The cumulative effect of the policies of the post 1966 regimes was the effective denationalization of national capital. The economic and social policies of the PNDC which have been summed up in the various policy packages under the Economic Recovery Programme (ERP) has the tendency to strengthen this process of externalizing national capital and thereby intensifying the imperialist domination of our country. The growing national debt and, consequently, the high debt-service ratio are unimpeachable evidence of this.

The persistence of foreign economic domination has serious implications for the ruling classes, and also for the economy. It not only means the loss of capital to the advanced capitalist countries. but that the national bourgeoisie will continue to lack the means for exercising the leading role expected of them in the economic and political life of the country. It is these two factors which underpin the constant intervention of the state (i) in the accumulation process; (ii) to create and recreate the social and political conditions necessary for capitalist accumulation; and (iii) to contain all forms of attack on capital, or acts which may endanger the freedom of the market.

Hence the authoritarian tendencies within the state which is manifested in constant violations of the basic democratic rights of the masses of the people, and also in the inclination to rely on the use of what Gramsci[9] calls the political means to ensure obedience. The direct use of the military to intervene in politics is only the extreme form of this tendency of the ruling classes to resort to authoritarian measures, to maintain their rule.

CHARACTER OF THE LABOUR FORCE

By the time the country became independent the labour force was extremely amorphous. Government figures which were released in 1952[10] show that the labour force was dominated by agricultural workers — mainly peasant cocoa farmers and farm labourers. They were followed by commercial workers and then by public servants. By 1960 the sectoral distribution of labour had not changed[11]. It was still dominated by employment in agriculture which accounted for 61.8%, and was followed by commerce with 14.5%.

The changes that occurred between 1960 and 1970 could only be described as modest even though there had been increases in both the total labour force and total employment. For instance, the share of agriculture and commerce in total employment had declined; but these two sectors still retained their leading position in total employment. And rather significantly, the share of such crucial industries as mining, construction and electricity in total employment had declined even though that of manufacturing had improved from 9.1% to 12.0%.

But as Graham points out (in this volume) there had been other significant changes in the sectoral and geographical distribution of the labour force. For instance, as a result of the big import substitution industrialization programme of the early 1960s the size of the labour force engaged in manufacturing had by 1970 increased by 4.8% while the corresponding labour force engaged in mining and quarrying had declined by 4.5%. Thus 'by 1977 workers in medium and large scale manufacturing numbered almost 89,000 as against a combined total of slightly more than 55,000 miners, dock and railway workers.'

Accompanying this was a similar shift which changed the geographical concentration of workers from the Sekondi-Takoradi area to the Greater-Accra Region, mainly the Accra-Tema area. This followed the growth of the Greater-Accra region as the principal industrial heartland of the country. Accordingly this region accounted for 60.0% of gross manufacturing output and about 55.0% of total industrial work force in 1977[12].

By 1982 this pattern had become pronounced. Manufacturing workers numbered 67,661 as against the 24,427 engaged in mining and quarrying. Out of those engaged in manufacturing the Accra-Tema area alone accounted for 37,589 followed by Ashanti Region with 11,788 and then the Western Region with 8,252[13]. Therefore, despite the prevailing numerical dominance of the agricultural labour force it is clear that by 1982 the industrial working class had become the main and dynamic political pivot of the labour force. Combined with their counterparts in the mining and the tertiary sectors of the economy they constituted a formidable political force. Even so the labour movement had not entirely overcome its ideological limitations which, according to Peil[14], was due to the overarching influence of rural values, sentiments and attachments. Yet no regime from the CPP to the present could afford to ignore labour's potential to act as the political barometer.

Since the time of the CPP this power had been demonstrated on several occasions: namely, in its tendency towards populism during the 1960s[15] and in the prolonged struggles it waged against the Progress Party government, the Supreme Military Council and the People's National Party regimes. By 1982, therefore, labour had become a significant political force which the PNDC had to deal with for good or evil.

THE RISE OF STATE CAPITALISM

At the time of independence in 1957 the backwardness of the economy and the weakness of the embryonic national bourgeoisie had created a situation of severe scarcity of capital. That situation called for vigorous efforts by the state to attract foreign capital as a means to facilitate industrialization. The main theoritical and empirical justification had been furnished by Sir W. Arthur Lewis[16a] who had based his propositions on his model of 'industrialization-by-invitation'.[16b] The state, according to this view, had to confine its intervention in the economy to the provision of essential social and industrial infrastructure and an investment climate that was good enough to attract foreign investors. For the incipient national bourgeoisie the state's support would be indirect: it would come through the Industrial Development Corporation (IDC) which had been established in 1948.

By the close of the 1950s the futility of the Lewis model had become evident: the inflow of foreign investments had not been overwhelming; the country was in the throes of trade and budget deficits and its liquidity position was extremely precarious. It was experiencing negative terms of external trade; and the government had to resort to massive borrowing to cover its deficits[17]. In effect, the neo-colonial character of the economy was becoming quite clear.

The response to this crisis was the redirection of the state's intervention in the economy which, thenceforth, took the form of capital accumulation and investment directly under the control of the state. The means to this end was the state enterprise which was regarded by the CPP government as the answer not only to the neo-colonial economy's crisis, but also as a preparation towards socialism[18].

Contrary to these claims, however, state enterprises became avenues for private accumulation for fractions of the national bourgeoisie which were either located in the CPP bureaucracy or in a position (operating even from outside the party) to manipulate the party and state bureaucracies for their private benefit[19].

In a neo-colony this outcome is inevitable. Because the national bourgeoisie can accumulate only under the aegis of the state the latter becomes the instrument of growth for the private capital of the nascent national bourgeoisie which capital is often nurtured directly by the state as public capital. But more especially, the economic policies of the 1966-79 regimes-particularly of the NLC government, show that in a situation where private capital is determinate, and where labour is politically weak, it is possible to privatize public capital or property for the benefit of the national bourgeoisie[20].

Given the fact that the building of state capitalism during the 1960-65 period did not proceed simultaneously with the strengthening of the political position of labour within the state this transfer of public property to the national bourgoisie became much easier to accomplish. Significantly, the ideologues and intellectuals of this class were the most vocal during the 1966-69 period in opposing and denouncing any sale which, in their view, compromised the national interest[21]. But to the extent that much of their opposition was directed against sales to foreign buyers, we would argue that for them what constituted the national interest was coterminous with what was beneficial to the national bourgeois class. In effect, the policy of promoting state capitalism was in the long-term interest of the national bourgeois class. In a more general sense, it prepared the ground for the post-1965 policies of promoting the growth of Ghanaian private capitalists.

Concurrent to this development was the growth of industrial enterprises of considerable size in the joint enterprises sector. In 1962, for example joint enterprises produced only 11.9% of total industrial output. This increased to 21.4% in 1966 and to 38.0% in 1970. In 1969-70, they accounted for 22.6% of all approved projects; 14.5 million cedis (out of a total invested capital of 35.1 million cedis) and 5 out of 22 projects approved for that period. The corresponding figures for the 1971-72 period show significant increases: 59.1%; 24.2 million cedis (out of 32.9 million cedis) and 13 projects (out of 22). And in 1977-78 alone joint enterprises accounted for 18 of the 19 projects approved by the Ghana Investments Centre.

GROWTH OF PRIVATE GHANAIAN CAPITALISM

A corresponding development throughout this period was the growth of indigenous capitalism. Under the free enterprise and indigenisation policies of the post 1966 regimes, Ghanaian investors of various qualifications could extend their operations in the economy. The result was an appreciable increase in the number of indigenous private investors. For example, Ghanaian private investments accounted for only 7 (out of 22) approved projects in 1969-70; 4 (out of 13) in 1970-71; and 6 (out of 22 in 1971-72). The figures for approved projects by the close of the next decade shows an impressive increase in the share of private investments held by Ghanaians.

The following figures illustrate the transition of Ghanaian capitalists from a minority to a majority group of investors. In 1977, they accounted for 65 of the 105 approved projects. In 1978, it was 73 out of 88; 1979: 67 out of 87; and in 1980: 10 out of 11. In aggregate terms it means that between 1977 and 1980 they accounted for 77.0% of total investments in all approved projects. An equally spectacular growth was recorded in the small scale sector of the economy. Investments in this section also jumped from a total of only 46 in 1977 to 235 in 1980. Between 1977 and 1980, there was a total of 524 separate investments with estimated total investments in buildings and machinery of 5,524 million cedis.

CAPITAL AGAINST LABOUR

These levels of state and private capitals' involvement in the economy altered state — labour relations. Under the CPP government it had become necessary to impose institutional or political and legal controls over labour. The National Liberation Council and Progress Party regimes adopted a policy of total confrontation with labour; the Supreme Military Council made futile attempts to co-opt the leadership of the labour movement; and the People's National Party tried to use the law courts to combat labour's militancy. The PNDC government on its part first tried to use the Committees for the Defence of the Revolution (CDRs) to bolster its rule; and it is now relying more heavily on the coercive arms of the state. These various attempts to cope with labour agitations seem to reflect the level of crisis in which capital and the bourgeoisie find themselves.

The statist policies of the CPP government had been prompted by the severe economic crisis which was already showing signs in the late 1950s. By the early 1960s the country was experiencing serious trade and budget deficits, negative terms of trade and negative capital flows[22]. The political situation was also rife with violent agitations by opposition elements[23].

The government responded to the overall situation in various ways. To improve upon the finances of the state it resorted to deficit financing[24] and to the extensive use of suppliers' credit with all the implications for the future financial and monetary administration of the country. Other stringent fiscal and administrative measures were introduced to salvage the situation. Politically however, the party and government embarked on a policy of centralizing power and total control of the political life of society. Party and government leaders developed an essentially monist view of society in which the party was monolithic and pervasive[25].

From 1961 onwards the party was acclaimed as the government and vice versa. Accordingly all existing associations, especially those which were engaged in the production process — urban industrial, commercial and clerical workers as well as rural workers and peasant farmers — all became members of the CPP through their respective organizations. By this they were deemed to have come under the discipline of the party. Consequently, the leaders of the key auxiliary wings of the party such as the Ghana Trades Union Congress (TUC) and the United Ghana Farmers Co-operative Council (UGFCC) were made members of the central committee of the party and given top government appointments.

It was in the wake of these transformations in the structure of authority and power that the Industrial Relations Act of 1958 was amended. The Industrial Relations (Amendment) Act 1960 (Act 7) provided for a more centralized control of trade unions by the TUC. It also provided for an adequate financial base through the mechanism of automatic deductions of union dues from the salaries of workers. Earlier in the same year the Civil Service Act 1960 (C.A. 5), enacted by the constituent Assembly on June 29 1960, had provided under section 24 that Civil Servants would be qualified to form a trade union. This meant, in effect, that they would also come under the control of the TUC and through it the CPP.

Also, the state's position as the largest employer became crucial in the efforts to control labour. It placed the state in a position from which it could exercise direct and effective control over the conduct of the entire labour force that was engaged in work either in the urban or rural sectors, especially where the activities of such workers impinged on the state's effective access to the surplus generated by the entire working people of the country. A classic example is the case of cocoa farmers who had to shoulder an average tax burden of 23.0% during the 1960-65 period[26] as a result of the effectiveness of the Cocoa Marketing Board and the UGFCC in controlling the choices that farmers had to make[27].

Labour's experience was similar to that of cocoa farmers. Through its control over trade union activity the state was able to impose all manner of taxes and simultaneously keep down wages. Up to 1964 for example, the monthly income of workers could be described as reasonable. But after this date they dropped in real term. For public sector workers, real incomes had fallen by 15.0% while their counterparts in the private sector experienced only 8.0% loss in real earnings[28].

In contrast foreign investors recorded handsome returns on their investments. A total of £160,482,000.00 was repatriated from the country during the 1960-65 period. The figure comprised £62,236,000.00 for profits and interests; £77,544,000.00 for freight and insurance on imports; and £20,702,000.00 for private remittances[29]. And yet this is the period which is generally regarded as having marked the beginning of the country's balance of payments and debt problems, and when money for national development was increasingly becoming very scarce.

It is possible that the amount of money which could have been repatriated during this period would be much higher than what was recorded in the national accounts but for the growing anti-imperialist posture of the CPP government and the tight exchange controls that had been imposed since 1960[30]. The apparent restraint on the externalization of foreign capital is one benefit which accrued to the country from the statist policies of the CPP government. For the same reason labour seems to have lost its independence for political action and could therefore not react to its losses in real earnings by engaging in strikes and other forms of protest.

A more tangible explanation for the relative industrial peace during this period can however be found in the socialist underpinnings of the CPP government policies. This socialist undercurrent summarised not just the anti-imperialism of the party and government but also the protection of the right of every Ghanaian citizen to work and earn a reasonable wage[31]. As the leader of the party and government was to restate later at the launching of the Seven-Year Development Plan in parliament, 'Our national wealth must be built up and used in such a way that economic power shall not be allowed to exploit the worker in town or village, but used for the supreme welfare and happiness of our people.'

This, we would argue explains why strike actions were quite sporadic. They were concentrated in the capital intensive enclaves of the economy. During the 1960-65 period the timber industry accounted for 17.4% of all strikes; manufacturing accounted for 18.8%; construction, 13.2%; commerce, 14.5%; and communication and transport 13.0%. Together they accounted for 76.9% of all recorded strikes during the period.

One observation is necessary here. With the exception of the 1961 strike by the railway and harbour workers of Sekondi-Takoradi which was the first industrial stoppage since the miners's strike of 1955-6, there was no major political challenge from labour. But even in this case it just happened that the agitations of a section of urban workers were effectively exploited by the opposition groups which were fighting to dethrone the CPP. This supports our earlier contention that the monolithic structure that the government and party had erected had enabled the state to control more effectively the conduct of all social groups which were strategically situated in the economy.

Arising from this control is the ability of the state to exploit labour. Clive Thomas has argued[32] that the role of the state as employer and appropriator of surplus underlines its intimacy with 'national and international capital, particularly their common interest in containing the growth of the share of wage income in national output, and in increasing the surplus generated by the workforce.' In the case of the CPP government the state's interest in controlling part of the wage income, and in increasing the surplus generated by the workforce did not arise from its alliance with international capital: it arose from the regime's commitment to increasing the nation's stock of capital for the purpose of national development.

In the period following the overthrow of the CPP government this emphasis on building national wealth would be modified to take into account the need to enhance the interest of international capital; and this would have the effect of pushing the class struggles to a much higher level than before.

THE PERIOD OF CONFRONTATION

Between 1966 and 1971 there was a concerted effort by government to reverse the policies of the CPP government. It was widely believed that the statist policies of that government was responsible for the economic crisis generally, and specifically for the trade and budget deficits, the negative flow of investment, and for the poverty of the private sector — especially of indigenous entrepreneurship.

Therefore with the support of the IMF and the World Bank stringent measures were enforced to make the Ghanaian investment climate attractive to private sector investors, both international and national. The measures included liberalization of trade and prices, and devaluation of the Ghanaian currency. Even though by themselves the policies were bound to undermine the living conditions of the working people, additional measures were taken which were directed specifically against labour. These included a wage freeze and retrenchment of labour. About 60,000 workers were retrenched by the National Liberation Council government within one year. As the government's deflationary policies further undermined whatever growth potential existed within the private sector, the unemployment situation worsened and compounded the plight of workers who were already faced with a situation of rising prices.

This desperate situation was exacerbated by the government's conservative wage policy which meant that increases in wages and salaries would be kept at the barest minimum. Thus even though the NLC granted increases in wages and salaries twice during its tenure, the first on July 8 1966 and the second after the publication of the Mills Odoi Report of 1968, the levels were such that by 1969 the real minimum wage for workers in Accra for example was as much as 38.1% less than its 1960 level[33]. And yet government was determined to take strong measures against workers in an effort 'to contain the strong social pressures...... (which were) emerging under the impact of stabilization'; because 'early or excessive wage increase' would undermine the 'objectives of devaluation.'[34]

During the euphoria of the immediate post-CPP years it was generally argued that the spate of workers unrest was reminiscent of the democratic opening which the overthrow of that regime had created. This explanation is farthest away from the truth. The only plausible explanation for the growth in workers unrest is the intensification of exploitation of labour under the NLC and the PP governments which was backed by state-sponsored repression against labour. For workers normally would resort to a strike to demand better working conditions, including just wages and moderate market prices for consumer items. Besides, that argument overlooked the fact that workers could resort to strikes even under the monolithic control of the CPP government.

At any rate the rising intensity of exploitation both through the mechanism of the free market and the production process provoked workers to embark on a number of strikes during the 1966-69 period. The records show that the number of strikes was more than what was recorded for the 1960-65 period; and these were concentrated in those sectors where the government's retrenchment and wage policies had been felt most. Agriculture, for example, recorded 10.6% of all the strikes that occurred in 1966-69 as against 1.4% in 1960-65. Other figures are as follows: timber, 17.4% in 1966-69 against 3.7% in 1960-65; manufacturing: 19.3% and 18.8%; construction: 14.9% and 13.2%; commerce: 4.3% and 14.5%; transport and communications: 16.1% and 13.0%; and services: 16.1% and 4.3% for the 1966-69 and 1960-65 periods respectively[35].

In all, these sectors accounted for 98.7% of all recorded strikes for the 1966-69 period as against 68.9%. for 1960-65. Among the 1966-69 strikes were some of the most violent in the recent history of the labour movement; namely, the Tarkwa and Obuasi Gold Miners' strikes. The seriousness of those strikes could be determined from the number of man-hours lost which was 289,971, and by the extent of worker participation which added up to 85,429.

The vehemence with which workers resorted to strikes undermined the self-confidence of the government to the extent that when the Obuasi miners strike broke out the government resorted to brute force to quell it. The degree of force used by the government was so high that it rather united the entire labour movement behind the striking miners of the Ashanti Goldfields Corporation.

It was in reaction to this development that the General Secretary of the Trades Union Congress found it necessary to issue a strong warning urging the government to refrain from further acts of brutality against striking workers anywhere in the country or risk facing a nationwide strike action.

When the PP government assumed office in September of 1969 the economic crisis had not been resolved, despite the stringent measures that had been implemented by the previous government upon the recommendation of the IMF and the World Bank. The PP government, whose members shared the same economic and political philosophy as the NLC, therefore assumed office with a greater determination to continue the liberalization policies of its predecessor. Armed with that commitment the government encouraged employers to lay-off many more workers so that by 1970 unemployment stood at 20.0% of the labour force.

Meanwhile the deflationary wage policies also remained in force. For instance, while in 1971 wages went up by just 4.5% over the level for 1970 the Consumer Price Index (CPI) rose by 90.0% for the same period. When the TUC asked for an increase from the 0.75 minimum daily wage to 1.50 the government adopted the same attitude as its predecessor: it refused.

The confrontation over the demand for a living wage for workers soon exploded into a full-scale political confrontation. Apart from the usual strikes which were on the increase, the TUC leadership embarked on a nationwide campaign to mobilize popular support against the government. The TUC even went to the extent of forming an alliance with the National Union of Ghana Students (NUGS) against the government. The climax of those confrontations came when the PP government rushed through parliament in just one day to enact the Industrial Relations (Amendment) Act, 1971 (Act 383) which dissolved the TUC.

Quite significant of the prevailing political situation is the fact that on the same day as this law was enacted (September 10, 1971) all the 17 labour unions which constituted the TUC met to reconstitute it. *The Spokesman* expressed the mood of labour when it declared in an editorial that the PP government was out to 'milk the workers dry and to do this with impunity'. Accordingly it urged workers to oppose the 'anti-worker conspiracy' of that government.

WEAKNESS OF THE STATE: STRENGTH OF LABOUR

Between 1972, when the National Redemption Council (NRC) — later to be renamed Supreme Military Council (SMC) came to power in a military coup, and 1974 the economy appeared to be recovering. But the signs were quite superficial. The regime had been blessed with a good weather during this period. And it was shrewd enough to exploit it through its short-lived anti-imperialist stand, particularly on the debt question. The regime linked this to a policy of self-reliance to mobilise and direct mass enthusiasm into food production.

By 1975 the crisis of the economy was beginning to resurface. According to the Economic Survey, 1977-78 published by the Central Bureau of Statistics (now Statistical Service of Ghana) the level of the crisis was unprecedented as output in all the major sectors showed a precipitous decline. Accordingly exports dropped sharply at the same time as the terms of trade also worsened. Inflation ran high, and the economy moved rapidly towards the brink of disintegration. Urgent measures had to be taken to arrest the situation. This took the form of what has now come to be known as the indigenization policy.

With regard to labour two complimentary strands of policy responses may be identified. These are (i) the democratisation of capital and (ii) the suppression of workers rights in support of capital. The policy of democratising capital was motivated by the propaganda that it would make even the smallest share-holder and worker a capitalist. In an address to a meeting of the business community on January 10, 1973 the Head of state, Colonel I.K. Acheampong explained that such a policy would 'create a greater sense of belonging and promote a higher sense of responsiblity among the workers.' The policy was directed mainly at foreign companies in an effort to give foreign capital greater security in the Ghanaian economy and society. The Investment Policy Decree, 1975 NRCD 329 and the Ghanaian Enterprises Development Decree, 1975 NRCD 330 provided the legal framework for implementing that policy.

But rather than resolve the economic crisis and thereby reduce the pressure on workers' incomes as well as their living conditions, their situation continued to get worse. In particular workers became target of numerous flagrant violations of their rights, especially where the factories had to change ownership into Ghanaian hands. Among the anti-labour practices are arbitrary salary reductions; retrenchment of sections of the workforce; sending workers on long periods of leave without pay; loss of employment benefits where workers had been secretly dismissed; and so on[36]. In all such cases the state remained aloof. In fact the state was responsible for these anti-worker policies and could not possibly intervene to stop them.

At the same time salaries remained low even though inflation continued its upward movement and basic items became increasingly scarce on the open market. According to the *Economic Survey, 1981* (at pages 188-189) nominal wage index numbers rose rapidly from 100 in 1974 to 302 in 1979. But the real wage index numbers declined equally rapidly because of the very high rate of inflation — from 100 in 1974 to as low as 17 in 1979.

Workers responded to the continued hardship in their lives with wide-spread strikes. Between 1974 and 1979 strikes escalated in number and duration. They increased in number from 8 in 1974 to 11 in 1976, 10 in 1977 and 23 in 1978. Similarly the strikes lasted longer after 1975; that is, as workers felt more sharply the pangs of the economic crisis. From the lowest of 4 days in 1974 and 3 days in 1975 some of the strikes could last as long as 11 days (in 1979), 14 days (in 1976), 20 days (in 1977) and 25 days (in 1978).

In most cases the long strikes involved workers in some of the most strategic and sensitive sectors of society. Among them were workers of the Ghana Rubber Estates Limited whose strike lasted 14 days in 1976; workers of the Ghana National Manganese Corporation at Nsuta: 20 days in 1977; workers of the Electricity Corporation of Ghana who staged a 10-day nation-wide strike in 1978; workers of the Ghana Oil Refinery Company at Tema: 11 days in 1978; workers of the Ghana Registered Nurses Association: 25 days in 1978; and the workers of the Ghana Railways Corporation who also staged an 11-day nation-wide strike in 1979.

Of special significance however, is the six day nation-wide strike action by the Civil Servants Association of Ghana. This strike paralysed the entire state machinery and so unruffled the government that out of panic it dismissed the entire workforce of the civil service only to re-employ them within days of their dismissal.

The foregoing figures represent developments in the public services alone. Nonetheless, available figures for both the private and public sectors confirm the fact that the industrial scene was quite tense with widespread labour unrest. Between 1976 and 1979, for example, there was a total of 186 strikes out of 237 recorded industrial disputes. In all a total of 551,000 man-days were lost to the economy through these strikes[37]. By 1978 the full extent of the mismanagement of the economy by the government had become clear to most Ghanaians.

Strikes by workers were therefore bolstered by nation-wide protests and agitations by students of the three Universities and of colleges throughout the country, by professional associations, as well as professional politicians. What were obviously different, often contradictory, tendencies in the anti-government political movements were forced into what later became the People's Movement for Freedom and Justice (PMFJ) by the common experience of the crisis. The SMCs response was not open suppression of political opposition despite the legitimacy crisis that confronted it. Rather it engaged in open though violent confrontation with all opposition elements. Furthermore no single social group or groups were singled out for attack. Just as the regime had lost any claim to represent either capital or labour as a result of its gross mismanagement of the economy so did it find itself fighting even some of the leading spokesmen for capital.

The worsening of the economic crisis considerably weakened the state and the ruling classes. At the same time, over one decade of struggle against the state and capitalists (employers) had strengthened organised labour both politically and organisationally. This advantage was further boosted by the three and a half months rule of the Armed Forces Revolutionary Council (AFRC); because this regime's intervention in Ghanaian politics did a great deal more to undermine the self-confidence and unity of the ruling classes and state institutions.

Organised labour received additional political impetus from militant political organisations which had sprang up or resurfaced as a result of the political situation created by the AFRC government through its attacks on the ruling classes for their unjust social and economic practices during the regime of the SMC. These two developments bolsted the militancy of labour as expressed in the strikes they carried out during the 1979-81 period when the PNP government was in power. For example, the number of industrial strikes rose to 66 in 1980 (from 43 in 1979).

And even though the number of strikes fell to 51 in 1981, the number of man-days lost in 1981 was more than the previous year's: 234,000 man-days in 1980 against 242,000 in 1981. The causes of those strikes were identified as (i) demand for payment of leave claims; (ii) demand for payment of overtime claims; (iii) demand for payment of new minimum wage rates; (iv) non-payment of salaries and wages; and (v) unilateral rescheduling of the effective dates for Collective Agreements.[38] These are some of the usual trade union demands against capital. Their resurgence should therefore be seen as indicating the extent of the contradictions which were prevailing between capital and labour at the time.

Compared to the situation of the preceeding period, there were fewer violent scenes. But the mood of workers, which was to struggle relentlessly against the state, was epitomized in the action of the striking workers of the Ghana Industrial Holding Corporation (GIHOC) who went to the extent of invading parliament house to express their anger and determination to go to every extent in their confrontation with the state.

By the time the PNDC came to power therefore, the growing ineffectiveness of the state in the face of the growing militancy of labour had underscored the need to strengthen the institutions of state power if the conditions conducive to capitalist accumulation would be successfully created.

FROM ANTI-CAPITALISM TO ANTI-LABOUR

Capital-labour relations under the PNDC has so far gone through two phases: the period of alliance and the period of conflict respectively. The first lasted from January 1982 till the end of 1983 while the second has lasted from that date to the present.

When the PNDC came to power it set itself the task of mobilizing the political and organizational power and militancy of organized labour. The political function of that was the establishment of legitimacy in the phase of the stiff opposition that was pouring out from the ruling classes. It could achieve this objective through the CDRs which instantly became a formidable bridge between labour and the government. Within the conditions created by the revolutionary and anti-imperialist pronouncements and actions of the government organised labour exploded into a state of almost total rebellion against the prevailing political and economic arrangements of society.

Under the leadership of the CDRs and radical political organizations like the JFM, NDM, KNRG, PRYLG the working people through their spokesmen attacked the imperialists and their internal collaborators; they assailed the capitalists for their anti-labour practices; and exposed and attacked what they regarded as negative management practices which in their view accounted in part for the economic and social malaise into which the country had been plunged.

The objectives of the worker's struggles may be divided into three. All three of them were responses to various sub-levels of the crisis which engulfed the country. First, as the economic crisis assumed morbid proportions the culture of the state bureaucracy also degenerated; and the work ethic of leading functionaries of the state bureaucracy became depraved, warped, extremely parasitic, lazy, careless, inefficient and corrupt. Under the PNP this work ethic which was originally associated with the SMC government appeared resurgent.

Second: at the level of policy the monetary and fiscal policies of the SMC government had ensured that public resources were allocated to benefit a commercial sector that was being invaded by waves of rentier and parasitic elements who made a fortune at the expense of the productive sectors. After the inter-regnum of the AFRC government this practice was also clearly on the ascendancy once more. Finally, these developments in the economy had reinforced and widened the gap between the rich and the poor. Workers were among the groups that suffered most under those conditions.

Regarding the first and second, labour concentrated its energies within individual factories, offices, enterprises etc, and exposed the corruption, inefficiency, mismanagement, and other unpatriotic practices of management personnel — like hoarding and diversion of basic consumer goods. They called for the dismissal of management personnel who were implicated in such acts; for the setting up of committees to investigate allegations they made against management; or they often took the initiative in dismissing such top management personnel themselves and appointed an interim management committee to run such enterprises; or they seized hoarded goods or those diverted into wrong channels and sold them at the official price and then subjected the offending persons to 'revolutionary' discipline.

Throughout 1982 and 1983 the PNDC supported workers in waging such attacks on management personnel in various enterprises. Even where it disapproved, it did not say so openly. But soon after the structural adjustment programme had come into force the government started to criticise these and other acts more and more openly and vehemently on the grounds that they were undermining support for the revolution and creating more enemies instead.

The second objective of workers struggles may be described as anti-imperialist; it took the form of actual or attempted take-over of existing manufacturing enterprises which were jointly owned by the state and foreign companies. With the support of Interim Coordinating Committees of Workers Defence Committees and factory CDRs the workers would occupy a factory, dismiss the management and announce a take-over. Labour succeeded in taking-over only two enterprises; namely, the Ghana Textile Printing Company Limited (GTP) and Juapong Textiles Limited (JTL). In other cases such as Allied Foods (a member of Cadbury Schweppes) even the attempt to get the government to take a majority share in it failed.[39] Finally, workers struggled against capitalist industries which were notorious for indulging in unfair labour practices; and they did so irrespective of the nationality of the capitalists involved. The revolt against the Pioneer Food Cannery based at Tema which is recounted in detail by Graham (in this volume) is a classic example.

These struggles differed from previous ones in a number of ways. We will concentrate on just three distinguishing features. First, workers struggles had a clear political motive of being anti-capital and opposed to the decadent capitalist culture that had developed in the course of the economic crisis within top management circles in industry, commerce, and the public services. Because of this workers agitations involved workers other than those of the enterprise in question. They were truly collective labour actions.

Second, they were organised and led by defence committees of the various work-places in collaboration with zonal and district offices of the defence committees. District Councils of Labour were also involved in mobilizing labour in key urban centres like Tema and Kumasi. But as Graham argues in this volume, the defence committees had become for the workers, a new weapon of militant political practice against capital, capitalists and their collaborators as well as the manifestations of capitalist culture which were regarded as offensive to the value and dignity of labour. For in contrast with the old TUC leadership the defence committees represented the independence, autonomy and militancy of labour. On the other hand, the old TUC leadership had come under suspicion as being corrupt, bureaucratic and undemocratic in its methods of work; and it was also accused of having subordinated the larger interest of workers to its own selfish political and economic aspirations and those of previous regimes. It is in the light of these that a group of militant workers calling itself the Association of Labour Unions (ALU) emerged in the early part of 1982 to take over the leadership of the TUC.

Third, workers hardly raised the conventional trade union demands. In addition to the demands and actions, instances of which I have oulined above, workers got themselves organised either in their work places or in their neighbourhoods and villages; and they either acted directly or invited the PNDC to take-over traditional councils, and stool lands which had become the subject of protracted litigation. They either destooled or suspended traditional rulers; or they would independently investigate allegations of corruption, economic sabotage etc, and act on them. In several other instances, they set up 'People's Courts' to try cases independently of the existing judiciary; and their actions or decisions were not subject to any higher body. They were guided by the revolutionary morality which they were struggling to uphold.

This distinctively political character of labour's struggles also affected the methods of struggle. The strike as a traditional labour weapon was abandoned. Instead workers resorted to mass demonstrations; open confrontations with people in authority; and collectively implemented what they had decided at defence committee meetings in defiance of whatever authority might have existed. Or they held mass meetings and rallies at which they issued statments of political intent, or statements that expressed their views or positions on pertinent political issues or developments.

One could therefore say that the 45,200 man-days lost (from 16 strikes) recorded for 1983 totally misrepresents the situation of almost permanant crisis into which workers mass agitations had plunged the country during 1983. These methods underscored the fact that the objective of their struggles were not restricted to individual management groups and enterprises or to parochial economic interests; but that they were goals of general social relevance just as the forces they were struggling against were neither private nor parochial.

The other equally important reason that determined the mode of struggle was the mere fact that there was now in power a government that was supposed to protect workers against capital. The PNDC's pronouncements and specific acts were proof of this confidence. For instance, in the *Provisional National Defence Council (Establishment) Proclamation, 1981* the new government had provided under Section 5, for the establishment of a National Defence Committee whose primary function was to advise the PNDC 'in the exercise of its functions'.

This function was later amplified in the *Provisional National Defence Council (Establishment) Proclamation (Supplementary and Consequential Provisions) Law, 1982 PNDCL 42*. Under Section 31 of this law it is provided that the National Defence Committee shall be responsible for developing, promoting and executing through the defence committees a programme of national education on the objectives of the revolution and do so in pursuance of the political programme of the PNDC for the revolutionary transformation of Ghana.

Apart from these constitutional provisions, the PNDC had enacted a corpus of laws which affirmed its commitment to restructure, at least, the existing political and legal institutions of society while it prepared to tackle the problem of the economy and prevailing social relations. For in the final analysis a 'revolution' is first and foremost a political act. The laws in question dealt with the establishment of a Citizens Vetting Committee, National Investigations Committee, low tariffs and other guidelines for urban rents backed by very punitive measures, and Public Tribunals[40]. All of them were enacted during the first six months of the government's existence. And to affirm its commitment to defending workers' interests the PNDC remained opposed to the retrenchment of labour throughout 1982 and 1983. Because of this conducive political situation labour regarded its struggles not simply as being in consonance with the government's overall political position and objectives; but more especially, as reinforcing them and giving government the much needed political support for carrying through its revolutionary programme.

As the political implications of those struggles became clear the PNDC started to recoil from its original commitment to defend workers' political positions against the ruling classes. The government attacked labour, as organised into the defence committees and other militant organisations, for their alleged misplaced enthusiasm and excesses. Apart from the storm of denunciations that engulfed labour and their cadres the government further acted in very concrete ways to restrain labour from taking over any more firms, whether local or foreign. The failure of workers to secure the partial nationalization of Allied Foods clearly shows the governments's determination to pre-empt or contain further 'revolutionary' actions against capital.

Peter Anyang Nyongo has argued, with regard to state interventions of this kind, that 'When all capitalists are threatened with destruction of their capital or its appropriation by the popular masses, it is the interest of foreign capital that the state must, in the final analysis, preserve.'[41] But we must recall that in the case of Pioneer Food Cannery the regime actually intervened to stop labour from destroying capital through its agitations and other claims.[42] That intervention shows that the state is prepared, under conditions where its interests are identical with those of both national and international capitals, to act in defence of significant national capitalist interests against threats of destruction from labour.

By the middle of 1984 government and labour were moving farther apart. The coming into force of the government's Structural Adjustment Programme (SAP) marked the beginning of the transition from the period of alliance to the period of confrontation. It must be recalled that when the initial phase of the SAP was implemented in the 1983 budget which was announced in April of that year workers were the principal defenders of the regime against massive criticism and opposition from representatives of the ruling classes. They did so knowing fully well of the serious implications that the first budget under the SAP meant for their incomes and for consumer prices generally. They nonetheless believed that ultimately the government was committed to defending and enhancing their interest. However, the government's subsequent wage, price and employment policies following the 1983 and 1984 budget and other fiscal policies sufficiently exposed the anti-labour posture of the regime.

The PNDC's anti-labour policies may be grouped into two; namely, the political and economic. Before the regime came out with the full extent of its anti-labour wage, prices and employment policies it moved rapidly to weaken the defence committees as independent, autonomous and militant organizations for labour's political struggles.

By the close of 1984 the denunciations had been translated into reorganization measures. The defence committees were renamed Committees for the Defence of the Revolution (CDRs) and were brought under the political 'command and control of the respective District and Regional Secretaries.'[43]

Following that the Interim Management Committees, which had been set up in all but a few public enterprises and corporations to include the representatives of workers in the highest decision-making organs of such public establishments, were also abolished. They were replaced by Joint Consultative Committees which have no executive powers. Simultaneously the National Defence Committee was abolished and replaced by a National Secretariat of the CDRs headed by a Political Counsellor for the Economic Development of the CDRs. These changes ushered the defence committees into a new non-political role; namely, mobilizing communities for communal work and educating factory workers to increase productivity.

Of equal significance is the fact that the CDRs have in recent times been employed by the government as a tool for dividing the ranks of workers and thereby preventing collective labour action against the government. This is because, in contrast with labour agitations of the 1982-83 period current ones are almost always in direct opposition to government policies. For example, between February of 1986 and July 1987 the TUC and the government openly differed on (i) workers' allowances and whether government could cancel or tax any of them without first consulting the TUC leadership; (ii) the government's wages, prices and employment policy; and (iii) the freedom of the labour movement to express itself in a democratic manner on matters affecting the rights of workers, the economic policies of the government as well as its political direction.

On two occasions the TUC threatened to bring its members out on a general strike: the first during the month of April 1986 and the second during the May-July months of 1987. During the latter period of confrontation the CDRs were mobilized on one occasion to invade TUC Headquarters as a sign of opposition to the stand of the TUC leadership on the subject of the controversy between them and the government.[44] On another occasion the CDRs were deployed to counter the TUC leadership's mobilization of the rank and file in preparation for a show down with the government. It was widely reported with satisfaction how CDR executive members in various establishments had held rallies to counter such moves by the leadership of the TUC.[45]

The government's anti-labour economic policies — on wages, employment and prices — are the factors which underpin the government's conflict with labour. Already the series of devaluations which were initiated with the SAP in April of 1983 had cut deeply into the incomes of workers in the form of higher prices. Therefore the deflationary wage policy coupled with the policy of massive retrenchment of labour in the public services as well as the freedom that the private sector now has to engage in similar retrenchments were bound to antagonize labour.

There was also the general policy of removing subsidies on social services and utilities such as education, health, electricity and water supply.[46] Suddenly workers begun to realise that the government's policies were after all not designed to protect their rights and make life better for them. Hence the rising level and incidence of conflict between organized labour and the government.

Compared with the policies of the NLC regime of 1966-69, one sees a great deal of similarities. Both of them worked out the details of their policies in close collaboration with the IMF and the World Bank; and they pursued similar policies which were based on the same economic thought that by redistributing incomes in favour of capitalists (i.e., the private sector) this sector will reinvest its higher incomes in new industrial ventures and thereby boost employment opportunities.[47]

But, as happened under the NLC, the private sector cannot easily overcome its structural limitations in order to create more job avenues for the teaming masses of unemployed peoples.[48] Invariably therefore the unemployment situation became severe while the incomes of those who were lucky to remain in employment continued to lag behind rising prices of consumer items.

Like the situation which prevailed during the regime of the NLC, organised labour reacted vehemently to the stringent anti-labour policies of the PNDC. But unlike the 1966-69 period labour's strategy in struggling with the government is no longer to use the strike weapon. Workers are no longer relying on the CDRs to wage their struggles against the government; for the CDRs do not seem to command the confidence of the rank and file and the leadership of the labour movement any longer. Nor are they engaging in mass demonstrations, mass rallies, open confrontations with people in authority or unilateral actions to establish the power of labour in the political economy of the country. Instead they are using conventional meetings, congresses, workshops etc, organised by the various unions of the TUC to challenge and denounce the regime's policies.

They have also responded directly to specific government policies and statements with counter statements which tend to be critical of government. For example, the General Secretary of the Local Government Workers Union reacted to the government's financial statement of 1984 by warning the government against a further deepening of the poverty of the working class while clamping down on workers legitimate activities.[49] Later on the Executive Board of the TUC issued a statement on the same subject after an emergency meeting held on October 24, 1984. In that statement the TUC leadership lamented 'the grave and critical economic and social situation in the country' and further warned against the continued implementation of the IMF and World Bank inspired SAP which was having deleterous effects on worker's incomes and living conditions.

Other instances have been May Day Rallies when workers have taken the liberty of celebrating this international workers solidarity day to express their displeasure with government policies. For instance at the 1985 May Day Rally in Kumasi workers carried placards some of which read: 'PNDC we are hungry' '70.00 wage not enough'.[50]

The PNDC has nonetheless responded to such forms of opposition from labor with a firm hand and often with severe reprisals. Government has resorted to the threats to employ the full force of the state or has actually used such force against workers agitations. Examples are the use of armed personnel against the workers of Assene Household Enamelware Limited in Accra,[51] and the dismissal of the leaders of striking workers of the State Gold Mining Corporation's Dunkwa mines.

During the 1966-69 period if the government had handled labour unrest in a similar manner it could easily have provoked serious confrontation with workers. But under the PNDC, the case of the Assene Household Enamelware Ltd and of the Dunkwa mines have passed without any concerted support from the other unions of the TUC. This is an indication of how the regime has succeeded in clamping down on the traditional forms of labour struggles.

At the same time, the labour movement cannot return to the forms of struggle which evolved during the 1982-83 period. The success of government in clamping down on workers strikes, and in forcing unions to resort to press releases (which have a very restricted circulation because of the official control of the media) have ensured the creation of the external conditions necessary for capital to operate peacefully and profitably.Hence the government is for example able to continue its policy of laying off workers in the public services — a policy which has been emulated by the private sector; pursue its deflationary wage policy; and continue to accord the market the necessary freedom to determine prices of consumer items. In short, the reverse side of the government's success in suppressing the demands of workers is the freedom which capital is currently enjoying in the Ghanaian economy. The former is a condition for the success of the later.

CONCLUSION

The central issues in economic development are how best to create wealth and how equitably to distribute this wealth among the productive sectors of the economy and among the different social classes engaged in the social economy for private consumption. In all societies the bases for resolving these issues to the satisfaction of all has been a source of contention between capital and labour. The problem is severe in a dependent economy like Ghana's where the bourgeois class has great difficulty in spearheading national capital accumulation. In such cases the state assumes a leading role in promoting capitalist accumulation.

In pursuit of the goal of capital accumulation for national development, the state forges various alliances with international capital through both bi-lateral and multi-lateral agencies and arrangements. In a number of cases the state becomes just an intermediary between international capital and the national bourgeois class. At any rate, the state eventually develops identical interest with both national and international capital and so tends more to defend capital generally against labour and other non-capitalists.

State intervention in the economy is intensified during periods of severe economic crisis. The depth and duration of the economic crisis have determined the extent of external involvement in the domestic economy. The deeper the crisis, the easier it becomes for foreign capital to assume almost total control of the economy through the mediation of the state.

During the 1960s when the country's economic crisis was at an incipient stage, state intervention was directed against both foreign and national capitals. The goal was the building of state capitalism as the first step on the road toward socialism. To this end the state merely sought to control labour through institutional and legal means in order to ensure capital accumulation under its aegis. Within the monolithic political order that emerged the state was less repressive of labour. The level of exploitation, measured by real income, public subsidy for social and utility services, and consumer goods, was also much lower compared to what was to follow in the wake of a worsened economic crisis.

The NLC initiated the process of closer collaboration with international capital under close supervision, if not dictation, by the IMF and the World Bank. Given the consensus between the regime, the IMF and the World Bank on the necessity to revive and strengthen the private sector as the basis for economic growth the state's full coercive power had to be pitched against labour. This was to ensure that stringent wage, employment, trade and price liberalisation policies would be implemented for the benefit of investors. Despite labour's aggressive struggles against such degradations, subsequent regimes continued to pursue the same anti-labour policies with varying emphasis.

By 1981 the economic crisis had become uncontrollable. As a result the state had not just become a capitalist; it had also become more deeply involved in managing the economy for purposes of promoting national capital accumulation. Furthermore, its interests had become more intimately interwoven with those of local and foreign capitalists. In particular, it had come to rely extensively on international capital in finding solutions to the economic crisis.

As the 1974-81 political and economic crisis showed, the state was also becoming increasingly arbitrary and repressive in dealing with workers demands for a just wage and improved working conditions.

This metamorphosis of the bourgeois state toward authoritarianism is a condition for the more efficient suppression of labour so that appropriate social conditions would prevail in which capitalism could operate freely and successfully. Since 1982 the maturation of this authoritarian state has taken on the form of populism (i.e. the populist authoritarian state) in order to ensure the successful co-optation of the masses, into the state apparatus and the subordination of labour to the power of capital and the state. But as Thomas has argued state intervention is contradictory in character: 'as the interventionist character of the state grows, the class struggle is increasingly (propelled foward and a common class bond is forged among the fragmented groups of the public and non-public sector workers; and the two invariably come to constitute a formidable force standing in opposition to the bourgeois state)'.

The overwhelming working class rebellion against the SMC regime illustrates such contradictions. The merit of the populist authoritarian state which has come into being since 1982 is, however, that it has been able to divide and intimidate the working class movement after effectively cultivating their confidence and winning their support during the 1982-83 period.

NOTES

1. Cruickshank, B. *Eighteen Years on the Gold Coast of Africa* (London: Hurst and Blackett, 1853.) and Reynolds, E. *Trade and Economic Change on the Gold Coast, 1807-1874*. (London: Longmans, 1974.)
2. See Kimble, David. *A Political History of Ghana, 1850-1928* (Oxford: Clarendon Press, 1963.); Foster, P. *Education and Social Change in Ghana*. (London:

Routledge and Kegan Paul, 1965.); and Priestly, Margaret. *West African Trade and Coastal Society*. (London: Oxford University Press, 1969)

3. Republic of Ghana. *The Proposals of the Constitutional Commission for a Constitution for Ghana*. (Accra: State Publishing Corporation, 1968.)
4. Accumulation in the agrarian sector was possible only through the cocoa industry that had been established through the hard work of the country's peasant farmers, and sometimes against the displeasure of the colonial government. See the documents assembled on this subject in Kay, G.B. *The Political Economy of Colonialism in Ghana: (A Collection of Documents and Statistics, 1900-1960)*. (Cambridge: Cambridge University Press, 1972.)
5. For a discussion of the impact of colonialism on the industrial capacity of the colonies generally and with reference also to Ghana See Hymer, S.S. and S.A. Resnick. 'A Model of an Agrarian Economy with Non-Agricultural Activities.' The American Economic Review. Vol. xix (No.4) September 1969. Pp. 493-5061. Also Resnick, S.A. 'The Decline of Rural Industry Under Export Expansion: A Comparison among Burma, Philippines and Thailand, 1870-1938'. *Journal of Economic History*. Vol. XXX (No.1) 1970.
6. Jonah, Kwesi, 'Imperialism, the State and the Indigenization of the Ghanaian Economy, 1957-84' *Africa Development* Vol. X (3) 1986.
7. Killick, T. *Development Economics in Action*. (London: Heinemann, 1978) Pp. 126
8. For an analysis of the indigenization policies of that government refer to Jonah, Kwesi. 'The Politics of Economic Decolonization: The Case of Ghana's Indigenization Policies.' Unpublished M.A. Thesis. Department of Political Science, University of Ghana, Legon, 1980.)
9. See Femia, J.V. *Gramsci' Political Thought*. (Oxford: ts Oxford University Press, 1981.)
10. The figures will be found in Ghana (Gold Coast) *A Survey of Some Economic Matters*. (Accra: Ministry of Finance, February 1952.)
11. Ewusi, Kodwo. Economic Inequality in Ghana (Dakar: CODESRIA, 1977) Pp.18-20.
12. Graham, Yao. In this volume.
13. Republic of Ghana. *Industrial Statistics, 1982-1984*. (Accra. Statistical Service, July 1986.) Table 2.4. A *worker* is defined here as 'the total number of persons engaged in the activities of the establishment during the reference period. The 'persons' include production workers as well as professional and managerial staff, proprietors, active business partners, etc. Ibid. p. 3.
14. Peil, Margaret. *The Ghanaian Factory Worker*. (Cambridge: Cambridge University Press, 1972.) Pp. 219- 221.
15. Jefferries, Richard. *Class, Power and Ideology in Ghana. The Railway Men of Sekondi-Takoradi*. (Cambridge: Cambridge University Press, 1978).

16a. Ghana (Gold Coast) *Report on Industrialization and the Gold Coast* (Accra: Government Printer, 1953)

16b. See for example Lewis, W. Arthur. *The Theory of Economic Growth*. (London: Allen and Unwin 1955.)

17. Killick op cit; and Krassowski, *A. Development and the Debt Trap*. (London: Croom Helm, 1974.)
18. See Republic of Ghana. *The Seven Year Development Plan 1963/64 — 1969/70*. (Accra: Office of the Planning Commission, 1965.)
19. The Reports of the numerous Committees and Commissions of Enquiry appointed during the aftermath of the 1966 coup provide ample factual evidence on this.
20. A good number of public enterprises were sold to the private sector after 1966.

It was regarded as one of the ways of promoting the growth of the national bougeoisie.

21. Their position in the famous *Abbot Case* which centred around the intended sale of what is now the GIHOC Pharmaceuticals Company Limited is a classic example of their agitations. For a summary of their arguments, see *The Legon Observer*. Vol. II No. 23, 10-22 November, 1967 to Vol. II No. 25, 8-21 December 1967.
22. For a discussion of these developments see Killick opcit., Krassowski op.cit. and Birmingham, Walter et al. *A Study of Contemporary Ghana*. Vol. I (The Ghana Economy) (London: Allen and Unwin, 1966).
23. For a succint account of the struggles between the political opposition and the CPP government, see Austin, Dennis. *Politics In Ghana, 1946-1960*. (Oxford: Oxford University Press , 1970.)
24. See Ahmad, *N. Deficit Financing, Inflation and Capital Formation. The Ghana Experience, 1960-65*. (Munchen: Welt-forum Verlag, 1970.)
25. In a speech to the 10th Annual Delegates Conference of the CPP held in August 1959 Nkrumah had likened the CPP 'to a mighty tree with many branches. The Convention Peoples Party constitutes the root and the trunk, and its branches include such organisations as the United Ghana Farmers' Council, the Trades Union Congress..... and other patriotic organisations which in their various ways are giving support to our party'. Quoted in Austin, op.cit. pp. 382-1.
26. For a study of the tax burden that cocoa farmers were called upon to shoulder see Dodoo, Sam Nii. 'Some Redistributive Aspects of the Tax on Cocoa Income in Ghana'. *Economic and Social Affairs*. Vol.3 July 1977 Nos 2 and 3. Pp.17.
27. The implications of the CPP government's effective control over peasant cocoa farmers through the UGFCC are discussed in Beckman, B. *Organizing the Farmers* (Uppsala: Scandinavian Institute of African studies, 1976.)
28. Ewusi, K. *Op.cit*. pp. 33-35.
29. Jonah, in *Africa Development; op.cit*.
30. See the Exchange Control Act, 1961 (Act 71).
31. Nkrumah, K., *Consciencism* (London: Heinemann, 1964) pp. 72-74.
32. Thomas, Clive. *The Rise of the Authoritariam State in Peripheral Societies* (New York: Monthly Review Press, 1984). P. 85.
33. Ewusi. *Op.cit*. p. 33
34. Republic of Ghana. *Ghana's Economic and Aid Requirements in 1968*. (Accra, 1967).
35. These data have been extracted from Krause, J. as quoted in Konings, P. *The Political Potential of Ghanaian Miners: A Case Study of the AGC workers at Obuasi*. (Leiden: African Studies Centre, 1980.) Research Paper No.9.
36. For a detailed description of such anti-labour practices see Jonah 'The Politics of Economic Decolonization...' op cit.
37. Republic of Ghana. *Economic Survey 1981*. (Accra: Central Bureau of Statistics, 1983.) p. 192.
38. Ibid.
39. A summary of labour's claims in the struggles against Allied Foods can be obtained from *Ghanaian Times*. June 22, 23 and 24 1983. See also Graham. In this volume.
40. The PNDC laws establishing these state organs are, respectively, *Citizens Vetting Committee Law 1982 PNDCL 1; National Investigations Committee Law 1982 PNDCL 2; Rent Control Law 1982 PNDCL 5; Compulsory Letting of Unoccupied Rooms and Houses Law 1982 PNDCL 7; and Public Tribunals Law 1982 PNDCL 24.*
41. Anyang' Nyang'o, Peter. 'State and Society in Africa' *Africa Development*. Vol. III (3) 1983, pp. 5-23.

42. Lokko, F.C.C. has done an excellent study of the confrontation between labour and Pioneer Food Cannery as well as the role of the state in suddenly resolving the conflict in order to save the enterprise. See his B.A. Long Essay 'The State, Capital and Labour in Ghanaian Politics, 1975-85. The case of Pioneer Food Cannery, Tema.' (Legon: Department of Political Science University of Ghana, 1986). Also Graham in this collection
43. *PNDC Statement on Reorganization of the CDRs*. (Accra: PNDC Secretariat, The Castle, Friday December 7, 1984).
44. Refer eg. to 'Cadres accuse TUC Leadership' in *The Ghanaian Times*. Saturday, 6 June 1987 p.2
45. For examples of such reported interventions see 'TTL-CDR calls for Disciplinary Action against DCLs'. *Peoples Daily Graphic*. July 21, 1987 p. 4-5 and 'Government Will Improve Lot of Workers'. *Peoples Daily Graphic*. July 22, 1987.
46. The extent of the retrenchment exercise is discussed by Jonah, Kwesi. 'The Social Impact of Ghana's Adjustment Programme, 1983-1986'. Paper Presented at the IFAA conference on the Impact of IMF/World Bank policies on the People of Africa. September 7-10 1987, London; and Ninsin, K.A. 'The IMF/World Bank in the Politics of Ghana 1982-87'. Mimeo (Legon: Department of Political Science, University of Ghana, 1987)
47. One of the exponents of this view during the last 4 decades was Sir W. Arthur Lewis. See for example his 'Economic Development with Unlimited Supplies of Labour' in A.N. Agarwala and S.P. Singh (eds) *The Economics of Underdevelopment*. (London: Oxford University Press, 1958).
48. One scholar who remained a consistent critic of the assumption that deflationary policies of the sort being pursued by the NLC would stimulate growth in the private sector is G.K. Agama. See his '*The Budget and the Economy*'. *The Legon Observer*. Vol. 3 1966.
49. The General Secretary of the Local Government Workers Union was addressing a Divisional Conference of his union in Kumasi. For the report on that conference see *The Pioneer*, Monday October 1, 1984. p.1
50. Reported in The Pioneer, May 3 1985. p. 1.
51. For details of the Assene workers struggles with their employers and the reactions from state functionaries and certain branches of the state apparatus, see Speech by the General Secretary of the Industrial and Commercial Workers Union (ICU) to the Union's 4th Quadrennial Delegates Conference in Kumasi, March 2-4, 1987. See also Graham's contribution to this volume.

2. FROM GTP TO ASSENE: ASPECTS OF INDUSTRIAL WORKING CLASS STRUGGLES IN GHANA 1982-1986

Yao Graham

INTRODUCTION

On December 31, 1981 the 3rd Republic, under the government of the People's National Party (PNP) led by Dr. Hilla Liman was overthrown in a coup d'etat led by Flight Lt. J.J. Rawlings, and replaced with the Provisional National Defence Council (PNDC).

The coup initiated a great upsurge in the class struggles with the dominated classes challenging the foundations of neocolonialism in Ghana. In such times of fierce class struggles,in the practice of both the working class on the one hand and the State and capital on the other, the line between so called 'legitimate' trade union concerns and political issues completely disappears. This point, which has often been overlooked by many analysts, was highlighted by Jack Woddis[1] in his study of the role of different social classes and forces in the overthrow of British colonialism in Africa. In the case of Ghana, he noted that,

> the general strike of 1950 did more than arouse the national movement. It was in fact the biggest single action undertaken by any section of the Ghanaian people and proved to be decisive in paving the way for the election victory of Kwame Nkrumah and the Convention People's Party (CPP) in 1951, the attainment of internal self government and so inevitably to the attainment of an independent Ghana in 1957.

Those whose perceptions of working class struggles are rooted in a narrow 'industrial relations' framework easily miss out on the kind of political and ideological impact Woddis ascribes to the 1950 general strike. Thus Kraus, who has done valuable work on the history and practice of industrial relations in the country, for example, takes the position that the 1950 general strike was 'successful only in its size' even as he acknowledges its overtly political purpose.[2]

This chapter discusses aspects of working class struggles in Ghana in the period 1982-86. It is primarily concerned with the manufacturing working class and focuses on a number of struggles around enterprises in the Accra-Tema area. Those struggles had socio-political implications and effects far beyond the 'industrial relations issues' which provoked them. They involved the use of forms of organisation and struggle novel to the Ghanaian working class. They also exposed the limits of the institutionalised industrial relations mechanism centred on the trade unions and the Labour Department as far as the advancement and defence of working class interests are concerned. The cases discussed also throw some light on the evolution of the relationship between the PNDC and the working people of this country.

THE BACKGROUND

The decade preceding the December 31, 1981 coup d'etat was one of deepening socio-economic crisis, a process which accelerated from 1977. Between 1970-80 the Gross Domestic Product (GDP) grew at a rate of 0.2%. This was far below the rate of population growth, which was about 3% per annum. Per capita GDP fell by 30% over the period. The materially productive sectors i.e. agriculture and manufacturing declined by an average of 1.2% annually. Between 1979-1982 alone the GDP declined by 6.1% yearly.

The annual rate of inflation averaged almost 55% throughout the 1970s. Real wage also fell by over 13% annually. The manufacturing sector reflected these trends. Average capacity utilisation fell from an annual average of 47% — from 43-52% between 1970-1977 to less than 25% in 1982 while actual production declined by an annual rate of 13% between 1977-1981. The contribution of this sector to the GDP fell from 14% in 1970 to 6% in 1981. Real wages in the sector also fell by about 50% between 1977-1981. For the working class the economic crisis also threatened jobs. Reliable statistics on the size of the manufacturing labour force since the early 1970s are not available. A 1983 estimate put the number between 365,600 and 415,000 with 300,000-350,000 employed in small-scale manufacturing (i.e. in enterprises employing less than 10 persons).

While those in small-scale manufacturing represent the majority of the labour force in the sector, historically and in the period under discussion it has been workers in the medium and large-scale enterprises who have had a significant impact on industrial relations and national affairs. The labour force in small scale enterprises are largely not unionised and the enterprises are widely dispersed. It is the struggles of the labour force of the medium and large scale enterprises which are of concern here.

The CPP regime (1957-1966) initiated a policy of rapidly expanding the manufacturing sector with heavy investments being made in modern factories between 1961-1966. In the 1960s, manufacturing output grew by 13% and the labour force by 8% yearly. On the other hand the mining labour force declined by 4% annually over the same period. This rapid growth of the manufacturing sector produced a strategic shift in the geographical concentration and composition of the industrial working class. By the mid 1960s, the manufacturing component of the industrial working class was larger than what was historically the core of the industrial proletariat, i.e. the miners, railway and dock workers.

By 1977 workers in medium and large scale manufacturing numbered almost 89,000 as against a combined total of slightly more than 55,000 miners, dockers and railway workers. Accompanying this was a shift in concentration of industrial workers from Sekondi-Takoradi and the mining towns to Accra-Tema. In 1977, over 60% of manufacturing output and around 55% of the manufacturing working class were concentrated in the Accra-Tema area. Since the PNDC came to power the workers of Tema have emerged as the most militant and combative segment of the workers' movement around both industrial relations and broader socio-economic and political issues.

The era of CPP rule also saw the definition of the industrial relations laws and institutions operative in the period covered by this paper. The Industrial Relations Act, 1965 (Act 299) (IRA) which amended and consolidated a law first passed in 1958 is the most important of these. Various writers like Kraus, Sawyerr and Crisp[3] have documented the history and character of the efforts of both the colonial and post-colonial state acting on behalf of capital, to constrain the independence of, and demobilise the organised working class either through repression or co-optation. For example, Sawyerr has shown how the state's 'carrot and the stick' policies found expression in the labour laws enacted since the Trade Unions Ordinance (Cap 91) of 1941.

But it must be acknowledged that the 1965 IRA is the product of a period when the State stressed the co-optation of, and political horse trading with, organised labour in preference to confrontation and repression. This approach reflected the CPP's origins, mass support base and genuine concern about the advancement of the working people. In exchange for a legally institutionalised place in industrial relations, a recognised voice in national policy formulation, security of jobs and a certain assurance of socio-economic policies beneficial to the working class and guaranteed flow of trade union dues through the check-off system, the trade union leadership of the time accepted an industrial relations framework and principles which, in their essence, bound the muscles of the trade union movement.

In a national situation where the political economic context and trade-off which underlaid the 1965 IRA is absent, its cumbersome dispute settling provisions and mechanisms are likely to be ignored by workers at the risk of state repression. This increasingly proved to be the case after the overthrow of the CPP regime in February 1966 especially in the period 1968-71 and 1977-81 when markedly anti-labour regimes were in power. Also where avenues which workers consider more facilitatory become available, naturally the IRA procedures are likely to be ignored. The latter was exemplified in the 1982-86 situation.

It is also noteworthy that most of the strikes during the pre-1982 period were spontaneous and had little publicity or solidarity outside the particular plant. Usually they were organised from the shop floor, were at times led by the local unions and in the vast number of cases, were without the knowledge of trade union leaders and officers beyond the plant. Labour Department officers normally came in together with trade union officials to urge a return to work pending the investigation of the grievances.

This isolation of the wider trade union organisation from the shop floor struggles was only one face of the gap between the rank and file of the workers' movement and the top hierarchy. The TUC's inability to make decisive interventions at the level of national politics to protect worker's interest also compromised its integrity among the rank and file. Other acts which isolated the TUC from its base included its taking over the distribution of scarce consumer items to workers without adequate machinery, and sponsoring a political party — the Social Democratic Front — to contest the 1979 general elections without consulting the rank and file.

All these produced deep disenchantment within the ranks of workers and turned them against their national and TUC leaders. The December 31, 1981 coup took place against this background of spontaneous, fragmented and localised workers' struggles, and an organised labour movement under the leadership of persons co-opted by the ruling circles and who commanded little grassroots loyalty and respect.

1982-1986: ISSUES AND STRUGGLES

Three broad phases can be discerned in the evolving political character and policy orientation of the PNDC. First, the year 1982 was a period of free ranging class struggles; and during this phase there was no concrete overall programmatic framework of government policy but several dominant themes within the governing circles.

Among these were anti-imperialism; national independence and economic reconstruction; democracy; accountability of public officers and anti-corruption; popular power and the need for restructuring the social and political relations; the leading role of the working people in the building of a new society; open acknowledgement of the existence of classes and class struggles; and government support for the initiatives and struggles of the working people. In spite of all the tumult of the period no systematic steps were taken to transform the inherited state institutions so as to make them reliable instruments for the realisation of the PNDC's proclaimed goals.

The second phase, lasting from the latter months of 1982 till the beginning of 1985 — saw a sharpening of the latent conflict among the different tendencies in the ruling coalition: it resulted in bitter struggles centred around an Economic Recovery Programme (ERP) announced in December 1982 and initiated in the 1983 Budget backed by IMF credit and access to OECD resources. During this period the group that advocated no more than reforming the Ghanaian neo-colonial economy and political institutions increasingly strengthened its position in the government. Government policies and practices increasingly diverged from orginal promises; and quietly the patriotic and democratic elements of the 1982 period were abandoned. Ultimately the ERP was reduced to a classic IMF stabilisation programme that would promote neo-colonial capital accumulation.

The period since the beginning of 1985 marks the third phase. The ruling classes became more brazen in pursuing their interests. The rights of the working people, the legitimacy of their interests and organisation came increasingly under attack; and neo-colonial economic policies were implemented with greater determination and vigour.

Corresponding to these three broad phases, the workers' movement moved from a posture of open assertiveness and increased challenge to the social relations of neo-colonialism in 1982-83, through a period of confusion; and from 1985 to 1986 it was increasingly on the defensive while it was locked in a growing conflict with the PNDC regime.

In his broadcast announcing the overthrow of the 3rd Republic,

Flight Lt J.J. Rawlings informed the Ghanaian people that the seizure of power was not a coup; he was calling for 'nothing less than a revolution.' In a fuller policy broadcast on 5th Janurary 1982, he laid out the goals of the new rulers: a broad and radical programme of national economic reconstruction and the democratisation of political and social life. He called for the formation of Local Defence Committees at all levels of society — in the towns, in the villages, in factories, offices and work places and in the barracks. These Defence Committees were to defend the democratic rights of the people and expose corruption and all tendencies which undermine 'the revolution'. In his view there was 'no alternative' to popular initiative in 'these national responsibilities'.

The coup uncapped the hitherto subdued class struggles. Various factors accounted for this. They include deep popular dissatisfaction with the failure of the 3rd Republic to ameliorate the economic crisis; the popular symbolism of J.J. Rawlings as leader of the halcyon days of the AFRC era which gave vent to some of the pent up popular discontent; and the early policy promises of the new regime.

Within days of the coup there were outpourings of workers' approval. Support demonstrations took place all over the country. The day after the coup a Tema based 'Workers Solidarity Council' expressed its support for the new regime and made concrete demands. Two days later workers in Accra took over Parliament House and declared it the headquarters of the defence committees. On the same day workers in Sekondi-Takoradi, the old centre of working class militancy, came out in support of the new regime while the Accra branch of the Public Utility Workers' Union (PUWU) also demonstrated in support of the overthrow of the PNP regime. A few days later there was a massive support march of Tema workers to the barracks headquarters of the new government. The leadership of the various segments of the organised labour movement also expressed their sympathy for the PNDC though in terms more restrained than the street activism of the rank and file.

Eight days after the coup the Ghana National Association of Teachers (GNAT) pledged to cooperate with the new regime 'in line with GNAT's constitutional provisions and traditions of cooperating with the ruling governmment'. On 11th January the Civil Servants Association (CSA) declared its willingness to support 'meaningful steps' by the PNDC. On the 19th January the leadership of the Trade Union Congress (TUC) announced a seven-point Plan for involvement in the 'Revolution'.

Two strands, which have important implications for industrial relations, were discernible in the early post coup political tumult: (i) workers' dissatisfaction with the state of the trades unions and (ii) the emergence of defence committees.

Virtually all the early workers' statements on the coup expressed a desire to see the trades union movement reformed. The Tema Workers' Solidarity Council statement described the TUC as 'inept and disappointing'. During their 8th January demonstration, the workers of Tema made the explicit point that their march was not in response to thc TUC's call for a demonstration on that day. And during the rally which was addressed by Flt Lt Rawlings, the Secretary General of the TUC, A.M.Issifu, was heckled and manhandled. In their statement of support for the PNDC the Tema workers criticised the poor coordination and lack of effective communication between the top hierarchy of the TUC and the rank and file of the workers whose interest they were supposed to serve and guard. On various grounds, including sponsoring the Social Democratic Front party in the 1979 elections, they declared that they had lost confidence in the TUC leadership. They called for the immediate and unconditional resignation of the leaders and the democratisation of the labour movement; and furthermore urged workers to form defence committees in their work places.

These declarations of workers' antagonism to, and loss of confidence in, the TUC leadership set in motion a process of turmoil and struggle within the trade union movement which induced the resignation of Issifu and his successor and some national union leaders. They culminated in the forcible overthrow of the TUC leadership.

By February, an Association of Local Unions (ALU) which was to spearhead the fight for trade union reforms, had been formed in Accra. ALU organised various actions, including kidnapping five national trade union leaders among whom was the acting Secretary-General. Following this incident the powerful Association of Financial Institutions (ASOFIN) — a section of the Industrial and Commercial Workers Union (ICU), called on all national union officers to go on leave to 'prevent violence, misinformation, confrontation with the law and wanton destruction'.

On April 29th, hundreds of workers stormed the TUC Hall, the ALU leadership announced the dismissal of the leadership of the TUC, the setting up of Interim Management Committees (IMCs) for both the Congress and the national unions, and pledged to initiate a full process of trade union reforms and democratisation. These struggles within the trades union movement weakened its already limited effectiveness in defending and advancing workers' interests in a period in which Workers' Defence Committees (WDCs) were emerging.

Following Flt Lt Rawlings' call on 5th January, Defence Committees began to spring up all over the country before full guidelines on their character and functions were issued and an official coordination structure set up. (District and Regional coordinating structures were also spontaneously created in district and regional capitals). The first reported WDC inauguration was at the Ghana Cargo Handling Company on 7th January with the Managing Director as the Chairman. Announcing the first set of guidelines in mid-January 1982, Chris Atim, then member of the PNDC, explained that the WDCs were to function parallel to and in cooperation with the unions and not to take over their functions. The existing industrial relations negotiating machinery was also to remain intact. Atim stated that the WDCs were not to undermine authority but at the same time should fight all instances of waste, corruption and malpractices and generate higher productivity.

A few days after the first guidelines were issued, a PNDC statement, which among other things warned management personnel not to be involved in WDCs and to desist from impeding their formation, explained that the 'committees are expected to defend the rights of ordinary people, expose and *deal* with corruption and other counter-revolutionary activities at their various workplaces and communities, to maintain collective national discipline and supervision over national resources and to afford everyone the opportunity to participate in the decision-making process in the country'. Thereafter, the guidelines were restated and elaborated in succeeding revisions and underlined in official speeches during the first two years of PNDC rule. Thus Flt Lt J.J. Rawlings[4] in November 1982 observed that:

> The people's defence committees are the democratic bedrock of the new people's power that the revolution is building ... The PDC's must see themselves as mass organs of the oppressed sections of society. Organs through which the oppressed must organize and educate themselves and mobilise the people to destroy oppressive power relations and institutions and undertake productive activity which transform their material lives.[4]

But the potential for WDC/Union conflict was not helped by the provision in a revised WDC guidelines of mid-1982 that 'WDC's would supervise the activities of local unions and other bodies that are supposed to work in the interest of workers and the nation, to ensure that the proper interests of the nation and the working people are catered for'. Speaking on May Day of that year the PNDC Chairman[5] summed up offical concern as follows:

> Whilst it is clear that workers have a legitimate basis for their anger at their union leaders, it is a dangerous and incorrect attitude to see the unionisation of workers as

> a problem. Unions have historically served specific and important functions and will continue to do so... The newly created workers' defence committees have not come to replace unions. Some union leaders have unfortunately adopted a hostile attitude to these committees. Such people fail to realise that a strong democratic union actively pursuing the interests of workers, will necessarily be a complement to a revolutionary defence committee.

The challenge from the WDCs to the traditional industrial relations role of the unions at enterprise level was matched outside the plant by the emergence of the co-ordinating structures of the WDCs. On 3rd February 1982 a 16 member Interim National Co-ordinating Committee of PDCs (INCC-PDCs), under the Chairmanship of Chris Atim, was set up by the PNDC to serve as the apex body of the co-ordinating structures, both mass-based and state-appointed which emerged in the early months of 1982. In July 1982 the INCC was replaced by the National Defence Committee (NDC).

The co-ordinating structures increasingly intruded into the roles hitherto served by the national unions and the Labour Department of the Ministry of Labour and Social Welfare. With the full support of the new regime, enjoying the undefined authority conferred on it, and employing non-bureaucratic and flexible processes the WDCs established a role for themselves in the area of industrial relations which hitherto the Labour Department, together with the national unions and the TUC, dealt with through mediation, conciliation and arbitration. The scale of this WDC intervention kept tempo with workers' confidence in the PNDC regime and the strength of the DC movement as a whole. In the major towns the traditional mobilising functions of the unions and the District Councils of Labour (DCLs) were eclipsed by the activism of the WDCs. The emergence of novel forms of workers' cooperation and action under the aegis of the defence committees made the difference between success or failure of some of the struggles discussed in this paper.

The principal immediate gain of the working people from the coming to power of the PNDC was the greater latitude, as symbolised by the WDCs, for organisation and struggle in defence or advancement of their interests, and in the majority of cases with government support.

Struggles of the First Phase

In 1982 and 1983, the decline in the national economy continued. The situation in the manufacturing sector worsened as the supply of raw materials and spares deteriorated further in those two years. In the textile industry for example only 10% of installed capacity was in use in 1982. The steady decline in the manufacturing labour force since 1977 also continued. From 88,947 workers in 1977 the figure fell to 77,600 in 1981, with a further 12,000 reduction in the labour force in 1982.

In that year, according to the records of the Labour Department, 37 establishments, including major manufacturing firms such as the Valco and a number of textile companies formally applied for permission to lay off over 4,500 workers. Informal investigations carried out in October/November 1982 suggested a larger figure of threatened lay-off in Tema alone. Accordingly, struggles against job losses became an important facet of working class activism in the manufacturing sector during 1982/83.

The PNDC responded to the threat to jobs by discouraging any rash reduction in the labour force of the private sector. During its first few months in office, the PNDC regime on its part announced its intention to reduce the huge public sector labour force through a redeployment of redundant workers into materially productive ventures rather than simply laying them off. It urged the private sector to emulate it. As this call run counter to the established practice in the country, the resort to mass political interventions proved important in holding back the desire of private employers to continue with the old policy of simply laying off workers. Thus in June 1982, protests by Tema workers forced the Volta Aluminium Company (Valco, a subsidiary of the American aluminium trans-national companies, Kaiser and Reynolds Metal) to shelve a plan to lay off a section of its work force.

In July 1982, the IMC of the TUC expressed concern about the threat of lay-offs and the determination of the labour movement to fight that threat. The workers action in the case of the Ghana Textiles Printing (GTP) Limited and Allied Foods Limited (AFL) convincingly demonstrates this determination.

THE GTP TAKE OVER

In February 1982 Ghana Textiles Printing (GTP) Limited at Tema, one of the biggest textile firms in the country, informed the Ministry of Labour and Social Welfare for the third time in a year of its dire economic situation and its plans to close down and lay off the work force.

At normal levels of production the firm employs around 1,200 workers. According to the management the company had subsisted on bank overdrafts since 1979 and had accumulated a debt of 31 million cedis. The Labour Ministry asked the firm to submit a redeployment plan. GTP proposed to redeploy about half its workforce into agriculture. Individual workers were to be granted loans for vegetable farming. The workers leadership informed the National Defence Committee (NDC) of the crisis at their plant, and management's proposals. A section of the affected workforce disagreed with their leaders' acceptance of the company's proposals arguing that any redeployment must seek to tackle the problems of raw material shortage facing the company. They argued that the company should capitalise a cotton farming venture into which the workers would be redeployed.

In the ensuing struggles within the ranks of the GTP workforce the leadership of the union and WDC were ousted and the proponents of redeployment into cotton farming took over. The latter had acquired legitimacy for their leadership through their opposition to the management's proposals.

Under the leadership of the Interim Co-ordinating Committee of Tema WDCs (ICC-WDCs), the GTP issue soon became the hub of the job-protection struggles of the Tema workers movement. The ICC-WDCs had also spearheaded earlier protests against VALCO's lay off plans and until its dissolution in June 1984 it was to stand out as the most militant and strategically most important central organisation of WDCs in the country. According to its own informal census in 1982, the ICC-WDCs was the umbrella organisation of WDCs in 127 establishments with an estimated total workforce of 41,000.

After several victorious struggles, the organisation became increasingly confident of its political clout, given the strategic importance of Tema in the national economy. The GTP-centred struggles against lay-offs was important in the organisational development of the ICC-WDCs and its emergence as a force in national politics.

The ICC-WDCs supported by the NDC, organised meetings of workers from all plants, especially those faced with lay-offs. The discussions at these meetings brought to the fore the wider political economic roots of the crisis facing the manufacturing sector and its consequences for manufacturing sector jobs. Redundancy came to be understood by the affected workers as involving more than a routine industrial relations issue to be considered within the formal terms of CBAs. The set pattern of union-employer — Labour Department negotiation of redundancies on plant by plant basis came under pressure from the political economic demands generated by this new awareness.

The pressure was reinforced by the inter-enterprise solidarity generated within the organisational framework provided by the ICC-WDCs which were by now linked with local unions. Isolated and spontaneous protests against lay-off were thenceforth replaced by a co-ordinated process. The militant section of the divided GTP workers, gained strength and support from this united front of the Tema workers. Therefore when the workers realised that management was uncompromising, and suspected that top officials of the Ministry of Labour were behind that tough posture of the GTP management they exercised this new political leverage to declare a takeover of the factory and the dismissal of the top management on 5th November, 1982.

In a statement explaining their action the workers accused the United Africa Company (UAC) — the management agent and biggest minority shareholder in the State-foreign private joint venture, of having deliberately discouraged the development of local cotton production as this would cut into UAC's earnings from cotton imports.[6] The statement demanded from government, among other things:

> (a) the abrogation of the agreements under which UAC became involved in GTP and also the agreement under which UAC run a cotton ginnery at Tumu.
> (b) the involvement of the textile industry in cotton production through either direct engagement in its production or support for small scale farmers.
> (c) the review of joint venture agreements with foreign firms especially in the textile industry; and
> (d) the formulation and implementation of a self reliant industrial policy based on an integrated relationship between agriculture and industry.

Though there had been instances of workers' self-help since the beginning of 1982, the GTP take-over raised major political economic issues. For example: to what extent would the regime support mass initiative and self-help, especially in a case which also raised issues about the PNDC government's attitude to foreign investment and the integrity of private property rights, etc.? The regime found itself trapped because any decision on the GTP takeover implied the definition of its attitude not only on the question of lay-offs but also on these other issues.

Between 5th November and the 16th November, when the GTP workers' statement was published in a national daily, *The Ghanaian Times*, there was no formal indication of an official policy except one from a PNDC member who was reported to have supported the workers' action.

Another state-owned paper the *Daily Graphic* later wrote an editorial supporting the broad principles raised by the struggles at GTP. It was however the mass action that forced the hand of the government. On 17th November, a massive solidarity march of Tema workers, led by the ICC-WDCs and the unions, was attacked outside GTP by armed police resulting in injuries to 23 marchers. The same day the PNDC announced support for the take-over, the deportation of an expatriate GTP manager, who allegedly incited the police, and condemned the police action with the promise of a probe into the day's incident. But to date, the government has not settled the issues raised by the workers take over despite persistent calls by the new GTP management; and so the company's Register still bears the GTP's old status.

In various statements of solidarity that followed the take-over less prominence was given to the jobs saved than the workers' victory over the oldest and most extensive foreign investor in the Ghanaian economy — the UAC. A powerful symbol of workers' power was thus created which gave impetus to a process of democratising power relations at the GTP and elsewhere. Within weeks of the GTP takeover, the workers of JTL also expelled UAC.

Furthermore, the Tema ICC-WDCs issued a circular calling a halt to all planned lay-offs. Managements complied. The ICC-WDCs had arrived as a political force. In the process it had succeeded in extending the frontiers of workers' action beyond the narrow limits of industrial relations actions.

THE OCCUPATION OF ALLIED FOODS LIMITED (AFL)

On 21st June, 1983, a section of several thousands strong workers, who were demonstrating in solidarity with the PNDC which had survived a serious coup attempt two days previously, occupied the premises of Allied Foods Limited (AFL) in Accra. The firm, formerly Cadbury (Ghana) Limited, is a subsidiary of Cadbury Schweppes, the food, confectionery and drinks transnational company.

The occupation which lasted six weeks dramatically transformed a month-long struggle between the firm's management and its workers, which had involved the Labour Ministry and the NDC over the company's attempt to lay off 165 out of the 212 workforce.

The AFL manufactures a range of cocoa based food drinks for which the principal raw material is cocoa powder. In January-February 1983, pleading raw material shortages, the management sent the workers on leave. The workers were later informed that the leave will be indefinite. The AFL management informed the Ministries of Labour, Finance and Economic Planning, Trade as well as Industries Science and Technology of the closure of the factory. The Labour Department, the Association of Ghana Industries (AGI), Ghana Employers' Association (GEA) and the TUC were also informed.

While on leave, the workers were individually contacted to consider applying for voluntary redundancy since the company's prospects of reopening its factory were poor for three reasons:

(a) low stocks of raw materials,
(b) lack of import licence, and
(c) the cancellation of an export order by Cadbury of Nigeria.

No worker applied. Then, in March the company served notice of its intention to declare 165 workers redundant, fixing 21st April as the day for the collection of entitlements by the affected workers. Early in April the union and WDC of AFL wrote to the management rejecting the lay-offs. It proposed that the workers be redeployed into farming in keeping with the PNDC's directive to employers. The AFL workers parent union, the Industrial and Commercial Workers Union (ICU), wrote to inform the management of its breach of the CBA provision requiring notification of redundancies to the union and requested a meeting of the Standing Joint Negotiating Committee (SJNC).The Greater Accra Regional Secretariat of the NDC, upon a report from the AFL WDC, asked the firm to suspend payment of terminal benefits while the NDC investigated the matter.

The AFL initially challenged the right of the NDC to dabble in industrial relations matters. It argued that the trade unions were the proper bodies to deal with the issue in question. But it subsequently attended a meeting convened by the NDC thus recognising the latter's role in labour matters. At a May meeting involving the AFL workers and management, the ICU, the Labour Ministry and the NDC and chaired by the PNDC Secretary for Labour and Social Welfare, AFL admitted not having followed the requirements of the CBA, and the government directive which required notification to the Labour Ministry before lay-offs were effected. It claimed to have followed GEA guidelines. It however pointed out that by early May, 15 out of 165 affected workers including 9 out of 10 executive members of the union had collected their entitlements. The workers' representatives on the other hand alleged that the management had forced workers to collect their entitlements by making it a condition for receiving their April pay. They also indicated a long history of management antipathy to the union and recently to the WDC.

On his part the PNDC Secretary made it clear that a) the Ministry of Labour and Social Welfare had had nothing to do with AFL's purported lay-offs; b) discussions between the Ministry and AFL management should have preceded the lay-offs; and therefore c) the AFL act was unilateral, improper and unlawful; and hence d) null and void. He however did not order the recall of the laid-off workers, but simply stated that the workers had a case against AFL and may explore all avenues open to them to regain their jobs.

The representatives of the ICU on the other hand demanded the immediate reinstatement of all the affected workers. The NDC representative supported the ICU's demand. He suggested in addition that if an immediate recall was not possible, AFL should redeploy the workers into agriculture as the workers themselves had suggested; or AFL should propose alternatives acceptable to the workers and all others concerned.[7] The meeting ended with an agreement for further meetings between the AFL management on one hand and the AFL union, WDC and the ICU on the other.

The management/union meetings that followed the May meeting had not made much progress prior to the occupation. Also the case of the AFL workers had received some publicity in the national mass media. In an editorial the *Ghanaian Times*, for example, expressed the view that:

> Where the logic of a given case proves the rightness of workers' objection to exploitation the workers will be supported at whatever cost even if this support means taking great risks of destroying to rebuild.

Soon before the occupation, the *People's Daily Graphic* had also started serialising an investigative article on the crisis at the AFL.

However, strong media sympathy together with support from the Ministry of Labour and Social Welfare and NDC for the AFL workers did not have a corresponding level of overt support from the mass of workers, especially in the Accra labour district. The ability of AFL militants to mobilise the mass support and solidarity of Accra workers was hampered by several factors.

The Accra WDC movement lacked a central co-ordinating organ with the coherence and mobilising capacity of the Tema ICC-WDCs. Especially, there was the problem of greater intra-class diversity of the Accra working class and its geographical spread: the industrial working class was concentrated in four different parts of the city; and it included a sizeable segment of commercial and clerical workers. These represented an objective difficulty. Efforts by the NDC in 1982 to create a co-ordinating framework for Accra WDCs, which had shown some promise, came to grief in the turbulent struggles within the PNDC regime during the period of October-November. A meeting of one of two zonal co-ordinating committees was the site of a false announcement on October 29th that a PNDC member, Sgt. Alolga Akatapore had displaced Flight Lt J.J. Rawlings as Chairman of the PNDC.

The fall out from the problems of the period included the dissolution of the zonal co-ordinating committees of the WDCs and the detention of some of its leaders. Subsequent efforts to reconstitute an all-Accra co-ordinating committee were not very successful. The other problem was the location of the AFL factory, situated on Accra's principal financial street, High Street. AFL is quite outside the geographical areas covered by the area co-ordinating committees of industrial WDCs that were functioning. These were based mainly in the Accra North and West industrial areas. Even though the workers in these areas strongly sympathised with the AFL workers, mass action of the GTP type posed more complex tactical and organisational problems. Hence the mass turn out and 'freedom of the streets' action that was afforded by the pro-government demonstration of June 21st 1983 resolved many of these problems at one sweep.

In a statement issued at the inception of the occupation to oppose the lay-offs the workers also made the following demands:

(a) the government should take over 55% of AFL's shares, pointing out that since 1981 the owners of the firm have had plans to divest themselves of some shares;
(b) the dismissal of the top management of AFL;
(c) a national policy on redundancy;
(d) a probe into AFL's use of import licences; and
(e) the provision by AFL of offices for the union and WDCs.

The occupation and the workers demands again presented the PNDC regime with a delicate political problem. Mid-1983 was the low point of the regime's battle to stay on top of a number of potentially destabilising developments. The nation was in the throes of an unprecedented food shortage; and the hardships of the situation had been worsened by the very austere budget the government had announced in April. The support of the workers' movement had been an important factor in ensuring the regime's survival through the various political challenges it faced during the period.

On the other hand the regime, following the budget, hoped to mobilise credit from Western sources such as the IMF and the World Bank to support its economic reform programme. The AFL occupation had the potential of sending out the wrong signals about the government's attitude towards private capital.

After a series of behind-the-scenes contacts with Cadbury-Schweppes International and the AFL workers, the PNDC Secretary for Labour and Social Welfare announced the government's stance on the principal issues at stake on 16th July; namely retrenchments in general. All redundancies in industry which had been undertaken without prior consultation with the Labour Ministry were declared null and void. (By implication this included the AFL action.) The statement expressed the PNDC's concern about indiscriminate and unfair lay-offs and also the disregard for the government's directive which required Ministry of Labour approval for all lay-offs.

The statement further noted that these practices by employers were causing increased hardship for workers, sowing seeds of dissatisfaction with the government, and thereby contributing to the destabilisation of the 31st December process. A plan for government and employers to share the burden of redeployment, where there were legitimate grounds for retrenchment, was also said to be in preparation.

On AFL specifically, the statement described the occupation as a lock out of management, and therefore an issue to be resolved through the normal industrial relations process between the parties. Government-supervised negotiations were to take place and 2.8 million cedis worth of foreign exchange was to be made available to the AFL for the purchase of raw materials to lay a basis for future resumption of work. For the Labour Ministry, the statement concluded, the AFL incident:

> illustrated the dangers of conflict and confrontation that exist where workers are denied the right information about the state and operations of their factories and establishment. It is to prevent this kind of situation that the Ministry is calling for direct involvement of workers in all policy decisions and fundamental restructuring of production relations in industry, the object being to create a peaceful and healthy industrial atmosphere for increased productivity.

The AFL's initial reaction to the statement was to reject the idea of government supervised negotiations. It preferred to continue discussions with the unions. It however made some concrete proposals:

> (a) the AFL workers were to be redeployed into agriculture by the government with AFL paying their wages less what had been collected as redundancy pay;
> (b) those not affected would be taken back immmediately; and the redeployed hands would be taken back in batches as the firm's production position improved. In addition the company indicated its willingness to negotiate around these points.

On 26th July 1983 negotiations between AFL and the ICU re-opened in the presence of a government appointee who was also a member of the NDC. AFL documents found during the occupation were tendered by the workers.[8] These revealed that:

(a) the real reason for the lay-offs was a decision to restructure production rather than the alleged shortage of raw materials and resultant financial problems;
(b) there was a management policy to hamper the operations of the workers' organisations, especially the WDC, at the AFL;
(c) management had sought, on the basis of misrepresentations, to use armed institutions of the state and civil servants to harass worker's leaders and deny their demands; and
(d) there was a possibility that the AFL had engaged in foreign exchange and tax malpractices.

At the end of August 1983, on the basis of the report of its appointee at the negotiations, the Ministry of Labour and Social Welfare announced that — a) all laid off AFL workers were to be recalled, b) the redundancy payments to them were to be offset against their April-August pay with the remainder being offset against entitlements accruing to employees in the event of legitimate severance. A ten-day period was specified within which employees were to report at the plant. The issue of possible irregularities by the AFL on foreign exchange and fiscal matters were to be referred to the Attorney-General's Department. AFL accepted the Ministry's decision and all the laid off workers were invited to return.

Demobilising the Mass Movement

The AFL occupation occurred in an unstable political and economic situation marked by sharp class struggles. From late 1982 to mid-1983 the PNDC faced the most concerted efforts to overthrow it. It for example, survived five planned or attempted coups d'etat. In April 1983, the PNDC announced a very austere budget at a time when the inherited economic crisis had been worsened by unforseen, man-made and natural factors and most of the population were suffering serious material hardships.

The main elements of the budget, the regime's first definitive statement of its economic policy, improved the possibility of Ghana's access to financial and other resources from the OECD countries, IMF and World Bank. These countries and institutions pressed the PNDC to create a political atmosphere 'conducive' to a proper utilisation of such external resources once they started flowing. The creation of those conditions meant curbing the militant, anti-imperialist and democratic mass movement whose representatives within the regime had been weakened by the October-November 1982 political crisis. As the PNDC implemented the budget and related political measures it gradually exposed its essentially petty-bourgeois class character and orientation, and it increasingly opted for the path of compromise with imperialism especially in the area of economic policy. At the political level it committed itself to a policy of reconciliation with the internal exploiting classes.

Days before the Labour Ministry ordered the recall of the AFL workers, the Chairman of the PNDC made a seminal live broadcast, which, in the official volume of his speeches, is entitled 'Discipline and Productivity'. The speech addressed the issue of reversing the economic crisis which in his view entailed increasing productivity, hard work and descipline. That speech raised the pertinent and urgent political issue of who bears the brunt of the sacrifices required to revive the economy and who would be the primary beneficiary of the wealth to be created — the working people or the parasitic and propertied classes? This was not addressed. On the contrary, the basic political slant of that speech was an attack on the popular forces and their struggles. The PNDC Chairman criticised the 'militant minority' who, he alleged, pushed the process too fast and took actions without understanding the consequences; who saw the NDC as a parallel structure of government, etc., and warned that the regime would not countenance 'even for a brief moment, a situation where petty power brokers exercise authority without responsibility'. The government was not going to defend criminals and economic saboteurs under the 'power to the people' slogan. 'We are here to defend people who are strict, disciplined, intelligent and efficient whether we like them or not, whether we have common political views or not, we are not going to call men and women of this country reactionary simply because we cannot meet their mental and physical level of discipline'. Consistent with the emerging anti-popular line of the regime, the speech announced a policy of reconciliation towards the class enemies of the masses. Two days after the speech the PNDC Chairman personally led a squad of soldiers to arrest WDC activists whose wrong doings he claimed were being covered by their colleagues.

In retrospect, the PNDC Chairman's 'Discipline and Productivity' speech was effectively a trumpet call to the anti-popular and anti-democratic forces in Ghanaian society. In the following months as more and more representatives of these forces were appointed to high office and their influence in government grew, the popular forces —

especially the working class, became increasingly alienated from the PNDC regime and opposed to many of its key policies.

In December 1984, the PNDC announced a number of far reaching measures, including the dissolution of the defence committees and their replacement with an emasculated organ — the Committees for the Defence of the Revolution (CDRs).

In the course of these developments the TUC sent a strongly worded memorandum to the PNDC in February 1985, asking 'what had happened to the noble objectives of the December 31st Revolution'. The memorandum expressed concern about 'the present direction of national policy' especially 'threats of mass retrenchment of workers, cutbacks in subsidies resulting in increasing cost of social services and basic commodities, the non-recognition of the crucial role of the masses in revolutionary social transformation and therefore the absence of any proper and consistent channels of participation in decision making by the mass of the people through their organisations.'

It also noted the 'growing trend towards arbitrariness and lack of respect for trade union rights'. The epic four-month battle which erupted in April 1984 around the Pioneer Food Company (PFC) in Tema graphically illustrates the growing divergence between the working class and the PNDC and also the anti-popular tendencies of the regime. The PFC struggle also shows the evolving changes in the correlation of class forces, which underlay this and their reflection in struggles around seemingly industrial relation matters which 'spilled' beyond the bounds of employer-employee relations and assumed a distinctly political character.

PFC — WINNING THE BATTLE; LOSING THE WAR

Pioneer Food Cannery (PFC), a private foreign/Ghanaian joint venture processes and cans tuna fish mainly for export. It started operations in 1976. In 1984, it had a total workforce of 373, the majority of whom were women. On 18th April 1984 the management refused to allow the workers into the company's premises, and announced the dismissal of 259 of them. The management accused the workers of slowing down and stopping work on 17th April; of abandoning work before the end of the working day; and sabotaging the efforts of the company to save unprocessed fish from going bad. These acts, according to the management, amounted to an illegal and unwaranted strike contrary to the IRA of 1965.

The workers challenged this version of the events of that day and the management's act. They condemned the act as an illegal dismissal and lockout. For them that was the high point of the illegal, authoritarian, arbitrary and oppressive regime at the PFC. The workers argued that up till the 17th April incident there was no CBA governing industrial relations at the factory. The Company had separate contracts with each individual worker, although the Maritime and Dockworkers Union (MDU) had been granted a bargaining certificate for PFC in 1980.

The workers claimed that efforts at forming, and having the firm recognise, a union had been frustrated by management's intimidation of the workforce and victimisation of those who led those efforts. In September 1980, for example, the PFC workers informed the Chief Labour Officer that a lay-off, affecting 67 workers which the management claimed was due to a shortage of fish and foreign exchange problems, was in fact directed at destroying the emergent union. Five union officials were among the sixty seven, many of whom had been active in the struggle for the recognition of their union. (PFC had not got prior ministerial approval for the lay-offs.) Furthermore, union leaders had been put on what management considered the most difficult tasks in the factory. It was only in 1982 that the management of PFC recognised the union.

In the struggles that followed the events of 17th April, the workers publicised the poor working conditions and violation of labour laws and trade union rights at PFC. Notable among the charges they made against the PFC management are the following:

(a) compulsory overtime: the management's insistence that 'the working day is deemed completed only when the last of fish is canned' resulted in the workers labouring for almost 12 hours daily;
(b) the absence, and poor quality, of protective gear: workers used bare hands to work on frozen fish;
(c) women who go on 'maternity leave' without pay had to re-apply for their jobs. Many were not taken back;
(d) no worker was allowed to go to see the doctor on Mondays and Tuesdays no matter his/her condition;
(e) back pay due since 1980 was still outstanding.

The workers claimed that on 17th April whilst negotiations on their conditions of service were going on between officials of the MDU and PFC, a Director of the firm, Robert Ocran, walked in and insulted the MDU team. He then proceeded to the shop floor, just after the end of the normal working day, that is, 5.00p.m. and showered the workforce with insults and threats. The workers then walked out *en masse*, refusing to do overtime.

Management denied any such act by Ocran and disputed the workers right to walk off after 5.00p.m. They claimed that the act was premeditated as evidenced by threatening statements posted around the factory by the workers on the day. Until the dramatic end of the dispute in mid-July the positions of the two parties remained essentially unchanged with the workers insisting that all the 259 workers be reinstated; while the management claimed that the only issue was the settlement of severance payments.

Negotiations between the MDU and PFC management which also involved the Labour Department, the Secretary for Labour, the TUC, the NDC, the Acting Secretary to the NDC and the Tema ICC-WDCs, failed to break the deadlock. The parties traded positions in the mass media, which increasingly sided with the company. The *People's Daily Graphic* was particularly aggressive in attacking the workers and favourably presenting the management's side of the case.

As the negotiations were proceeding a process of mass mobilisation was initiated by the ICC-WDCs. On 27th April a mass demonstration of Tema workers delivered an ICC-WDCs ultimatum to the PFC management in which they called for the workers to be unconditionally recalled. Despite the resistance of the PFC management and the exasperated appeals from the Labour Department that the NDC should keep itself and the WDCs out of the dispute here again the ICC-WDCs became an accepted part of the negotiation.

Meanwhile propaganda and agitation by the workers' movement under the slogan 'Touch One Touch All' had drawn nation wide attention to the PFC struggle. By June their struggle was no longer an isolated Tema affair. A solidarity committee comprising the MDU, TUC, ICC-WDCs, Tema District Council of Labour (TDCL) and the Tema Interim Co-ordinating Committee of PDCs (ICC-PDCs) was formed. Messages of solidarity with the PFC workers were issued from the key areas of workers concentration — Accra, Sekondi-Takoradi, Ho, Tarkwa, by individual organisations such as the TUC, the New Democratic Movement (NDM), and the workers of Cargo Handling Company. All of them uniformly demanded the unconditional reinstatement of the PFC 259. In its solidarity statement, the Accra District Council of Labour (ADCL) said 'the PFC issue is now no longer an issue for only PFC workers or Tema workers, but a matter of concern to the whole working class of this country'. It declared the workers' readiness 'to use every possible means to ensure a speedy resolution of this matter'. Tens of thousand of cedis were paid into the PFC Solidarity Fund.

On 21st June, a mammoth rally of workers held in Tema, resolved that:

(a) the illegally locked out and dismissed 259 workers of PFC be immediately and unconditionally reinstated;

(b) steps be taken immediately after reinstatement to ensure that PFC workers labour under a legitimate CBA;

(c) the Ministry of Labour and Social Welfare, the NDC and the PNDC should ensure that the management of PFC respect international labour conventions and the labour laws of our homeland

(d) *The united working class of Accra and Tema shall impose sanctions on PFC and the Mankoadze Group of Companies if the PFC management should prove difficult in the matter of unconditional reinstatement of the 259 workers*. (emphasis added).

The resolution ended by calling on all workers, 'labouring under oppressive and backward conditions' to demand and fight for their legitimate and democratic rights as workers. These intense militant actions created considerable panic in high political circles; and in a comment made by the *Graphic* on the rally which it described as 'peacefully and maturely done', the paper expressed fear about the widening ripples of the dispute and pleaded that the responsible agencies intervene to stop the spread of the economic damage that was threatened.

The day after the solidarity rally, the PNDC dissolved the ICC-WDCs with the injunction that no organ with similar functions was to be constituted in its place until elections were held for that purpose. The PNDC statement made the unsubstantiated charge that the leadership of ICC-WDCs was terrorizing residents of Tema, causing dissatisfaction with the 'Revolution', and using the 21st June rally to hurl insults at responsible government officials and innocent citizens. The statement indirectly accused the ICC-WDC leadership of being 'demagogues' manipulated by 'imperialist agents' who sought to use the genuine feelings of workers in Tema for their selfish political ambitions.

In a press release the leadership of the dissolved ICC-WDCs described the contents of the PNDC statement as 'unfortunate and shocking'. They refuted the PNDC's charge, reciting the ICC-WDCs long record of struggle and activism in defence of workers and the national interest and also in support of the PNDC. They reiterated the justness of the fight for the reinstatement of the 259 workers and their determination to keep on fighting.

The dissolution of the ICC-WDC signalled the PNDC's sympathy for the PFC management and also the regime's fear of the growing independent strength of the Tema workers' movement. This did not however stop the battle for the PFC 259. In the backlash from the dissolution of the ICC-WDCs the Tema DCL gave notice of sanctions to be applied as already forewarned. On 11th July, the Ministry of Labour, declared the dismissals null and void on the ground that the Ministry's permission, which was required to lay-off more than five employees, had neither been sought or given. The statement said the parties were willing to negotiate.

This clearly was an attempt to defuse the growing confrontations. But it failed; and instead the state now rattled its sabre on behalf of capital. On 14th July it was reported that soldiers led by the Deputy Chief Operations Officer at the PNDC Headquarters had threatened the workers of the national oil refinery (GHAIP) for refusing to supply petroleum, and ordering that no supplies of petroleum products should go to the Mankoadze Group of Companies — Mankoadze being the umbrella for enterprises owned by PFC director, Robert Ocran.

Thereafter the conflict that showed all signs of escalating ended dramatically. The Chairman of the PNDC ordered the recall of the 259 workers. According to the news reports he had personally intervened and held meetings with the PFC Managing Director and Robert Ocran, following an appeal from the Secretary-General of the TUC. But the Chairman's intervention was objectively on the side of capital. On the one hand, as the news papers reported, the Chairman concluded after a briefing from the PFC bosses, that 'there was no way the *striking* (sic) workers would win in any legal resolution of the issues involved'.

On the other hand, workers did not have the privilege of an audience with the PNDC Chairman in his mediation effort. At any rate, the Chairman took the view that the sanctions against the Mankoadze Group were illegal since it was a separate legal entity from PFC and ordered that they be lifted.

The central aim of the PFC struggle, which was the reinstatement of the illegally sacked workers, was thus attained, but at a very high price. The process of achieving it had thrown up wider political issues. These included the balance of power between capital and labour; a severe test of and a further clarification of the class position of the PNDC regime; and the extent of the State's tolerance of an independent and combative worker's movement.

The workers movement emerged overall losers once these issues are considered alongside the original goal of reinstatment of the PFC 259. The PNDC's decision to concede on the issue of reinstating the 259 workers was tactical. Politically the dissolution of the ICC-WDCs was a major blow to the workers movement and its further growth but a boost for anti-working class forces. The process of demobilising the insurgent workers' movement was given a major boost by this event; and the months following it saw a growing assault by the

PNDC leadership on the NDC and its nationwide network of orgnisations. In separate incidents the staff of the NDC's regional secretariats in the Eastern, Central and Greater Accra Regions were brutally assaulted by troops from the PNDC headquarters and detained for varying periods without charge.

The attacks on the defence committee movement culminated in the PNDC's dissolution of the NDC and the Defence Committees in December 1984. They were replaced with Committees for the Defence of the Revolution (CDRs) which, unlike the DCs, are subject to the authority of management in the workplace and above all to the direct supervision and control by leading state organs. In the Armed Forces for example, the unit commanding officer is now the automatic chairman of the CDR.

From then on the neo-colonialist and anti-working class policies of the regime became more blatant; and were accompanied by a more overt use of state power in its various manifestations in support of capital against labour. The disregard for established trade union rights that the TUC had complained about in its 1985 memo to the PNDC became more widespread; and workers demand and struggles that received unqualified government support in 1982/83 now met with State repression. The case of Assene Household Enamelware Limited (hereafter referred to as Assene) illustrates these developments.

1985-86: CONSOLIDATING NEO-COLONIAL LABOUR RELATIONS

THE ASSENE CASE

On 3rd and 7th October 1986 a contingent of policemen, one hundred according to Assene's Executive Director, backed by two armoured cars (equipment that can be moved only on orders from the highest levels of the State) led by the Deputy Commissioner of Police in Charge of Operations, entered the premises of Assene. On the first occasion, they came in to arrest five out of six workers' leaders. On the second occasion, it was to arrest the remaining one.

After the first police invasion the company declared that it had dismissed 71 of the workforce who had been involved in a dispute with the company over the provision of protective clothing. The dispute was, at the time, the subject of negotiations between the ICU local union and the management. The CDR National Secretariat was involved. After being detained for a week the workers' union/CDR leaders were put before a circuit court on criminal charges of assault and threat of harm against the management.

Assene, owned by a Hong Kong Chinese, produces household

enamelware and employs around 220 workers. It has been operating since 1978. Its industrial processes generate heat, involve the use of acids and power presses, and produce lots of metal shards. From October 1978 the Factory Inspectorate Division of the Ministry of Labour and Social Welfare constantly sought to ensure that minimum safety standards, as demanded by the Factories, Offices and Shops Act, 1970 (Act 328) were observed at the factory. Until late 1986 the management, on their own admission, neither acknowledged receipt nor complied with most of the terms of any of the Inspectorate's directives. The Division's investigations showed that:

> (a) some of the workers were exposed to excessive heat;
> (b) lacked the requisite protective gear for their specific work; and
> (c) dangerous machines were not adequately guarded. In one of its many letters to the company the Chief Inspector noted that:
> (i) The tools of power presses are recognised as being among the most dangerous parts of machinery and knowledge of sheet metal industry should point to the fact that a high proportion of power press accidents in these industries result in permanent injury and severe mutilation. This is evidenced by the accidents in your factory most of which are caused by power presses ... and which result in permanent injuries, crushed fingers, amputation of hands, fingers, multiple injuries, etc to your imployees

The Inspectorate's letter asked for proper protective guards to be put on presses and lamented Assene's failure to report industrial accidents in accordance with the laws of the land. Another of his letters expressed the expectation of the firm's fullest co-operation in the effort to secure the health and safety of the workers 'which are considered essential for productivity and harmonious industrial relations at work places'.

And indeed the company had a high accident rate. Between 1978 and 1986 twenty-one workers suffered injuries in the machine section where the power presses are used; 1 lost an arm and 8 lost fingers. Out of the 21 only 4 were paid any compensation.

The dispute leading to the police invasion of Assene, the arrest of the workers leaders and so on was related to the supply of protective footwear to the workers. In 1984, the firm agreed with the Union to supply shoes twice a year. In July 1986, the management decided to supply only one out of six departments in the plant. The intervention of the union resulted in the number of benefiting departments being raised to four. The two departments that were not supplied refused to work outside their departments because the production process litters the ground with shards of metal which is dangerous to unprotected feet.

The management summarily dismissed the protesting workers. On 24th September the rest of the workforce refused to work in solidarity with their sacked colleagues. Management then agreed to supply the protective equipment. Another dispute errupted when the workers were marked as having worked half-day on the day of the protest although the work stoppage lasted less than two hours. Three days after this dispute which was taken up by ICU, two PNDC officials, visited the factory. One of them, in an address to the workforce is reported to have denounced them as economic saboteurs and threatened to lock them up. This was the immediate background to the display of the military might of the state — the kind of which had not been seen since the days of the National Liberation Council (NLC) and Progress Party regimes (1966-71).

The dispute over the dismissals was the subject of arbitration under the IRA of 1965 with the ICU claiming that the dismisals amounted to an illegal lockout contrary to the IRA. The arbitrator dismissed this claim. The ICU's appeal against this decision was pending at the time of writing.

Apart from an unfavourable arbtrator's decision and criminal prosecution of the workers' leaders there has been even more naked state support for the Assene management. On 15th July 1987 Geofrey Kumfu, a dismissed CDR secretary, and one of the leaders facing criminal charges, was arrested by state security police. An Executive Instrument signed by the PNDC chairman under the regime's Preventive Detention Law legalised his arrest and detention 'in the interest of national security'.

Two issues arise from this Assene case. First, the struggles of the Assene workers evoked no visible working class solidarity and virtually no open statements of criticism of the PNDC's anti-labour role in the dispute. The NDM issued a statement of solidarity with the workers in the early period of their struggle but the ICU was the only significant organisation which actively fought alongside the workers with the support of the Ghana Association of Democratic Lawyers (GADL) which provided free legal services.

Second it marked the full exposure of the petty bourgeois nature of the regime. Suppression of the Assene workers struggle confirms the inherent inclination of the post-colonial state to protect foreign capital. Above all, it shows the determination of the state to fully subordinate workers interest to capital in general and achieve this by any means. Accordingly, by the end of the Assene dispute there was little doubt among the mass of the working class about the petty bourgeois character of the regime. For, alongside the growing conspicuous consumption of the exploiting classes, workers faced severe economic hardship as the regime's policies threatened jobs and held down incomes relative to the escalating cost of living. The re-establishment of managerial autocracy has also been fully endorsed by the regime.

CONCLUSION

This chapter has sought, on the bases of specific instances of working class struggles, to demonstrate the unity of working class industrial relations concerns and political struggles. It has stressed that this unity is highlighted during moments of intense class struggles such as those which occurred between 1982 and 1986. The chapter has also tried to expose the changing character of the relationship between the working class and the state under the government of the PNDC, and has emphasised the determinate role of capital in shifting the balance against the working class.

Legitimate objections could be raised about the wide ranging deductions which have been made from the material presented here. But it is important to note that while the material is limited in one sense — it deals specifically with four cases in the struggles of the working class — it also covers a broad spectrum of issues which are of concern to the overall struggles of the country's working class which impinge on the crucial question of the nature of the relationships between them and the state. Above all, it examines at the micro-level the political experiences that are often not captured in their fullest detail by macro-type analysis that is pitched at a higher level of abstraction. From the persective adopted here it becomes possible to view the specific cases of struggle and their outcome as the microcosm of the larger political processes which have taken place so far.

For the moment, it is correct to conclude that the regime's untrammeled support for capital has firmly restored the hegemony of capital and rescued it from the battering of labour. However, this success has had another effect which is worthy of notice. Following the destruction of the defence committees, the trades union movement has regained the role it briefly lost to the former as the sole organisational vehicle of working class struggles. The process was helped by the fact that the disappearance of the defence committees gave a fresh importance to collective agreements and the IRA of 1965.

Furthermore, although the ALU reform movement had failed to

achieve all its objectives it had produced a crop of new union leaders alongside the old guard and shaken the established traditions of opportunism and bureaucratism that characterized the old style of trade union leadership. Thus currently the PNDC regime feels threatened by the very force which had been so critical to its survival during the crucial years of 1982-83. This accounts for the tendency towards frenzy and hysteria in its handling of workers opposition to its policies, especially since 1985: it is determined to break the back of the working class militancy. It is this which lay at the bottom of the unnecessary display of state power during the Assene workers struggles. Given the issues at stake the PNDC could not wait for the cumbersome processes of the IRA of 1965 to take their normal course. The genie which found form in the struggles at the GTP, AFL, and PFC had to be re-bottled so that the social conditions conductive for capitalist accumulation would prevail. But then the experiences and achievements of working class militancy of the period 1982-84 and the accompanying growth in working class confidence and consciousness cannot be wiped out that easily by administrative decrees or through state-sponsored violence.

NOTES

1. Woddis, Jack. *New Theories of Revolution*. (London Lawrence and Wishert, 1972) p. 121.
2. Kraus, Jon. *Strikes and Labour Power in Post Colonial African States. The case of Ghana*. Paper presented at the seminar on 3rd World Strikes. The Hague, 1977. p. 22.
3. For example, Kraus, Ibid. Sawyerr, Akilagpa. 'Thirty years of Industrial Relations Legislation in Ghana, 1941 — 1971.' Verfassuing U. Recht in Urversee, 1978. p. 331 — 45; and Crisp. J. *The story of an African Working Class*. (London: Zed Publications, 1984).
4. *A Revolutionary Journey* — Selected Speeches of Flight Lt. J.J. Rawlings December 31 1981 — December 31 1982. (Accra Ministry of Information) p. 74.
5. Ibid p.26
6. For Juapong Textiles Limited (JTL) the UAC was also the management agent even though it was here again the minority shareholder. It was the JTL which supplied the GTP with greybaft for printing.
7. Throughout the various stages of the negotiations the AFL management insisted that their company was a manufacturing and not an agricultural enterprise.
8. The possibility of bringing international pressure to bear on the PNDC, in the event of any development around the AFL issue which they considered negative, was a contigency the AFL management had worked out. This was revealed from those internal documents seized and published by the workers group that had occupied the factory.

REFERENCES

1. U.G. Damachi: H.D. Seibell & L. Trachtman — *Industrial* Relations in Africa. (New York: St Martin's Press; 1979)
2. J. Crisp — *The story of an African Working Class*. (London: Zed Press London 1984.)
3. A. Sawyerr — '*Thirty Years of Industrial Relations, Legislation in Ghana, 1941-1971*;' Verfassung V. Recht in Ubersee 1978, p. 331-45.
4. Jon Kraus — '*Strikes and Labour Power in a Post-Colonial African State: The case of Ghana*;' Paper presented to seminar on 3rd World Strikes; the Hague; 1977.
5. Yao Graham — '*The Politics of Crisis in Ghana*,' ROAPE No. 34 December 1985.
6. *Selected Speeches of Flight Lt J.J. Rawlings* Vols 1, 2, 7, 3, (1983, 1984, 1985) (Accra: Ministry of Information)
7. World Bank Reports:- *Ghana — The Policies and Programs for Adjustment* 1984 *Ghana — INDUSTRIAL POLICY PERFORMANCE* & RECOVERY 1985.
8. Central Bureau of Statistics — Ghana: Economic Survey 1977-79 (Accra: Central Bureau of Statistics 1980)
9. J. Woddis — *New Theories of Revolution* (London: Lawrence & Wishart; 1972.)
10. Various Records of the Labour Department — Accra.

3. WOMEN'S POLITICAL ORGANISATIONS 1951-1987

Edzodzinam Tsikata

INTRODUCTION

The six years of Provisional National Defence Council (PNDC) rule, following the overthrow of the 3rd Republic on 31st December 1981, have seen great activity around women's issues. This is comparable perhaps only to what occurred during the period of the Convention Peoples Party (CPP).

In the first half of 1982, two women's political organizations — The Federation of Ghanaian Women (FEGAWO) and the 31st December Women's Movement were inaugurated. A third organisation, the All Women's Association of Ghana (AWAG) was formed later, in 1984. By 1987, only the 31st December Women's Movement operated in any significant way. The AWAG had been virtually reduced to its market women's component, and the FEGAWO had stopped functioning altogether.

These developments — the formation and decline of two women's political organizations, and the survival and spread of a third, occurred in a wider context which brought the question of organization of the underprivileged in Ghanaian society to the fore. Different factors were important in shaping the situation of women's organizations in this six year period. These include the atmosphere generated, in the aftermath of the coup d'état, by the promises of the coup leaders; the responses of the new regime's early support base — the working class and other disadvantaged sections of the population; the changes that the political climate underwent; the strength of independent political organizations; and the character of the organizations under discussion.

What emerges from the discussion is that women's organizations in this period, in spite of their aims and objectives, were not able to tackle the important problems of women in the country. The reasons for this failure include the unfavourable political climate for independent struggles; the political character and practice of the organizations in question; and weaknesses arising from the lack of a tradition of independent political organization in the country. It is concluded, therefore, that women's political organizations would be stronger, more effective and relevant through the development of a different political culture — a culture of independence and the pursuit of objectives determined primarily by the conditions of women.

The paper does not cover all the relevant issues raised by a discussion of the organization of women. It does not discuss the Trades Union Congress, the Ghana National Association of Teachers, the Registered Nurses Association — labour organizations whose membership includes women, the increasing number of Ladies Association in workplaces, the organizations of wives of personnel of the Armed Forces and Police, the various Professional Women's Associations, women's self help associations and religious based women's associations. All these organizations are concerned with some specific issues in the life of Ghanaian women which are narrower than the more general women's liberation goals of political women's organizations.

THE GENERAL CONDITION OF WOMEN IN THE POST-COLONIAL PERIOD

Ghana's post-colonial economy is a typical neo-colonial one which shares the characteristics of the economies of most ex-colonies. They have been summed up thus:

> a backward and exploited agrarian sector dominated by a single export raw material crop — cocoa — the fortunes of which exert a decisive influence on the Ghanaian economy and politics, an industrial sector heavily dependent on imported raw materials and technology and therefore weakly linked with local primary production, and dominated by imperialism through a variety of mechanisms, a decisive presence of foreign capital, especially monopoly capital in key areas of economic activity such as banking, mining, timber production, manufacturing and large-scale commerce, a disproportionately large commercial and service sector with hundreds of thousands of unstable, insecure petty traders and commodity producers.[1]

It therefore suffers from the attendant problems of the neo-colonial situation — wretched and deteriorating living standards for the majority of the population, who are unable to afford social amenities like health, housing and education. These problems are exacerbated in the rural areas where over eight million of the twelve million population live, and in many areas considered urban where the poorer segments of urban workers live. In these rural and urban areas, the gross inadequacy of public utilities like electricity, piped water, and the underdevelopment of basic infrastructure such as schools, roads and health facilities is well known.[2]

The labour force of about 5.4 million has about 2.8 million women, over 50% of whom are in agriculture.[3] The majority of women in this sector are self-employed, aided by unpaid family labour in some cases. Only a few of them are employers or employees of any kind.[4] They are usually involved in foodstuff and vegetable production for subsistence. Problems such as access to, and the high cost of land, credit and technology result in low levels of productivity. In addition to these, the involvement of a large number of male farmers in cash crop production leaves virtually the whole burden of food production for subsistence in the hands of women. This additional burden of unpaid work seriously undermines their capacity for economic independence.[5]

Women outside the agricultural sector who are engaged or employed in the manufacturing and service industries, such as trading, nursing, teaching, secretarial and clerical duties, also face serious problems. The majority of them are not unionised or otherwise organised. Therefore, the protection provided by the labour laws of Ghana such as the right to unionise, compensation in the event of accidents, social security and pension on retirement, the eight-hour working day, allowances for overtime, risk, health care and transport, maternity leave on basic pay etc, are denied to many of them.

The denial of basic labour rights are most widespread in enterprises where labour relations are affected by feudal and patriarchal ideology, and where employment is strongly influenced by family and ethnic affinity with the proprietor or management. Such enterprises — usually privately owned, are mainly involved in small-scale industrial production or in the provision of services.[6]

The unionised and otherwise organised minority of women[7] found mostly in the manufacturing industries, the nursing, teaching, and secretarial professions face problems like job segregation. The majority of them are engaged in the marginal aspects of production and support services — for example canteen and secretarial work, where they are employed on lower level jobs with correspondingly lower renumeration, and so do not enjoy protection against discriminatory regulations. These problems are reinforced by the lower levels of education among women particularly in the labour force. More than 50% of the labour force is illiterate; and 60% of them are women.[8] The gap in the level of education between the sexes sharpens at higher educational levels where females form about 14% of the university-educated component of the labour force.[9]

The weak, and often inferior, position which the majority of women occupy in the labour force is an aspect of their position in the wider society where women are dominated. Two factors are important in the domination of women — the sexual division of labour, and ownership of the means of production by males. The practices associated with the institution of marriage, as various studies have shown, is a useful illustration.

The payment of the bride price acquires for a man the unpaid labour of his wife and that of any children they might have in return for maintenance. Women's labour consists of reproduction, household chores and the production of goods and services. They do not own the means of production in most cases and males inherit such property, even in matrilineal societies. It has also been shown how socialisation processes, and practices like polygamy, levirate, widow inheritance, child marriage and various taboos support the inferior status of women.[10]

Outside the sphere of marriage, the exercise of political power is dominated by males — from the realm of traditional rule to that of central government. Queenmothers and old women who have retired from their 'feminine' roles, and the few women who get into government, although involved in the direct exercise of political power, do not make much impact on the male-dominated character of government. All these are a reflection of the patriarchal ideas, values and norms which pervade the dominant neo-colonial capitalist relations and the remnants of the pre-capitalist relations operating in the country. They are manifested in the existence and application of two complex systems of law: customary law on the one hand, and inherited common law as well as post-colonial legislation on the other.

On the one hand, colonialism resulted in the spread of wage labour, modification of some institutions, norms and practices, and the introduction of some rights that had been won by women in Europe — for example, the right to vote, membership of trade unions; the right to equal pay for equal work; and the possibility of monogamy with improved property rights for women and children. However, these gains have been limited by the difficult material conditions in the country. On the other hand, colonialism reinforced some negative aspects of the culture and practices of Ghanaian society. An example is the prevailing system of formal education which discriminates against women in terms of numbers, levels of educational attainment and job segregation thus reinforcing traditional notions about the role of women in society.

In sum, it is fair to say that women in Ghana, like women all over the third world, face a specific form of oppression arising from their economic dependence and their inferior positions in all areas of life in spite of their important contributions to society.

WOMEN'S POLITICAL ORGANISATIONS — THE CPP PERIOD, 1951-1966

Women in Ghana have had a long history of organization. It has been recorded that there were women's associations and groups for social, ritual and military purposes in the traditional setting. During the colonial era, many benevolent and mutual associations, credit unions and market women's voluntary groups sprung up.[11] But these forerunners did not tackle the wider question of the oppression of women.

Women were very active in the anti-colonial struggle. One area in which their contribution was important was the cocoa — holdups which date as far back as the 1917-1918 period. The participation of women in those early protests stemmed from their work as retail traders. As such they also felt the threat posed by the monopolistic activities of the European trading firms. Apart from these, women traders became staunch supporters of the Convention People's Party (CPP) and contributed generously to its funding and organization. There were also outstanding women to whose work and support Dr. Nkrumah attributed 'the solidarity, cohesion, and success of the CPP...'.[12]

It is to the credit of these women, who toured the regions of the country alongside the men, that women's sections developed in the party's branches. The CPP's women's sections were important in mobilising women to participate in the final phase of the anti-colonial struggles.[13]

They were also active in organising the party's youth League. The women's sections sponsored rallies and made various contributions such as providing speakers and forming singing bands and cultural groups which performed at CPP functions. Madam Yeeye, one of the enthusiastic women supporters served water at CPP rallies from mid-1949 on her own initiative.[14] By May 1951, the party had appointed four women — Letitia Quaye (PG),[15] Miss Doku, Hannah Cudjoe and Ama Nkrumah as propaganda secretaries charged with the duty of organising women. The CPP constitution made provision for an inner party organization to be known as the CPP Women's League, under which all women members were to be organised into women's sections at branch and ward levels. Duties which were assigned to these sections were the organisation of rallies, dances, picnics and other functions through out the year. The constitution also established a special Ghana Women's Day which was held at Easter.[16]

During this period women were also involved in struggles which were not directly anti-colonial but political in very significant ways. For example, they organised demonstrations to protest against the suspension of the Ga Mantse, chief of the Ga in Accra, whom the women said was being victimised, 'because he refused to let the headmen of various houses continue misusing the State's revenue'.[17] Also, market women fought against forced removals to obscure points in Accra, and against frequent and unjustified increases in market tolls as well as rents on stalls which they regarded as too small for them.

By 1960, there were two prominent women's organizations operating in the country — The Ghana Women's League, led by Mrs Hannah Cudjoe and the Ghana Federation of Women led by Mrs Evelyn Amarteifio.[18] The latter was founded in 1953 as the National Federation of Gold Coast Women[19] and was described as a non-political body, working within the confines of colonial law. By 1960, it was involved in activities which were similar to those of the League and the Women's section of the CPP, and which can only be described as political. For example, the two organizations supported protests against the French Government's plan to test an atom bomb in the Sahara.[20]

In addition to talks and demonstrations on nutrition, childcare, and the distribution of clothes to needy children, the League was involved in explaining government policies. In 1960, for example, its census education unit undertook a ten day tour of the Northern Region to explain the purpose of the Government's proposed Population Census.[21] It also adopted resolutions supporting the government's proposals to turn the country into a Republic.

The Federation on its part carried out a house-to-house educational campaign on the government's census in areas in the Central Region. A Women's column in the CPP paper, *Evening News*, under the pseudonym Akosua Dzatsui supported these activities with articles discussing government policies and attacking opponents of the party and government. However, it did not have many articles on women's problems.

A merger of the League, the Federation and many small women's groups all over the country was proposed by the CPP and overseen by the party's general secretary, Tawia Adamafio, assisted by Sophia Doku — secretary of the Bureau of Women's Organizations at the party headquarters. Adamafio reports that the differences between the two organizations, manifested in 'wordy combat' between their leaders — Hannah Cudjoe and Evelyn Amarteifio, were easily resolved by shouting at them and pretending anger at their behaviour.[22]

The result of the merger, The National Council of Ghana Women (NCGW), was inaugurated by Dr. Nkrumah on 10th September 1960, as the only recognised body under which all Ghanaian women were to be organised to contribute their quota to the political, educational, social and economic construction of Ghana.[23] As Dr. Nkrumah said on another occasion, 'in the factories, shops, on farms, in the universities, in departments and ministries, and all aspects of our national life, and at all levels of party activity, the Ghanaian Woman must make her presence felt. The NCGW gives a great opportunity to all women to serve their party and country and to make a useful contribution to the total African struggle![24]

The NCGW replaced the women's section of the Party. It became an integral wing of the Party and had representation on its Central Committee. The post of secretary to the Council, and presumably other executive positions were held on appointment by members of the Party's Central Committee. Successive secretaries — Ms. Doku, Ms. Stella Abeka, and Mrs. Margaret Martei were described as party stalwarts.[25] The Council established branches throughout the country. Many of its young members were sent abroad to study, or were assisted to find employment. Its market women members controlled the allocation of space and goods in the market. Like the CPP Women's wing, the Council organised rallies, and undertook programmes like the building of daycare centres in the towns to cater for working women. It also established and maintained links with women's organizations outside the country through visits and conferences.

The organization of women in this way was a reflection of how the CPP saw women's problems and therefore their resolution. Dr. Nkrumah's desire to improve the condition of women comes out clearly in Adamafio's account of how the task of organising women fell to him. There was a recognition of the contributions of women to the anti-colonial struggle, and the implications for development of a backward female population.[26] Government policies reflected these concerns. An assessment of the CPP government's policies towards women has noted that it consciously encouraged the participation of women in politics and public life with the result that a few women held high political offices as members of parliament, deputy minister, and district commissioners; and that these were not acts of tokenism, but a recognition of their abilities.

Educational measures such as the Accelerated Plan for Education of 1952 and the Education Act of 1961 which made education compulsory for all children of school going age, led to higher enrolment figures for women in basic education. New facilities for post-basic education, and the removal of some of the most blatant discriminatory practices in employment enabled women to enter new occupations hitherto closed to them. These facilities, however, were not uniform all over the country and figures for educated females still lagged behind those for males.

In the economic sphere, policies under the Seven-Year Development Plan (1964 — 1974) and the CPP's Programme for Work and Happiness promised to provide employment avenues from which women would benefit. The establishment of the Ghana National Trading Corporation during the economic conditions of the 1960s resulted in the flourishing of petty trading for many women. Policies in agriculture however, did not make any special provisions for women's problems and therefore did not significantly improve their conditions in this sector.

In the area of social reform, the government passed a law on the maintenance of children, which tried to resolve the problem of neglect of children; but the law did not tackle the problem adequately. Moreover, the government failed to pass its Uniform Marriage, Divorce and Inheritance Bill into law. Admittedly the bill was controversial, but that failure meant that the government was leaving the problem it wanted to address intact.[27]

However, the undemocratic character of the government's intervention in the organisation of women, and the negative attitudes to women in government circles were limitations to the attempts at addressing women's problems. For example, the General Secretary of the CPP in that period saw an organization of women as a potential threat to the position of men, and thought that the task of organising them which had been assigned to him by the Party was a great inconvenience. Therefore, he only grudgingly acknowledged the militancy of women and the great promise the Council had.[28] The Council was abolished along with its parent organization, the CPP following the government's overthrow in 1966.

THE APOLITICAL PHASE, 1966-81

In the period between the overthrow of Ghana's First Republic and the coup d'etat of 31st December, 1981, the only political women's organizations were the women's sections of various political parties which had a very brief life span. The organisations which dominated the field were non-political, and were mainly self-help or charitable organizations. There was the Ghana Assembly of Women, founded in August 1969, as 'a voluntary women's body which served as a central women's organization in Ghana.' It seemed to be the successor of the Ghana Federation of Women in terms of its aims and membership. By 1976, it had 25 affiliates, made up of ten religious groups, and other self-help organisations. Its activities in that period included encouraging its constituent bodies to go into income generating activities like soap and crafts-making, and 'leadership training' workshops. It ran a newsletter that covered issues like the work of the various affiliates, guidelines about how to choose a project, problems of inequality, other women's organisations outside Ghana, cooking recipes, home making, marriage and religion.[29]

There were also professional women's groups like the Ghana Business and Professional Women's Association, the Ghana Branch of the International Federation of Women Lawyers, (FIDA) and the ZONTA Club. Following the International Women's year a statutory body, the National Council on Women and Development (NCWD) was set up in 1975 by the ruling National Redemption Council (NRC). It was in response to a UN Resolution calling on member states to 'establish the appropriate government machinery to accelerate the integration of women in development and the elimination of discrimination against women on grounds of sex'. The NRC Decree establishing the NCWD gave this new body advisory and research functions as well as a liaison role between government and national and international organisations.[30]

This low tide of political activity on the women's front was a reflection of the state of paralysis that characterised mass political activity during the 1966-81 period. In those fifteen years, eleven of which were under military rule, mass political activity was virtually non-existent except for a period of mass protests by sections of the working class, students and professionals against the deteriorating economic and political situation in the country during the latter stage of the Supreme Military Council's (SMC) rule.[31]

The absence of independent political organisations of the underprivileged on the political scene was a factor which ensured this continued marginalisation of mass politics. For example, a relatively old organization like the TUC had had its independence threatened by past governments and had even once been dissolved by an Act of Parliament.[32]

RESURGENCE OF POLITICAL WOMEN'S ORGANISATIONS, 1982-87

By 1982 new independent mass political organizations had come into existence. They included the New Democratic Movement, June Four Movement, Kwame Nkrumah Revolutionary Guards and the African

Youth Command. But they were young, and therefore weak mass organisations. Nonetheless, they became quite important in the resurgence of mass politics during the early period of PNDC's rule. That period saw them engaging in more intensive mass political agitation and organisation than had hitherto been possible.

The period was also a different experience for the country's underprivileged groups, including women. The new government declared a revolution and in response to its directives, Peoples Defence Committees (PDCs) and Workers Defence Committees (WDCs) were formed all over the country — in communities and workplaces respectively to express the interests and power of the people and to protect the '31st December Revolution'. A National Youth Organising Commission was also set up; and existing organizations like the TUC and the NCWD had their old methods of operation questioned.[33]

Attitudes to women in this period were contradictory. Market women were held responsible for the economic problems facing the country, shortages in the supply of basic consumer items like soap and sugar were attributed to their speculative practices, popularly called 'hoarding and profiteering', and a few women were prosecuted for these trade malpractices. Markets in some regional capitals — Accra, Takoradi, and Tamale were destroyed, and traders in the Ashanti and Central Regions were threatened with the demolition of their markets if they did not lower their prices.[34]

When market women went to Burma Camp, the seat of the PNDC, in the early days of its rule, to demonstrate their support for the regime, as was being done by other groups, they were chased out. Young women were also accused of having 'taken advantage' of their gender to acquire favours from past regimes, and practicing prostitution in neighbouring countries.

Although some government officials were involved in stating these criticisms against women, the official position of the government was that the anti-social practices of these women had deep roots in the socio-economic conditions of Ghanaian society which required changing if women were to change. There was a certain tendency to feel that the declaration of a revolution meant that women had been instantly 'liberated'. Thus at a rally in Bolgatanga, in the now Upper East Region of Ghana, the PNDC Chairman presented a rifle to a woman to symbolise the emancipation of the Ghanaian woman, and called on women to accept the challenge to become equals of men.

Political mass organizations and the Defence Committees discussed women's issues during this period, and on a few occasions invited women to speak on these matters. This, in addition to the government's recognition that the roots of economic crimes lay in the problems of women, and the organizational possibilities of the period, favoured political work among women.

On the negative side, the intimidation of market women, which assumed startling proportions during the AFRC period was resumed with the coming to power of the PNDC. There was also the more fundamental fact that interest in women's issues was marginal compared with the interest shown in issues concerning the working class and other sections of the underprivileged. These factors meant that the task of convincing women about the need to get organised would not be easy. Above all there were few women during this period who were interested in political work among women. Some of them were members of, or were associated with, either the June Four Movement or the New Democratic Movement. There were others who did not belong to any such organisations. The political work of these few women activists drew attention to the oppressed conditions of women and created the momentum for their mobilization into organisations.

The Federation of Ghanaian Women

The Federation of Ghanaian Women (FEGAWO) was the first organization to be inaugurated — on March 8th 1982. Among its aims and objectives, as set out in a draft constitution, were to struggle for equal rights and opportunities for women in economic, social and political matters, and to struggle against the structures, laws, norms and practices which oppress women. There was also a provision about encouraging women to participate actively in the political processes of the period, especially participation in the work of the defence committees.

The FEGAWO was intended to have a national spread but started organising in Accra, where its foundation members lived. Its earliest branches were established at three workplaces — namely Accra's two main markets, and the Ghana Broadcasting Corporation. They were followed by community based branches in Accra suburbs like Madina, Nungua, Mamprobi, Osu, Dansoman, New Fadama, and at Asofaa, a small village on the outskirts of Accra. Later, branches were started in Kumasi, Sunyani, Tamale, Bolgatanga and Navrongo — all of them regional capitals.

Its mode of operation differed, depending on the character of the branch. At Asofaa, for example, where its members were illiterate farmers, it established a vegetable farm, and women's problems were discussed after work on the farm. At Madina, it worked with the kenkey makers association. Side by side with discussions about the problems of acquiring maize (the raw material in kenkey making), there were educational programmes on subjects like childcare and nutrition, the government's budget statement, its Economic Recovery

Programme etc. There were also visits to market branches to discuss problems faced by the market women. The Nungua branch started a soapmaking project as a viable economic alternative for its petty-trading members displaced by the PNDC's ban on trading in some items like cloth, sugar, milk, canned fish and meat which were in short supply. That project was also to serve as a supplementary source of income for other members of the branch.

In addition to work with the branches, the organization launched a campaign against the contraceptive, depo-provera, exposing its side effects in the newspapers, and demanding its banning. It also started developing links with women's organisations outside the country. The Soviet Women's Committee, for example, donated some equipment and provided scholarships to enable some members of the organisation to study in the Soviet Union.

The organization soon began to face problems that retarded its work. Its short gestation period resulted in the absence of a strong core of conscious cadres to consistently direct and sustain its work in the various branches. This problem was faced by the two other organisations which will be discussed presently. There was also the problem of finance for political work and economic projects.

Another problem was the diffuse sense of loyalty and attachment to the organization showed by the women among whom political work was done. This problem was manifested in some of the women joining as many women's organisations as had tried to mobilize them. For instance, a few months after the formation of the FEGAWO a new women's movement, the 31st December Women's Movement, was inaugurated by the Chairman of the PNDC. This new organization also started to organise from the main markets. Among at least one group of market women, it was shown during an independence day parade of voluntary organizations that the same leader and members of the FEGAWO also belonged to the 31st December Women's Movement. These same women were to become important members of the All Women's Association of Ghana (AWAG) when it was formed.

In late 1982, merger talks between the FEGAWO and the 31st December Women's Organisation were initiated by Mrs Aana Ennin, PNDC member and honorary president of the FEGAWO — a position she held before becoming a member of the government. The purpose of those discussions was to put an end to what was regarded as the duplication and waste of energies by the two orgnisations. The talks dragged on until 1984. Even though they failed, they nonetheless generated considerable rancour between certain key members of the two organisations. The failure of the merger attempt has been put down to political diffferences between the two organisations. It is alleged that the FEGAWO regarded itself as independent of the government while the 31st December Women's Organisation was seen as a government — sponsored organisation. There have also been allegations of 'subjective differences' between some leading figures in the two organisations.

These problems were still unresolved when the political situation deteriorated making independent mass political work impossible to undertake. During this period independent working class organizations like the TUC and WDCs came increasingly under severe criticism from government. In December 1984, the WDCs which had become the leading organ of mass political struggle were redesignated as Committees for the Defence of the Revolution (CDRs) and their role redefined. With that change, the era of independent political work, organization and struggle seemed to have ended.[35] All these factors contributed to the demise of the FEGAWO.

The 31st December Women's Movement

In its regulations, the Movement stated as its first objective the mobilisation of women to participate actively in the 'revolutionary process', contribute towards national reconstruction, and fight for a complete change in the social and economic conditions of women. The regulations set out areas of interest — literacy campaigns, economic ventures, social services, educational programmes, protective legislation, and the abolition of discriminatory laws. By 1987, the movement had grown from a few branches in Accra into a national organisation with branches in all the ten regions of Ghana. Its membership was reported to have increased from an estimated 50,000 (4,000 of them being registered members) in 1983 to about 250,000 in April 1987.[36] The movement is run by a three member national executive. Its work is not funded by membership fee; and its various branches appear to be quite autonomous, especially outside Accra. This is probably due more to lack of adequate number of cadres, rather than a deliberate policy of the leadership.

Also the branches are not involved in policy making; and by 1987 it had not been known to elect its leadership. Nor had it held a national conference of its members. The leadership has changed in composition as the years went by and become the preserve of urban middle class women. This contrasts with the earlier leadership which comprised younger more radical urban women.

The branches have been involved in various economic activities chosen from the national executive's broad guidelines to suit local conditions and to enable them to become self-sufficient economic units.

For example, one of its first branches, located at Burma Camp in Accra — the main barracks of the Ghana Armed Forces, was awarded contracts to supply bread and kenkey to the Armed Forces. Other branches were involved in soap making and pottery. But farming and baking have become the two most popular activities. The national organisation has been involved in organising workshops on food processing and conservation; and educational campaigns on personal hygiene, family planning, maternal and childcare, health and nutrition.[37]

In 1986, the movement declared as its priority, the construction of daycare centres, and encouraged its branches to put up structures for the purpose. Two such centres were constructed and recently commissioned in Accra. Members of the movement have been participating in community development projects in many parts of the country. In addition to these economic and social activities, the movement has been involved directly in current political activities which define its political character as well as its relation with the government. In 1987, it was described as a 'non governmental and self supporting voluntary organisation, one of the organs the revolution gave birth to';[38] but its aims and objectives according to its leaders were identical to those of the PNDC,[39] and so the two ought to work together, to build the nation.

The association's priorities so far have been to publicise, and educate women and the rest of the population on, the policies of the government, and mobilise women to participate in what it regards as nation-buidling. For example, the government's educational and political reforms were extensively publicised by the leadership of the movement. It endorsed the government's 1987 budget, calling it the best since independence.

Contrary to the claims of some of its founding members the movement has been closer to the government and enjoyed great official support than the FEGAWO ever did. From 1984 onwards it has worked in close cooperation with PNDC Regional and District Secretaries, as well as other government appointees, who sometimes accompanied the President on her tours of their areas of jurisdiction. It also cooperated with the CDRs, especially in the propagation of PNDC policies, and at least one of its projects has been funded by a district CDR secretariat.[40]

Traditional rulers, a power block which was challenged by the formation of PDCs during the 1982-1983 period, have also become a support base for the movement, organising durbars to welcome its president when she toured the regions — especially in 1987. The President has accordingly declared that all queenmothers are patrons of the movement[41] and she has given them the task of educating women in their areas on government policies.[42] Perhaps this transformation from seeming independence to active collaboration with and dependence on the government has been facilitated by the fact that the changes in leadership that occurred in 1984 resulted in the assumption of the post of National President by Mrs Nana Konadu Agyeman-Rawlings, wife of the PNDC Chairman.

The general membership, on their part, have occasionally participated in public marches to express their solidarity with the PNDC on issues such as apartheid, or to support the regime's policies; for example, marching to the Osu Castle, the seat of Government to thank the PNDC for passing a law reforming the rules of Interstate Succession. These activities are however mainly symbolic and do not commit the general membership to struggles around the fundamental causes of the oppression of women that have the potential for conflict with the PNDC.

A direct result of the movement's political practice is the easy access to State facilities and resources which it enjoys for its work; and this has enabled it to reach out to all parts of the country, transforming itself from an Accra-based organisation into a nation-wide movement by 1987. It has also succeeded in establishing links with women's organisations in socialist countries such as the Soviet Union, and Cuba. These links have provided it with scholarships and equipment like sewing machines and toys for the benefit of its work. Nearer home, it has established links with women's organisations in Burkina Faso and Algeria to enable it to learn from their experiences.

The All Women's Association of Ghana (AWAG)

The AWAG was formed in August 1984 after the collapse of the merger talks between the FEGAWO and the 31st December Women's Movement and inaugurated in March, 1985. This Association was sponsored by the PNDC Member who had initiated and coordinated the merger talks, as an answer to the problems of disunity in the women's movement. Although its aims and objectives did not differ significantly from those of the FEGAWO and the 31st December Women's Movement, the AWAG was conceived of as a non-governmental, non-partisan coordinating organisation. It was to act as an umbrella organisation capable of accomodating the varying aspirations of existing women's organisations.

Members of the FEGAWO and the 31st December Women's Movement never became members of the AWAG. Its membership was made up of various women's groups — business, religious, labour, market women and individuals who did not belong to any of the existing groups. It claims to have established branches in four regions — Greater Accra, Eastern, Central and Western. These branches were supposed to organise activities like farming; workshops on soapmaking, tie and dye manufacture, and other cottage industries; and seminars on health, legal issues, civic rights and responsibilities, etc.[43]

But it is not clear how many women's organisations were active in the AWAG, or how many of its branches were functioning. By 1987, its Accra market branch seemed to be the only functioning section; and it was involved in struggles with the Accra City Council over what it regarded as the imposition of exhorbitant market tolls at two Accra markets. These struggles culminated in the setting up in 1987 of a government probe into allegations of corruption in the allocation of market booths. It was also active in campaigning to get its members and other market women to register during the government's voters registration exercise in November 1987. The prominence of its market branch was probably the result of the fact that its president, Madam Laryed Commey, is also the leader of a section of Accra's market women.

CONCLUSION

The foregoing discussion of the goals and character of political women's organisations raises an important question; namely, that given the limits of the neo-colonial situation, what organisational forms will advance the interests of Ghanaian women? An assessment of the character, political practice and achievements of the 31st December Women's Movement, the survivor of the various attempts at political organisation of women between 1982-1987 is important in satisfactorily answering this question. A comparison of the movement with the experience of the National Council of Ghana Women (NCGW) shows instructive parallels in character and practice.

It must be noted at this point that the two organisations belonged to different historical periods of the country's history. The mass character of the anti-colonial struggle, the existence of a mass party even if it had limitations, and the militancy of women in that period fostered by their long and extraordinary role in the anti-colonial struggle created conditions quite different from the spontaneous mass enthusiasm generated by the PNDC government when it assumed power.

The two organisations, the NCGW and the 31st December Women's Movement, however share a similar position in the power structure of the county: they were coopted, and taken over by ruling groups. Both the CPP and PNDC rule produced some benefits for women. The PNDC government has recently enacted laws which are favourable to women.[44] These laws have given some formal advantages to women. However, problems like lack of adequate machinery for publicity and enforcement, and hostility to some provisions of the laws and many others have not ensured the desired effect. More especially, the laws did not make any fundamental changes in the social, economic and political conditions of the majority of women whose spouses do not own any property.

The CPP, as has been shown, in spite of the defeat of its proposed legislation on marriage and inheritance went further than the laws in its policies especially those related to educational, economic and political rights. Both organisations generally share a common heritage of intimate state support which has come to them in the form of financial help, media promotion and access to other resources. It is this official support that has ensured their successes and high achievements. But that relationship has been maintained at the expense of the women's struggle; for ultimately both of them have had to devote much of their attention to mobilising support for their respective governments. In so doing women's issues have been shelved; or at best, they have received very casual attention.

Thus in her assessment of the NCGW, Manu concluded that though it was a truly national organisation its leaders seemed to have been more concerned with party activities and with the monumental task of nation-building than specific women's questions.[45] That judgement, with some modifications, would apply to the 31st December Women's Movement.

An equally important political consequence of the cooptation by political leaders of a women's organisation is the marginalization of all other womens organisations. In the First Republic, the General Secretary of the party decided to use administrative means to kill the Young Women's Christian Association for refusing to merge with what became the NCGW.[46] Currently, it is the 31st December Women's Movement which is projected as the only women's organization in the country.

In the final analysis, it could be argued that cooptation and control was possible in the two cases because the leadership of the organisations shared identical political and class aspirations with the ruling groups. Thus currently the 31st December Women's Movement has not shown concern about the deteriorating conditions of working class peasant and petty-trader women. Rather it has been jubilant about marriage and inheritance laws which are of little consequence for poor women in the cities, towns and villages. Because of such gaps in values and aspirations between the leadership of such women's organisations and ordinary women, the leaders lead but do not represent the mass of women. This credibility crisis accounts for the lack of a deep sense of loyalty and commitment to women's political organisations, and for the apathy and cynicism among women in the country. It also accounts partly for the rapid turnover among women's organisations and their failure to gain roots in either the long or short run among women; and partly for the proliferation of non-political women's associations.

It is possible therefore that the inability of the NCGW to survive the fall of the CPP might be replayed in the case of the 31st December Women's Movement. Should this happen it would have grave consequences for the women's struggle just as the demise of the NCGW did. It would show once more the problem of lack of a deeply rooted women's political organisation, an organisation that is operated in accordance with the real interests of the majority of women who are underprivileged. Furthermore it would bring to the fore the problem of lack of continuity in the building of independent political organisations for the women's struggle.

NOTES

1. Graham, Yao, *Ghana — the Politics of Crisis: Class struggles and organisation, 1976-1983* Paper presented at a ROAPE seminar at Keele, 1984. p.2.
2. Four million out of the six million females in Ghana are in the rural areas. All figures on the population are unpublished data from the 1984 Population Census.
3. 1.5 million.
4. Although women are more than one half of the agricultural labour force, they are about a third of the number of males in the sector who are in wage employment of any kind — in for example, central government, public boards, cooperatives, private enterprises and international organisations.
5. Manu, Takyiwa, 'Law and the Status of Women in Ghana' Paper prepared for the E.C.A. 1984 p.57. See other studies about female peasant farmers elsewhere — example, Jacobs, Crehan and Feldman in the *Review of African Political Economy*, No.27/28, 1984; and Cutrufelli, M. *Women of Africa: Roots of Oppression*. (London: Zed Press, 1983) pp.115-123.
6. For a discussion of the conditions of women in two service industries see M. Safo: 'Women at Risk:' *The Mirror* October 3rd and 10th, 1987.
7. Trade union membership is estimated at 733,196. Women make up about 25% of that figure. There are other associations for civil servants, teachers and nurses.
8. The exact figure is 1.8 million.
9. There are 3,300 female to 22,000 male university graduates — a ratio of about 1:7.
10. See Christine Oppong (editor): *Family Research Papers No. 1 — Domestic Rights and Duties in Southern Ghana:* Institute of African Studies Publication 1974 and ROAPE Vol. 27/28 1984
11. Manu, T., 'Women and their Organisations During the CPP Rule in Ghana 1951-66' in Kwame Arhin (ed.). *The Life and Works of Kwame Nkrumah* (forthcoming).
12. Nkrumah, K. Ghana: *The Autobiography of Kwame Nkrumah*. (Edinburgh: Thompson Nelson and Sons,1957).

13. By 1951, there were women's sections in Kpandu, Ododen, Dzodze, Westend Arena, areas of the Western Province Brakwa, Manya Krobo etc. all in the southern part of Ghana. — *Evening News* 1951.
14. *Evening News*: May 29, 1951.
15. *Evening News*: May 29th 1951. P.G. stands for prison graduate, a title given to those who had been imprisoned for their anti-colonial activities.
16. Nkrumah, op.cit., 1957, P.301.
17. *Evening News*: October 24th, 1951.
18. Other members of the executive committee were Mrs A.M. Akiwumi — National President and Elsie Ofuatey Cudjoe — executive member. *Evening News*: January 15th 1960.
19. It worked through church organisations, benevolent societies and market associations, with branches in the Colony, Ashanti, Trans Volta Togoland. It sent many petitions to the Colonial government on discriminatory practices affecting women in employment, marriage and social life, and published a periodical, *The Gold Coast Woman*. Manu op.cit.
20. The League was involved in demonstrations and the Ghana Federation of Women presented a cheque to the Ghana Council for Nuclear Disarmament. See *The Evening News* January 15th, 1960.
21. *Evening News*: March 9th, 1960.
22. Adamafio, T. *By Nkrumah's Side: The Labour and the Wounds*. (Accra: West Coast Publishing House. 1982.) p.113-120.
23. Manu, op cit; also *Selected Speeches of K. Nkrumah* vol.2: *On his assumption of office as general secretary and chairman* of the central committee ofthe CPP on May 1, 1961. p.102.
24. Speech by Nkrumah: ibid.
25. Adamafio, op.cit.
26. ibid
27. Manu, op.cit.
28. Adamafio, op.cit.
29. *The Ghanaian Woman*: (Quarterly of the Ghana Assembly of Women) — January — June 1976. Vol.2 No. 1 & 2.
30. *Annual Report of the National Council on Women and Development (NCWD) 1980 — 1984*. The NCWD stated in the report that it had set itself the task of raising the consciousness and living standards of women, by getting them involved in economic activity. It had set up economic projects for school drop-outs, school leavers, working women, farmers, traders and women in food processing, and run educational programmes on nutrition, childcare, family planning and sanitation. It also made representations to various regimes on issues such as prostitution, proposed laws on intestate succession, the plight of displaced market women following the demolition of markets, on government ratification of the UN Convention on the Elimination of Discrimination against women etc. However, only a few women have felt the impact of its existence: and it was regularly criticised for not doing enough for women. The Council put its lack of effectiveness to the lack of resources and governmental support. Its governing body was dissolved in June 1986 and replaced with an Interim Management Committee. The 31st December Women's Movement was heavily represented on it.
31. In 1975, the NRC changed its name to the Supreme Military Council (SMC) which then became the highest organ of state power.
32. Refer to the Industrial Relations (Amendment) Act 1971 (Act 383).
33. In the TUC, there was the Association of Local Unions (ALU) takeover. In this action, some local unions expelled the old leadership of the TUC, accusing it of

not serving the interests of the membership. (*See People's Daily Graphic* January and February 1982 issues) The NCWD reported that a workshop on alternative economic activities for some women it had organised at the Kwame Nkrumah Conference Centre was picketed by a group of young adult women calling themselves 'concerned women of Ghana' who 'marched into the foyer and distributed leaflets calling the Council names and alleging that it had been involved in malpractices...' *NCWD Annual Report. 1980-1984*.

34. For reports on these developments refer to *People's Daily Graphic* — January to March 1982.
35. For a detailed discussion of these changes and their implications for working class politics see the contributions by Graham and Ninsin in this volume.
36. Interviews with a founding member of the 31st December Women's Movement; also *The Post* (Accra: Information Services Department Publication April 1987).
37. Ibid
38. Ibid
39. *People's Daily Graphic* — November 10th 1987 — The President of the Movement at a durbar of chiefs, people and members of the Kassena-Nankani District held in her honour at Navrongo.
40. The Manya Krobo District Secretariat of CDRs — *Ghanaian Times* October 22 1987.
41. *The People's Daily Graphic*, 30th November, 1987.
42. *The Ghanaian Times*, 9th October, 1987.
43. Information about the AWAG is from an interview with a founding member.
44. The Intestate Succession Law PNDCL 111 had made inheritance laws uniform irrespective of the character of marriage contracted by the deceased, or system of succession prevailing in his area. The aim is to improve the marital conditions of widows and children. The Customary Marriage and Divorce (Registration) Law makes it mandatory for all marriages to be registered. Its purpose is to ensure the equitable distribution of property on intestacy. The government has also enacted a law banning widowhood rites which in most cases humilate and degrade widows. In addition to these, it has ratified the UN Convention on the Elimination.
45. Manu, op.cit., 1988, p.33.
46. Adamafio, op.cit., p.119.

REFERENCES

1. Adamafio T: *By Nkrumah's Side: The Labour and the Wounds*, (Accra: Westcoast Publishing House, in association with Rex Collings, London 1982).
2. Cutrufelli, M: *Women of Africa: Roots of Oppression*. (London Zed Press, 1983).
3. Daniels E.W.C. E.W.C. and Woodman G.R. (eds), *Essays in Ghanain Law*. (Accra: Ghana Publishing Corporation 1976.).
4. Davies, Miranda. (ed) Third world; *Second Sex: Women's Struggles and National Liberation*. (London: Zed Press, 1983).
5. Development Dialogue: Another Development with Women: *Journal of International Development Cooperation* (Uppsala: the Dag Hammarskjold Foundation, 1983.).
6. Economic Commision for Africa Law and the Status of Women in Ghana. Prepared by Manuh, T. (Adis-Ababa, 1984).
7. Graham, Yao. Ghana — *The Politics of Crisis: Class Struggles and Organisation — 1976-1983*: Paper presented to a ROAPE Seminar at Keele, 1984.
8. *Journal of African Marxists*: Issue 8: January 1986.

9. *Journal of Southern African Studies*: Vol. 12 No. 1 'Transforming the Foundation of Family in the Course of the Mozambique Revolution' by Welch, Dagnino and Sachs. October 1985.
10. Manu T. *Law and the Status of Women In Ghana* Paper prepared for the E.C.A. Addis Ababa, 1984 Women and their Organisations During the Convention Peoples Party Period in Ghana: 1951-1966.
11. National Council on Women and Development: *Annual Report-1980-1984*.
12. Nkrumah, Kwame: *Ghana: The Autobiography of Kwame Nkrumah* Edinburgh: Thompson Nelson and Sons Ltd., 1957.
13. Obeng, S. (compiled): *Selected speeches by Kwame Nkrumah*. Vol 2. (Accra: Afram Publications Ghana Ltd., 1961.
14. Oppong C. (ed): Legon Family Research Papers: No.1. *Domestic Rights and Duties in southern Ghana*. (Legon: Institute of African Studies Publication, 1974).
15. *Review of African Political Economy*, vol. 27/28, 1984.
16. Newspapers:
    a. *The Evening News*: 1951, 1952, 1953 and 1960
    b. *Peoples Daily Graphic* — January-December 1982, 1986, 1987
    c. *The Ghanaian Times* — 1987

4. CHANGING RELATIONS BETWEEN THE IMF AND THE GOVERNMENT OF GHANA 1960-1987

Kwesi Jonah

INTRODUCTION

Ghana has had a long association with the IMF and the World Bank. In the 1960s, when the Ghanaian economy began to develop serious balance of payments difficulties tense relationship developed between the government and the Fund because of the former's stubborn resistance to Fund recommendations. After the overthrow of the Nkrumah regime in 1966 tension and resistance gave way to amicable collaboration which continued until the beginning of 1972. From that date when another democratically elected civilian government was overthrown there was a period of temporary defiance and non co-operation. In 1978 and 1979, there was a brief spell of co-operation which was disrupted by the June 4 uprising of 1979.

The election of the Peoples National Party (PNP) led by Dr. Hilla Limann in 1979 inaugurated a two year period of official hesitation and indecision regarding the government's relationship with the Fund to solve the persistent crisis in the Ghanaian economy even, though the government was facing acute balance of payments difficulties. In December 1981, a military coup, led by Flt Lt Jerry John Rawlings, brought to power a new government which opened a new era of close co-operation with the Fund.

This coup also ignited what perhaps amounts to the bitterest political struggle ever to occur in Ghana's history over the question of whether or not the government should seek the assistance of the Fund in solving the nation's economic crisis; and if it should, what form that co-operation should take. By March 1983 it was clear that the question had been resolved and Ghana had embarked on the closest and perhaps the longest period of collaboration between the Fund and any one regime in Ghana's history.

This close collaboration is taking place against the background of nearly two decades of economic decline. Since 1983 the PNDC government has been implementing a Fund-Bank sponsored Structural Adjustment Programme (SAP) which was divided into an initial stabilization phase lasting up to 1986 and a second phase of development. Consequently, between 1983 and 1987 the IMF made available to the government financial resources totalling about 1222.50 million SDR. More than half of this sum consisted of a series of stand-by credits approved up to 1987 while the rest consisted of an extended fund facility of about 550.50 million SDR.

The intensity of Ghana's use of Fund resources within this short period becomes obvious if one recalls that as the middle of 1986 Ghana's quota with the IMF was only 204.50 million SDR. The World Bank has also supported the government's efforts with various forms of credit to rehabilitate infrastructure, stimulate cash crop production for export, and assist industry and the improvement of the utilities. Bank and Fund assistance for the government is likely to be increased with the introduction of the Structural Adjustment Facility in 1986. This facility requires a much closer collaboration between the IMF and the World Bank in assisting developing countries with serious economic problems to design and implement a Structural Adjustment Programme (SAP).

The government's close collaboration with the Fund and the Bank, buttressed by its unyielding commitment to implementing SAP, has drawn substantial financial assistance from Western bilateral and multilateral sources as well. This is believed to be one of the benefits of close collaboration with the IMF and the Bank.

It could therefore be argued that Ghana's association with the Fund in the past was intermittent and brief; its impact was insignificant; and the volume of resource flow was too meagre; because the governments which had to implement those Fund and Bank recommendations lacked the political will and determination to impose them on the people. Currently, the Government is determined to carry through Fund and Bank recommendations far beyond the SAP phases. It is necessary therefore to direct some attention to the nature of this association and its political implications for the country.

The focus of this paper is on the relationship between the Government of Ghana and the IMF. Its primary objective is to show that Ghana's association with the Fund has entailed significant changes in political and ideological direction as well as in development strategy. We shall start by examining the nature of the relationship between each of the pre-1982 governments and the Fund, beginning with the government of the Convention People's Party (CPP).

THE CPP GOVERNMENT'S DEVELOPMENT STRATEGY

The CPP government led by Kwame Nkrumah was overthrown in 1966 following years of resistance to the dictates of the Fund. The tense relationship between the Nkrumah regime and the Fund was the consequence of the regime's refusal to compromise on what it considered to be its socialist principles and strategy of development. Ironically, however, even that resistance could not save the regime and its socialist policies.

When the CPP came to power in 1951 the country had the benefit of a prosperous export economy. Total foreign investment was about $151 million and her external reserves stood at a comfortable level of £182,622,000. Apart from agricultural production her economy was controlled by a handful of Western companies; her trade was largely with the West. The new government's development strategy was just an improved version of the colonial model. It was based on the laissez faire economic philosophy of minimum state involvement in the economy.

The government's economic policies soon began to show negative results. Prosperity soon gave way to dwindling reserves and budgetary deficits. The country's external reserves dropped from £211,165,000 in 1955 to £182,622,000 in 1957 and again to £150,280,000 in 1960. Foreign investments were not pouring into the country. Above all, the country's external terms of trade were deteriorating. To arrest the situation the government took measures to diversify the country's trading partners. It reduced her dependence on trade with the developed Western countries because that involved the use of hard currency. It rather signed, bilateral barter trade pacts with several socialist countries. The import licensing and foreign exchange policies were introduced to give the government greater control over foreign trade and the allocation of the country's meagre foreign exchange resources.

Import duties on certain goods originating from certain trading areas were raised to as much as two-thirds of their landed value in order to discourage excessive imports from such areas. The most important change ocurred in the government's development strategy. It abandoned its laissez faire policy for an interventionist role in the economy. From 1960 the state competed aggressively with the private sector in commerce, banking and industry.

By 1965 this new policy had produced very dramatic results. The Ghanaian economy which by 1957 was (apart from agriculture) almost completely controlled by foreign companies, mainly from Western Europe, had undergone substantial changes in terms of ownership and control[1]. The government succeeded in bringing a good proportion of the commercial and manufacturing sectors under state control.[2] Very important changes also took place in Ghana's external trade relations with a considerable volume of external trade being redirected to the socialist countries. Accordingly by 1965 the socialist countries accounted for about twenty-five per cent of Ghana's total external trade as against less than five per cent on the eve of political independence.[3]

The CPP Government And The Fund

By 1960 Ghana had already joined the World Bank and the IMF and started negotiations with the World Bank, the USA and the UK for loans to finance the Volta River Project. The government had, until then, depended on its own resources for investment in the economic infrastructure, public utilities and social services.[4] To stem the strain on the country's deteriorating balance of payments brought about by this and the negative terms of trade the government decided to seek the assistance of the IMF. In August 1962, it borrowed US $14.25 million to reduce the balance of payments deficit.[5]

However, by the following year it became clear that the government and the Fund were heading for a collision. While performing its normal consultative functions with the Ghana Government, the Fund had warned the government to reduce its deficits by either reducing public expenditure or increasing revenues. The Executive Board of the Fund advised that:

> determined measures are needed to reduce public expenditure or increase revenues so that any deficit can be financed from non-inflationary sources and so far as capital expenditures are concerned, from long-term foreign borrowing in order to reduce excessive demand and the strain on balance of payments.[6]

The government quietly ignored this advice. But in the face of the mounting economic crisis, it decided to enchance its ability to draw on more Fund facilities. It accordingly took advantage of a general quota increase to raise her quota in the Fund from US $35 million to US $55 million.

But the Fund became increasingly irritated by the government's unwillingness to adopt the prescribed corrective measures. Around the end of 1964 a Fund team arrived in Ghana to hold the usual economic consultations with the government. After the visit the Fund's

Executive Board issued a stronger warning to the government. It declared:

> In order to prevent a further deterioration in the domestic and external situation the Fund considers that there is urgent need to contain domestic, particularly government expenditure. Total government expenditure should be limited to an amount that can be financed from non-inflationary sources. Priorities for development expenditure should be established and resources should be allocated only to those which offer benefit to the economy. In addition overseas borrowing for capital expenditure should be confined to long-term finance.[7]

The government did not heed this second warning either; and therefore their relations continued to worsen.

1965 marked a turning point in the worsening relations between the Nkrumah Government and the Fund. With a view to drawing once again on Fund facilities to reduce the balance of payments deficit, the government invited a Fund mission to study developments within the economy and make the necessary recommendations. It was obvious what the outcome would be since the government had not heeded previous warnings to take urgent corrective measures. As could be expected therefore the Fund minced no words about the state of the economy. It observed:

> The Ghana economy is severely constrained, the balance of payments is in serious deficits, and the country's foreign exchange reserves are at a precariously low level. Foreign debt repayments are increasingly putting added pressure on the balance of payments. The cause of the difficulty is not only the fall in cocoa price but also the excess of total government spending; a period of consolidation is urgently needed; to delay action would make the inevitable adjustment onerous.[8]

As the Government had in the past shown no inclination to heed any such warnings, the Fund this time submitted to the government a number of specific recommendations on how to remedy the economic crisis. They are:

> 1. Government expenditure — recurrent and capital — should be limited to an amount that can be covered by government revenue and non-inflationary borrowing.

> 2. In general a temporary halt should be placed on the launching of new projects financed by suppliers' credit
> 3. Additional steps should be taken to cut domestic demand including a cut in the price paid to cocoa farmers.
> 4. The dependence of state enterprises on the budget should be terminated.
> 5. The control of the public purse and the commitment of public funds should be centralised and strengthened.
> 6. The liberal attitude towards foreign investment found in the Capital Investments Act should be made more manifest in public policies.
> 7. Import licensing should be based on a strict system of priorities; some global quotas should be introduced and licenses issued should be honoured promptly by all relevant agencies of the Government. Discrimination in shipping should also be eliminated.
> 8. The bilateral and barter arrangements should be reconsidered with a view to reviewing their harmful impact on the Ghanaian econoy.[9]

A World Bank team invited by the government to examine its economy and make recommendations for assistance repeated the Fund warning much more strongly.[10] By the end of 1965 it was clear that the government was not prepared to submit to the kind of financial discipline required by the Bank and the Fund. Accordingly Western sources of credit were closed to the government and the country's economic difficulties assumed very critical dimensions.[11]

Political Significance of The Nkrumah Government Resistance

The unwillingness of the Nkrumah Government to submit to Fund and Bank recommended measures posed a serious political problem. On the one hand, Ghana had ceased to be a viable part of the international economic system. With a huge balance of payments deficit and debt the country was no longer a good customer on the international market. The government could not buy and pay for goods and services: it lived on borrowed money. This was unacceptable to the international capital market and trading circles. But for the government to implement the recommended measures would mean reduction, or even total stoppage, of certain social and development programmes that had been started for the mass of the people; relaxing its control over the economy; and curtailing its economic links with the socialist countries.

The government's whole strategy of development, its socialism, its politics and sovereignty were at stake. From the viewpoint of the Fund however the government had become a big political obstacle to sound economic policies. Somehow this contradiction had to be resolved; and when it was finally resolved with the violent overthrow of the CPP government in the coup of February 24, 1966, the worst fears of the government were proved right: workers were dismissed by the thousands; state owned enterprises were sold or opened to foreign private participation; and socialism was buried alive.

THE NATIONAL LIBERATION COUNCIL AND THE FUND

In its relation with the Fund, the National Liberation Council (NLC) — the military government that came into office in February 1966, took the exact opposite of what the Nkrumah government stood for. It began a period of very close collaboration with the Fund and the Bank. The basis of this collaboration was a Rehabilitation Programme commenced in 1966 and divided into rehabilitation and stabilization phases.[12]

Within two weeks of the coup a Fund team arrived in Accra for discussions with the NLC. In May 1966, a stand-by arrangement, equivalent to $36.4 million, was approved for the country; and over the next three years four stand-by credits, totalling $78.4 million, and a compensatory financing facility of $17.25 million were approved for the government. The NLC also increased the country's quota from $55.0 million to $69.0 million. But the Fund's generosity towards the government was conditional. Concrete austerity measures had to be imposed on the country as the price. These included:

1. a thirty per cent devaluation of the cedi
2. liberalization of both internal and external trade
3. reduction of government expenditures
4. restriction of new loans to only long term ones
5. reduction of employment in the civil and public services
6. privatisation of some state enterprises.

Though at the time it would have been politically unwise to admit it, the programme was almost a complete flop. Subsequent analyses have been quite objective. Money supply increased, the balance of payments problem persisted, economic growth was marginal, the rate of inflation did not abate to the level expected and the production of all major exports apart from timber declined, though export receipts went up due to favourable World Market prices.[13]

The Fund and the Bank were aware of this poor performance of the economy during the stabilization phase of the programme. For in a review of the Ghanaian economy the Bank admitted that the stabilization measures brought no improvement in export performance despite a devaluation of 30% in 1967.[14] It has been observed by critics that the 1966-68 stabilization programme neither addressed the problem of the external environment nor dependency structures. Besides, inadequate attention was paid to supply bottlenecks while the devaluation itself had a neglible effect on import and export levels.[15] And one very close observer has gone so far as to suggest that in fact the NLC programme left intact the basic source of instability and crisis in the Ghanaian economy.[16]

From The NLC To The Progress Party Government

Contrary to what some observers at the time might have thought, one of the underlying reasons for the failure of the NLC's stabilization programme was political. Conflict between two of the NLC's main policy-making organs did not permit full and unimpeded implementation of the IMF sponsored programme. These two bodies — the Political Committee and the Economic Committee, were constituted by people with different political orientations and interests. The Political Committee consisted mainly of politicians who had been in opposition to the Nkrumah regime. They still harboured political ambitions, and were impatient for the NLC to withdraw soon for them to assume power. Much more than the members of the Economic Committee, they were inclined towards a measure of economic nationalism; interested in preserving some state owned enterprises while limiting the creation of new ones; openly critical of the worst aspects of private enterprise; and determined to preserve the positive gains of the Nkrumah regime which would be beneficial to the country.

Members of the Political Committee tended to criticise publicly the terms on which state enterprises were offered for foreign private participation. The technocrats of the Economic Committee, on the other hand, lacked the nationalism of the members of the Political Committee; had little or no political ambitions; and therefore tended to take a technocratic position on issues like those related to the economy. Accordingly conflict could not be avoided, especially over controversial economic matters which the NLC had to deal with.

The relationship between the short-lived regime of the Progress Party (PP), led by Kofi Busia, and the Fund is politically important because it illustrates the difficulties that democratically elected regimes encounter in implementing Fund programmes. Though freely elected by the majority of Ghanaian voters, its attempt to impose austerity measures on the people created so much political resentment and conflict which resulted in its overthrow in January 1972. The tenure of the PP government is politically important for a second reason: it provides an excellent example of how powerful multilateral institutions like the Fund and Bank can take over the bureaucracy of a weak Third World Country like Ghana and reorganise it as well as create within it what they consider to be an appropriate structural network for implementing their policies.

As we have already noted one of the main causes of the NLC's inability to implement Fund policies thoroughly was that its decision-making structure was riddled with conflicts emanating from the presence of divergent political interests. With this experience behind them, it was considered necessary to reorganise the PP government's decision-making machinery in order to facilitate the implementation of Fund policies. Principally, reorganisation meant placing in the economic ministries and in the cabinet secretariat a network of representatives — mainly Fund and Bank sponsored experts or advisers. These then consituted a co-ordinating body at the apex of the economic decision-making machinery from where they also shaped and directed economic policy. In effect, the effective decision-making power was co-opted and the sovereignty of the country compromised.[17]

The PP government accepted the Fund and Bank recommendations, and was prepared to implement it. It had also succumbed to the de facto control of the key government ministries and related departments by Fund-Bank staff. However, because of the limitations of an elected government in implementing austerity programmes, it was unable to carry them through: it was overthrown even before it had made the first major move to put those policies into effect.

The successor government of the National Redemption Council (NRC — later re-named Supreme Military Council — SMC) led by Acheampong, naturally found tangible political reasons to confront the Fund and the Bank and, indeed, the whole community of Western Creditor governments and institutions on the country's debt.

THE ACHEAMPONG GOVERNMENT'S TEMPORARY DEFIANCE

After the overthrow of the Busia regime the government-Fund relationship entered a new phase which was characterised by temporary defiance and non-co-operation. During this period the National Redemption Council (NRC) government that had replaced the PP government pursued policies which ran contrary to anything the Fund and the Bank had advocated since the overthrow of the Nkrumah regime in 1966.[18]

The regime pursued an active interventionist policy in the economy. For instance, during the early phase of its rule, the NRC acquired majority shares in foreign companies engaged in the mining and timber industries.[19] It also repudiated some of the country's debt, which in its view were contracted under dubious conditions, and unilaterally rescheduled the rest. This phase however did not go beyond the first three years.

The next phase began in 1975 when the position of the state in the economy was further strengthened at the same time as Ghanaian private capital was encouraged to take over part or the whole of foreign-owned enterprises engaged in a wide-range of economic activities. The period also witnessed the most militant expression of economic nationalism under the official slogan of 'capturing the commanding heights of the economy'. The policy of economic nationalism was implemented under the Investment Policy Decree 1975 (NRCD 329). The outcome of that policy was that the state could acquire directly 13,189,471 shares valued at 19,365,081 in twenty-four foreign companies.[20] It could acquire some more shares indirectly through parastatal organisations. In contrast, foreign companies lost to the state, Ghanaian entrepreneurs and individual shareholders 62,181,004, worth of shares.[21] Largely because of this policy the NLC's sale of some state-owned enterprises was nullified; and the state sector became vastly expanded once again. At the same time however Ghanaian private participation in the economy expanded considerably. And so did the joint enterprise sector.

The expansion of the state sector was evident from its share in total output of manufacturing enterprises and in employment. Table 1 illustrates this trend especially in the manufacturing sector. It shows that the state and joint state/foreign private sectors expanded remarkably during the 1972-78 period. Not even the Nkrumah years witnessed such remarkable growth of state involvement in the economy. As Table 2 indicates, the effect of the expansion of the public sector in the manufacturing industry has been to reduce the position of the foreign private sector in the economy.

In spite of these developments, which were against the interest of foreign capital, the country's foreign creditors were surprisingly accomodative and gave the country the best debt rescheduling terms she has ever had. The country's medium-term debt was rescheduled under an agreement in March 1974. Under the terms of that agreement all payments due after February 1 1972 in respect of pre-1966 debt obligations were to be paid over a period of twenty-eight years beginning in 1982 after a grace period of ten years. The interest was fixed at two and a half per cent per annum.[22]

TABLE 1: MANUFACTURING ESTABLISHMENTS' SHARE IN VALUE ADDED AND EMPLOYMENT, BY TYPE OF OWNERSHIP (per cent of totals)

VALUE ADDED					
	1964	1967	1973	1977	1979
State-Owned	13.3	17.6	17.2	29.4	27.1
Joint-Ownership	7.9	14.6	18.0	19.5	25.6
Private	78.9	67.8	64.8	51.1	47.3
	100.0	100.0	100.0	100.0	100.0
EMPLOYMENT					
State-owned	29.4	32.6	23.2	18.0	24.0
Joint-Ownership	3.2	7.6	19.5	26.0	29.0
Private	67.4	59.8	57.3	50.0	46.0
	100.0	100.0	100.0	100.0	100.0

TABLE 2: VALUE ADDED IN MANUFACTURING BY TYPE OF OWNERSHIP, 1979 (percentage shares)

State-Owned	27		
Joint State-Private	25.6		
Private	47.3		
		Private Mixed	12.7
		Private Ghanaian	12.7
		Private Foreign	22.9

Notwithstanding these favourable terms gross economic mismanagement and unfavourable external factors combined to plunge the economy in a deeper crisis. The most important of these external developments was the rise in the price of petroleum and declining export earnings. These exerted a severe pressure on the country's balance of payments position and fuelled domestic price inflation. In a situation of fast dwindling revenues and sharp monetary expansion, hyper-inflation set in.[23]

Furthermore, the production of almost all the major crops — both export and non-export, declined to abysmally low levels. The country's rating in the world economy dropped to an all-time low. As can be seen from Table 3, Ghana placed very low on the scale of economic performance in many respects.

TABLE 3: RANKING OF GHANA'S ECONOMIC PERFORMANCE, 1978

INDICATOR	No of Countries	Ghana Ranking
1. Av. Annual Growth of Per Capita income 1960-1976	89	82nd
2. Growth in per captia food production 1965/7 — 1974-76	89	69th
3. Av. Annual rate of inflation 1970/76	88	80th
4. Growth of Annual Agricultrual production 1970/76	79	60th
5. Growth of Industrial Production 1970/76	78	58th
6. Growth of domestic investment as % of GDP 1970	82	79th
7. Gross domestic saving as % of GDP 1970	81	68th
8. Av. Annual Growth in the volume of exports 1970-76	80	64th
9. Av. Annual Growth in the Quan-tum of imports 1970-76	80	53rd
10. Ext. Public Debt Servicing as % of exports 1976	74	21st
11. Gross foreign exchange reserves relative to imports 1976	73	61st

Source: World Bank, *World Development Report 1978*, Washington (Annex Tables)

SMC II AND THE FUND

This level of economic decline required urgent stabilisation measures which implied a change of economic policy. Whereas during the 1960s the entire Nkrumah regime had to be removed from office before the Fund adjustment programmes could be carried through, this time the dismissal of the head of state was the only condition. Thus on July 5 1978 a palace coup was staged to remove General Ignatius Acheampong as Head of State and replaced by General Akuffo. It is clear therefore that no major political and ideological differences were involved.

With the obstacle now removed the Fund returned into the country's economic life again; and a short-term stabilization programme was launched after which a stand-by credit of SDR 53.0 million spread over twelve months was approved for the country.

Again there were preconditions attached to the financial support the Fund was granting. The following policy measures had to be implemented: a 58% devaluation of the cedi; drastic reduction of the budgetary deficits; reduced borrowing from abroad; prompt repayment of external debt and a big increase in the producer price of cocoa.

But there was still a major political obstacle to the success of the programme. Worker dissatisfaction with deteriorating economic conditions had been rising for some time. With the announcement of an austerity programme that would impose greater austerity on them, industrial unrest escalated. At this stage the regime felt the need to demonstrate its political capacity to implement those measures even against stiff working class oposition. On 6th November, 1978 it declared a state of emergency. Workers were warned that:

> To resort to pressure, blackmail, strike action and damage, or the tampering with employers' property or installation by workers to secure redress outside the normal procedure shall be regarded as criminal acts against the security of the state and dealt with in accordance with the relevant laws of the country.[24]

At a time when the severe economic situation had mobilised almost the entire nation against the regime, the use of force to quell political opposition by the mass of the workers destroyed whatever legitimacy the regime had.

On June 4th, 1979, a Fund team arrived in Accra to assess the extent to which the government had carried out the prescribed policies. On the same day, the uprising by the ranks and the junior officers of the armed forces broke out. The regime whose capacity the Fund team came to assess had been overthrown but the new one had not yet settled down. No talks could be held and the team had to leave as soon as the airport was re-opened to traffic. Therefore only the first tranche of $32 million could be drawn. Another attempt to carry out the IMF programme had been politically frustrated and further contacts had to wait for the next elected government led by Dr. Hilla Limann.

POST-AFRC PRESSURES

The AFRC saw itself as an interim government. During its four months reign its main goal was to clean the society quickly of anti-social practices and leave. There was therefore no time for, and no concern with, the need to formulate a coherent set of policies. Its essentially piece-meal policies were aimed at fighting the high cost of living in the urban centres. With its rigid price control measures and punitive confiscation of private industrial and commercial enterprises and houses, it effectively breached the agreement which the SMC II, led by General Akuffo, had reached with the Fund and served as the basis for the stand-by credit granted by the Fund.

The failure of yet another attempt by the IMF to get the government of Ghana to undertake an economic stabilization programme must have been a matter of concern to the Fund and other western economic interests that have a stake in the Ghanaian economy, especially as the country remained a member of the Fund and so continued to enjoy the rights of membership throughout the 1970s without submitting to the necessary economic discipline and control.

During the second half of the 1970s Ghana utilized as much as it could all those Fund facilities which did not carry any conditions. In 1979 alone, the government utilized a total of SDR 68.6 million. As the Economic Survey points out:[25]

> Ghana made extensive use of IMF facilities; the total use of Fund resources for the period January-October1979 amounted to SDR 68.6 million. On February 1st, 1979 withdrawals under the stand-by arrangement of January 1977 totalled SDR 32.0 million.

A much fuller picture of Ghana's total transactions with the Fund can be derived from Table 4 below which is a summary for the six year period, 1975-1980.

TABLE 4: GHANA'S TOTAL TRANSACTIONS WITH IMF 1975-80 (amount in Million SDR)

No.	Year	Type of Transaction	Amount
1.	1975	Oil Facility	38.6
2.	1977	Earmarked gold	0.1
3.	1977-78	Distribution of Pro-fits from sale of gold	6.6
4.	1977-78	Gold Purchases	2.0
5.	1978-80	Oil facility Re-purchases	−24.0
6.	Jan-Oct. 1979	Use of Fund Reserves	68.6
TOTAL			91.9

Source: *Ghana, Economic Survey* 1977-80, CBS, 1981 P. 291.

In the face of the continuing deterioration of the Ghanaian economy and the lack of political capacity shown by the successive regimes either to implement a stabilization programme or sustain it, international pressure on Ghana mounted after the AFRC had handed over power to the elected government of the PNP. The most concerned bodies were the major donors and foreign investors with operations in the country. The World Bank was particularly concerned because after investing about US $208.1 million in Ghana between 1975 and 1980 the crisis of the economy was undermining every potential for positive results.

There was a critical shortage of competent managers; the government itself was unable to mobilize adequate domestic savings to support bank projects; the whole government machinery was on the brink of collapse; and dollars contributed by the Bank fetched inadequate cedis because the latter was overvalued. For these and, probably, other reasons the Bank closed its Accra mission in the latter part of 1980 and stopped lending money to the country.

The USAID was equally concerned about the severe deterioration in the Ghanaian economy. The agreement under which the US government supplied food to Ghana — the PL 480, gives the US government the option to receive payment for such aid in local currency at the highest prevailing legal exchange rate. At the prevailing exchange rate the value of the food aid in local currency terms was not high enough. The US government was so concerned about the situation that at the 1981 renegotiation of PL 480 Title 1 Agreements, the US delegation felt obliged to draw attention to the linkage between the macro-economic policies of the government and the performance of the economy and stressed the need to reverse the situation.[26]

Another organisation which had every cause to be interested in Ghana's acceptance of an IMF package was the Volta Aluminium Company (VALCO), a subsidiary of a giant American aluminium company. Valco was interested in the devaluation of the Ghanaian currency and had indeed been pressing the Government to give it a preferential exchange rate for its dollars because the company had been spending in Ghana a lot more hard currency than it would under a different exchange rate regime. For example:

> between 1978 and 1981... Valco had on the average to bring into Ghana about $15 million more per annum than if the exchange rate had been at a 'market level'.This largely explains Valco's initial position at the Ghana-Valco Renegotiations in 1982 which was to offer only a minor increase ... conditional on receiving a preferential exchange rate.[27]

The PNP Government's Response

The government of the PNP led by President Limann was surprisingly resistant to these pressures. And yet the capital-starved government stood to gain from the Fund about $400 million, i.e $300 million in stand-by credit and $100 million in Compensatory Financing Facility. All that the government had to do was to pluck the political courage to implement the economic stabilization policies that the Fund was recommending. These were normal IMF prescribed policies: a three hundred per cent increase in the producer price of cocoa; a sharp reduction in government expenditure; a subtantial devaluation of the cedi, etc. It was also reported that the Fund was prepared to offer another $1000 million in due course in support of a three year stabilization programme.

Even though the Limann administration increased the producer price of cocoa and the price of petroleum products, it was on the whole very hesitant and sceptical about the soundness of the entire IMF package of reforms. In view of the potential negative social and political repercussions of an IMF package this democratically elected government opted for caution and procrastination in its relation with the Fund.

On the whole, there was little support in the government and party for the Fund package. The government's opposition to the Fund policies was manifested in several ways. First and foremost, it showed glaringly in the constant reshuffling of Ministers in charge of the finance ministry. For example, under the cover of the first cabinet reshuffle, the pro-IMF Minister of Finance Dr. Amon Nikoi, was allowed to withdraw quietly from the government. He was followed in the next reshuffle by his two deputies Mr. Innocent Katsriku and Dr. E.L. Nyakotey, both of whom were reported to be 'favourable to the rigorous conditions proposed by the IMF before granting large financial support to Ghana'.[28]

The departure of pro-IMF ministers from the government confirmed the president's own public views on the question of IMF policies. On devaluation he was reported to have said that 'Ghana has had four devaluations and each was followed by social explosions including executions'.[29] The President believed that devaluation had failed to pass the test each time it had been tried in the country. Since not all forms of Ghana's productive activities were dependent on external resources he was highly sceptical of the relevance of devaluation to the country's economic problem. Cocoa, the major export crop, is not responsive to devaluations. Labour retrenchment could not be helpful in efforts to reduce government spending.[30]

Earlier the President had argued that, 'Every action must be related to the social climate... The government is a major employer and we are dealing with human beings, we cannot simply carry out a massive dismissal of workers'.[31] The refusal of the PNP government to comply with Fund prescriptions were based on hard political and social facts. But whatever the reasons were, an important reason was the weakness of the regime and other state institutions to administer such an austerity programme that was likely to provoke a severe social and political backlash. The conduct of the PNP government left the future of the foreign economic interests in the country as well as the country's role in the world economy extremely uncertain. The continued crisis in the economy coupled with this dearth of a strong regime to take bold corrective measures, did not inspire much confidence among the country's donors and trading partners.

THE PNDC GOVERNMENT

The task of reversing this situation fell squarely on the shoulders of the PNDC government. The PNDC inherited an economy in a shambles. The Ghanaian economy had reached an unprecedented level of economic decline. This was compounded by the outbreak of drought, famine, bush fires, and the sudden expulsion of about 1.2 million Ghanaians from Nigeria.

In the meantime, the structure of the economy had undergone further changes. The state sector had become much bigger as a result of the AFRC's punitive nationalisations. The question then was: would the PNDC be able to agree with the IMF on a solution to Ghana's economic problems? In 1982, it was not so obvious that the PNDC would wholeheartedly embrace the Fund's SAP with all its strict conditionalities. There were two main obstacles to an early collaboration between the PNDC and the IMF. These were (i) the compostion of the PNDC and its support base; and (ii) the attitude of the political opposition to the PNDC during the 1982-83 period.

The PNDC and its support base as well as the basis of political opposition to the government derived from the opposite camps of the great divide in Ghanaian politics. According to Hansen, two broad groups — the Left and the Right, can be identified in Ghanaian politics and these became polarised in the 1982-83 political struggles. The Left believes that there is:

> the need for revolution defined in terms of the transformation of the social and economic order. (Within the Left there is) consensus that (a revolution) involves (the) termination of the control of the local economy by foreign multinational companies, changes in the structure of production and production relations, changes in the class structure of control of the state, creation of political forms which would make the interest of the broad masses of

> people predominant and realisable and a programme which would initiate a process of improving the material conditions of the mass of the people.[32]

On the right are those who maintain the postion that:

> there was nothing basically wrong with the nature of the country's structure of production or production relations or the nature of our economic relations with the Western Capitalist countries as well asthe structure of power, class relations or the nature of state power and that only certain aspects of the functioning needed to be reformed.[33]

We would add that ideologically, the Ghanaian Left tends to revolve around the traditions of Kwame Nkrumah while the right as a whole gravitates towards the Danquah/Busia tradition.

As originally constituted the PNDC had a heavy representation of the Ghanaian radical Left — i.e. the militant sections of the student leadership, workers and soldiers as well as Left movements such as the June Fourth Movement. Indeed the PNDC's composition to a large extent also reflected its support base which was constituted by the Left movements — the June Fourth Movement, the New Democratic Movement, the Kwame Nkrumah Revolutionary Guards, the African Youth Command, radical students, workers and soldiers.

In general these groups, are even more suspicious of IMF solutions. The composition of the PNDC therefore would have to change and its support base controlled if it were to have close collaboration with the Fund. On the other hand the Ghanaian Right, was not opposed to IMF and its solutions. But it was opposed to the PNDC which it regarded as a usurper. The hostility of the Right towards the PNDC posed a grave security problem and did not give the government the congenial political environment in which it could immediately assume a pro-Fund posture. This security problem posed by the Right also had to be resolved before the regime could consolidate its power and tackle the country's economic problems.

The greatest political asset of the PNDC is its ability to take on and demolish one major politcal opponent at a time. First, with the support of the Left and workers, the Right opposition was brought under control. With that threat removed the PNDC then neutralized the Left and working class organisations. The defeat of the Left removed a major source of opposition to the IMF and enabled the government to embark on the total implementation of the Fund package of structural adjustment.

The PNDC's attitude to the Left was of particular importance.

It indicated to the Fund, Bank and the Western donor countries how the government viewed the private sector and its determination or lack thereof to promote the growth of private enterprise in the country. Hence, for example, the Bank would observe that 'the economic framework... would certainly be effective provided the general political and social millieu is favourable'.[34] Also until the close of 1984 foreign donor countries continued to express doubt about the government's capacity to control the Left effectively as a condition for the successful implementation of the SAP.[35] These political pressures had achieved the desired effect by the end of 1984.

To facilitate the implementation of the Fund policies the PNDC began to depoliticise its politcal structures and recast their role to ensure that they did not become an impediment to its economic policies. The sweeping changes in the structure and role of the CDRs which occurred during the last quarter of 1984 firmly established the government's commitment and determination to pursue the SAP. They effectively brought the CDRs under the control of the PNDC and changed its orientation from political agitation and mobilization to essentially non-political tasks. These changes culminated in the shift that occurred in the ideological and political orientation of the PNDC and increased its resolve to push through with the SAP.

During the first phase of the programme 1984-86 these changes enabled the PNDC to collaborate more closely with the IMF to implement its policies. The measures included a major devaluation of the Ghana cedi; a widening of the tax net; reduction of government expenditure; restricting bank credit; and removal of subsidies on utility services. With these measures and substantial financial assistance from external donors, the PNDC was able to stabilise the economy and stimulate its growth.

Ghana-IMF collaboration was further strengthened and carried to a higher stage when the government launched the second stage of the SAP. The best known elements of the SAP include a reform of state-owned enterprises; redeployment of redundant labour in the public sector; market determined exchange rate; and an income policy that provides adequate wage differentials to attract much needed skilled and professional personnel. These measures were meant to reduce significantly the state's share in wage employment and ownership of enterprises.

Thus at long last the role of the post-colonial state in the economy started reverting from one of active participation to one of providing the social conditions for the growth of the private sector, with the active support of multilateral agencies like the Fund and Bank. This trend is also evident from the investment pattern that has been unfolding since the government embarked upon the Structural

Adjustment Programmes. Increasingly private sector investment is outstripping state investments even though the pace is slower than the PNDC would have liked. Table 5 illustrates this pattern of investment which is symptomatic of the changed role of the state.

TABLE 5: OWNERSHIP STRUCTURE OF PROJECTS APPROVED BY THE GHANA INVESTMENT CENTRE IN 1986

		Cedi Million				
TYPE OF OWNERSHIP	No. of Projects	Total Invest ment	Foreign Currency Component		Local currency Component	
			Equity	Loans	Equity	Loans
100 % Ghanaian	89	11,750.9	109.9	5254.4	3646.1	2740.5
100% State	5	2,595.2	—	9973.7	506.3	1115.2
100% Foreign	1	6,806.3	1544.0	5262.3	—	—
Joint Foreign/ Ghanaian/Private	52	9,605.8	1179.0	4661.9	1764.3	2000.6
Joint Foreign/ State	3	1,858.5	97.8	1294.0	249.0	217.7
Joint State/ Ghanaian/Private	2	268.6	—	90.0	37.5	141.1
Joint State/ Foreign Ghanaian/ Private	2	926.3	70.5	581.8	83.5	190.5
TOTAL	154	33,811.6	3001.2	18118.1	6286.7	6405.6

SOURCE: Ghana Investment Centre *Annual Report 1986*.

CONCLUSION

It is evident by now that Ghana's relations with the IMF have passed through many stages. From an initial position of stubborn resistance to the Fund in the 1960's Ghana has now fully embraced IMF policies and collaborates with the Fund on almost every aspect of economic policy. This about turn in relations has come about largely because of many political and economic changes that have made it possible for a regime with a favourable attitude towards the IMF to emerge.

The PNDC could forge close collaboration with the Fund only because the economic crisis had reached a point at which the need for tough measures to reverse the decline had become paramount. The Right was determined to ensure that this would be accomplished. Foreign investors, trading partners, donor countries and agencies also shared this view. The merit of the PNDC is that it could create the necessary political conditions for a bold beginning towards reversing about two decades of economic crisis.

The relationship between the government and the Fund/Bank is therefore not merely an economic one; it is anchored to a very large extent in a solid political framework. The Fund and Bank may claim that they are not interested in the politics of the countries which it assists. In practice the right political environment is so crucial to any successful collaboration between the Fund and Third World Countries that neither government nor Fund/Bank officials can pretend that it can be ignored.

The ability of the PNDC to sustain its collaboration with the Fund and Bank into the future will therefore depend on the kind of political changes that would occur in its lifetime. That is, the key question about the future of Fund and Bank policies is not their acceptability either to a government, or to one or the other political group. The crucial issue is the kind of politics that will facilitate the acceptance and implementation of their policies.

NOTES

1. Esseks, J.D. 'Political Independence and Economic Decolonisation: The Case of Ghana Under Nkrumah', *Western Political Quarterly* 1971 Vol. 24 No. 1.
2. Jonah, Kwesi 'Imperialism, the State And The Indigenization of the Ghanaian Economy' *Africa Development* Vol.X Nos. 3 1986 p. 63-99.
3. Jonah Kwesi *'Ghana Under Nkrumah: The Struggle Against the Neo-colonial Trade Patterns'*. Paper presented at the Symposium on the Life and Works of Kwame Nkrumah, organized by the Institute of African Studies, University of Ghana, Legon, May 27th-June 1st 1985.
4. *Ghana Economic Survey* 1960 Accra: Central Bureau of Statistics, p.76.
5. *Ghana Economic Survey* 1962 Accra: Central Bureau of Statistics p.101.
6. *Ghana Economic Survey* 1963 Accra: Central Bureau of Statistics p. 108.
7. *Ghana Economic Survey* 1964, Accra: Central Bureau of Statistics, p.61.
8. *Ghana Economic Survey* 1965 Accra: Central Bureau of Statistics p.50
9. Ibid
10. Ibid
11. Ibid
12. Lindsay, John K. 'Ghana's Policy For Economic Rehabilitation' *Legon Observer* Vol. II No. 10 12-25 May 1967.
13. Ofori Attah, Jones 'Devaluation Versus Devaluation' Legon Observer Vol. X No.2 15-28 September 1978; also BANK OF GHANA, 'Ghana's Stabilization measures and the IMF: A Case Study' *Africa Development* Vol.X Nos. 1 & 2 1985 p. 134-144.

14. *Current Economic Situation and Economic Prospects of Ghana*, IBRD and IDA Washington DC 1972 p.1
15. Hutchful, Eboe, 'IMF Adjustment Policies In Ghana Since 1966' *Africa Development* Vol. X Nos. 1 & 2 1985 p. 122-133.
16. *Killick, Tony*, 'A New Economic Strategy for Ghana.' Part One, *Legon Observer* Vol. XI 18th-31st May 1979 and Part Two, *Legon Observer* Vol. XI No.9 8th-21st June 1979.
17. Libby, Ronald T. 'External Co. Optation of A Less Developed Countrie's Policy-Making: The Case of Ghana 1969-1972,' *World Politics* No. 1 October 1976.
18. Ofori Atta, Jones Op. Cit.
19. The acquisitions were made under the following laws: Timber operations (Government Participation) Decree, 1972 (NRCD 139) and Mining Operations (Government participation) Decree, 1972 (NRCD 132).
20. Jonah, Kwesi 'Imperialism the State and the indigenization of the Ghanaian Economy' *Africa Development* Vol. X No. 1985, p. 63-99.
21. Ibid
22. World Bank, Report No. P. 3554 *Report and Recommendation of The President of the World Bank To The Executive Directors on a Proposed Credit of SDR 37.0 Million to the Republic of Ghana for a Reconstruction Import Credit*. Report No. P. 3554. June 1983 Washington D.C. p.9
23. Steel, William F. 'Hyperinflation in Ghana' *Legon Observer* Vol. II No. 13 30th November-30th December 1979.
24. The Declaration of the State of Emergency by the Head of State General F.W. Akuffo in November 6 1978. Reproduced in *Legon Observer* Vol. X No. 6 10-23 November 1978.
25. Ghana. Economic Survey 1977-1980. (Accra: CBS 1981)
26. Minutes of the negotiating sessions of Title I Agreements Between the Government of the US and the Government of Ghana, 1982.
27. Sims, Rod and Casely Hayford L. 'Renegotiating The Price and Availability of Energy for an aluminium smelter: The VALCO Renegotiations,' in Tsikata, Fui.(ed.) *Essays from the Ghana-Valco Renegotiations 1982-1985* Accra VRA. 1986. p. 29, p.35.
28. *West Africa* 17th October 1981 p.2368.
29. *Africa Now*. October 1981 p.48.
30. Ibid
31. *Africa Now*. October 1980 p.45.
32. Hansen, E. 'The State and Popular Struggles in Ghana 1982-86'. In P. Anyang Nyongo. (ed) *Popular Struggles for Democracy in Africa*. London: UNU/ZED 1982.
33. Ibid
34. Mission Report from Paris, Meeting of the Consultative Group for Ghana, Paris December 11-12 1984.
35. Ibid

5. FINANCIAL INTERMEDIATION AND ECONOMIC DEVELOPMENT

Nii Kwaku Sowa

INTRODUCTION

It is the aim of every government to create conditions of stability and well-being and to ensure a minimum standard of living consistent with human dignity through economic and social progress and development. In persuance of this noble objective, member nations of the United Nations declared the decade of the 1960s as the First United Nations Development Decade. The following decade was subsequently declared as the Second United Nations Development Decade.

During these decades member nations of the world body pledged themselves to keep their economies growing at certain rates. For example, developing countries resolved to maintain a growth rate of 6 per cent per annum in gross domestic product (3.5 per cent in GDP per head). Towards this goal, it was envisaged that there would be an average annual expansion of 0.5 per cent in the ratio of gross domestic savings to the gross domestic product, so that this ratio would rise to around 20 per cent by 1980.

Ironically, the period of the sixties and the seventies were the times when most developing countries witnessed a slow-down in their growth rates. It was also the period during which most developing countries gained their independence from their colonial dominions. Was it, therefore, an accident of history that post-colonial developing countries found their economies slowing down? Or, did their economies just suffer most in a period of global recession? Were there any institutional difficulties that caused their economies to backslide so much?

In this chapter, we shall look at one particular set of institutions — the financial intermediaries — and the way they have helped or hindered economic development in Ghana. The chapter will examine the operations of Ghana's financial institutions regarding the mobilization of savings and rechanneling them into investible funds. It will also look at the relationship between successive governments and the financial institutions, and examine the extent to which some government policies have hindered or facilitated the smooth operations of the banking system.

The chapter starts off with an overview of the post-colonial economic situation in the country. The next section examines what is ideally regarded as the role of financial intermediaries. This sets the stage for the evaluation of the performance of banks in Ghana during which we first analyse the operations of the banks during the colonial period. The rest of the chapter analyses the operations of banking institutions in the post-colonial period.

THE POST-COLONIAL ECONOMIC SCENE

Ghana gained independence from Britain on the 6th of March, 1957 and was hailed as Africa's hope. The Nkrumah government which took over from the colonialists wasted no time with industrialization. The second half of the fifties saw a 50 per cent increase in Ghana's capital stock. The record for the first half of the sixties was even better with net capital accumulation in 1965 estimated at not less than 80 per cent of the 1960 level.[1]

Despite this massive initial investment which was expected to push Ghana into a period of sustained growth, the economy retrogressed. GNP (at 1960 constant prices) fell from about 140 million cedis in 1960 to about 125 million cedis in 1969. Between 1960 and 1970 GDP in Ghana grew at an average annual rate of 2.2 per cent. In addition the country became a net debtor. By the early 1980s the country was faced with a serious problem of stagflation: inflation run at 3-digits while output declined sharply. This trend in the country's economic development has been variously refered to by different authors as a period of 'development without growth', 'investment without growth', or 'modernization without growth'.[2]

One may argue that the growth rate for that decade was low because the investments were of a long term nature and needed time to mature. But it is remarkable that between 1970 and 1980, the growth rate of GDP fell to −5.5 per cent which was the worst in the whole world. Between 1980 and 1985 when the whole world economy was in a recession, the country's GDP declined at the rate of −0.7 per cent per annum.

By the 1980s, per capita income in Ghana had fallen below the $400 mark. It is no wonder that Ghana's economy, which in the early seventies was classified as a middle-income economy, was by the eighties classified as low-income economy. This continued fall in the rate of growth of the GDP seems to suggest deep-seated structural imbalances in the economy which make it difficult for the full realization of the fruits of these investments.

The decline in the Ghanaian economy reached its lowest ebb in 1983. That year went down as one of the worst periods in the country's history. Coupled with a severe drought and extensive bush-fires the economic crisis deprived the country not only of imported commodities, but also locally produced consumer goods. Everything was in short supply — food, water and fuel. In that same year thousands of Ghanaians were repatriated from Nigeria.

This protracted decline in the economy affected savings and investments too. In 1960, about 17 per cent of gross domestic product was saved; but by 1982 this had declined to a mere 1 percent. In other words, Ghanaians consumed all that they produced. Gross domestic investment in the economy also declined from a proportion of about 20 per cent of GDP to about 1 per cent by 1982. Thus, both savings and investment — the two essential elements in capital formation, fell sharply.

The question which should then be asked is: What happened to the third element in capital formation — finance? The purpose of this paper is to examine the role of the financial intermediaries on this subject. That is, to what extent have they contributed to the growth or decline in the economy?

THE ROLE OF FINANCIAL INTERMEDIARIES

We live in a world of surpluses and deficits. At any period in time there are people who have more than their immediate needs demand, and others who need more than their resources can provide. Those with excess funds would like to save their idle funds to earn some interest on them. On the other hand, there are those who need funds and would like to borrow some to use. A financial intermediary is that institution which interceeds between borrowers and savers. It collects funds from those who have excess supply and gives it to those with excess demand. In other words, it acts as an 'agent' between the savers and the investors. By performing this function, therefore, a financial intermediary can rechannel idle balances into productive sectors where they are most needed. One begins to see in this the important role that financial institutions must play in the economic development of a country.

As financial institutions grow, people stop hoarding money. With active intermediation taking place in an economy, savings and investment habits are promoted among ordinary people who may have no knowledge about investment behaviour. People are just encouraged to safely deposit their idle balances with the financial intermediary and receive interest payments as reward.

But a financial intermediary should function more than just as a 'pawn-house' for lenders and borrowers. Financial intermediaries should not be idle agents just collecting fees for helping investors. They should take the initiative of investing some of their funds in viable projects. In other words, they should take risks: they should be prepared to engage in venture capital, and invest in projects which are viable but not covered by collateral. They should, in fact, assume some of the risks that is usually borne by savers and investors and promote the pooling and sharing of risks among depositors.

Financial institutions specialize in gathering information about loan projects. They have the qualified staff to thoroughly appraise projects before loans are granted. Such activities help to reduce market imperfections and improve the allocation of resources. Thus, 'changes in the level of financial intermediation due to monetary policy, legal restrictions or other factors, may have significant real effects on the economy.'[3] Some economists are even of the view that the quantity and quality of services provided by intermediaries are important determinants of aggregate economic performance.[4]

Economic growth requires more investment. Investible funds can come from either foreign or domestic sources. But as Ahmad (1970) points out:

> foreign capital alone cannot create any permanent basis for higer standards of living in the future. Foreign capital can relieve initial foreign exchange shortages,stimulate domestic production and increase domestic incomes, but to ensure self-sustained economic growth, it is necessary to generate domestic savings, to mobilize them effectively and to canalize them into productive investments.[5]

The central institution for mobilizing domestic savings and canalizing them into productive investments is the financial intermediary. In Ghana, there are several institutions, formal and informal, performing intermediation functions. These include one central bank, five commercial banks, two merchant banks, three development banks, a cooperative bank, a building society, several rural banks, insurance companies, credit unions, and several 'susu-collectors', (see Appendix A).

BANKING IN PRE-INDEPENDENT GHANA

Banking normally develops where there is a monetary economy. There was an abortive attempt by the British colonialists to monetize the economy of the Gold Coast as early as 1825, by the introduction of British silver coins, here and in other parts of British West Africa. After that abortive attempt, it was not until about five decades later that the economy of Britain's West African colonies became monetized. Thenceforth, the colonial government considered the establishment of a bank.

The first bank in the Gold Coast — the Government Savings Bank — was set up in 1888. About a decade later, the first commercial bank opened its offices in the country. It was a branch of the British Bank of West Africa, then headquartered in Lagos, Nigeria. (This bank still operates in Ghana under the new name Standard Chartered (Ghana) Limited.) It has been claimed that this bank helped to abolish the barter system in Ghana, and promoted in its place a money economy — primarily, the expansion of trade by financing merchants. McPhee (1926) remarks that these banks:

> enhanced the circulation of coin indirectly by increasing the volume of trade directly. They advanced money to small traders who are notoriously energetic and venturesome on bills. The result was that small traders multiplied, competition grew and the demand for coin currency expanded accordingly.'[6]

In 1917, the monopoly of banking in the Gold Coast which the British Bank of West Africa enjoyed was broken by a new comer — the Colonial Bank, now Barclays Bank (Ghana) Limited. These two banks operated in the Gold Coast for a long time as the only commercial banks. In 1953, the first indigenous commercial bank — Bank of the Gold Coast, later to be known as the Ghana Commercial Bank — was established.

There was no central bank in pre-independence Ghana. There was however, the West African Currency Board which was set up in 1912 to issue and redeem the West African currency. The Board itself was housed in London but had local agents to see to its affairs.

In the absence of a central bank for the colony, the issuance and redemption of currency was done by the Bank of England. The Gold Coast economy did not, therefore, benefit from the seignorage arising out of the printing of money. In addition, practically no developmental direction was given to the commercial banks in the performance of their duties. These banks operated on just pure profit motives. As commercial banks, they invested their money where they could have the quickest turnover — merchant trading. Even so, in their intermediation process, they helped to get the economy monetized.

TABLE 1: FINANCIAL INDICATORS (1950-1957)
(Cedis million)

End of Period	(1) G.D.P.	(2) Money Supply	(3) Total Deposits	(4) (2)/(1) (Percent)	(5) Currency In Circ.	(6) Currency Ratio
1950	388.4	43.6	21.8	11.2	21.8	.5
1951	472.8	46.0	23.3	9.7	22.7	.5
1952	476.5	58.4	29.1	12.3	29.3	.5
1953	505.4	66.6	33.3	13.2	33.3	.5
1954	574.5	78.1	39.3	13.6	38.8	.5
1955	668.0	87.0	43.6	13.0	43.4	.5
1956	690.0	88.9	44.2	12.9	44.7	.5
1957	726.0	91.2	45.6	12.6	45.6	.5

Source: Kodwo Ewusi, Statistical Tables on the Economy of Ghana, (1950-1985), ISSER, Legon.

Table 1 provides a summary of financial indicators between 1950 and 1957. Within that period GDP at current prices grew from 388.4 million to 726.0 million , representing an average annual growth rate of about 9.3 per cent. During the same period the total money supply grew from 43.6 million in 1950 to about 91.2 million cedis by 1957, representing an average annual growth rate of 12.4 per cent.

Over that period currency in circulation seemed to be guided to maintain a one to one relation with total deposits. The currency-money supply ratio therefore remained constant at 50 per cent between 1950 and 1957. Whereas a constant currency ratio is good for effective operation of monetary policy,[7] a high currency ratio implies that money is functioning more as a consumption good than as producer good. In this kind of situation, there is likely to be idle balances around which could have been mobilized by the banks and rechanelled into productive ventures.

In Ghana, and other British West African colonies the monetary systems which were set up were an extention of the British monetary system. It has been argued by Hopkins (1973) that:

> it was related closely enough to the metropolitan system to ensure that international trade would not be unsettled by changes in the rates of exchange.[8]

The colonial government maintained tight control of the money supply of the colonies. To ensure the success of this credit control, money supply in the economy of the Gold Coast and other British colonies was tied closely to their balance of payments. The money supply was allowed to expand when the balance on the current account showed a surplus; and it was forced to contract when there was a deficit.

This situation forced on the Gold Coast a very tight monetary policy; but it had its advantages as well. For instance, there was practically no problem with inflation during that period. At the same time it encouraged the country not to incur deficits on the balance of payments, since a deficit will imply a reduction in the money supply.

However, this colonial monetary system also had its shortcomings. First, the tight monetary policy did not allow for growth of the internal exchange economy, except when there was an export surplus. This system imposed on the Ghanaian economy a compulsion to increase its exports as a condition for achieving any measure of growth at all. In a sense, therefore, one can argue that the colonial banking system helped to entrench the colonial economy.

The biggest shortcoming of the colonial banks was, however, that they did not do much to help the local economy build the internal capacity to generate growth. They failed to advance loans to local peasants and entrepreneurs because they lacked collateral securities. Credit was circulated only among big commercial houses which could afford to provide a 'good' collateral.

Moreover, the type of collateral demanded — life assurance policies, stocks, shares and bills — were not the kind that could be afforded by the local entrepreneurs and therefore kept them away from the banks. In this way the big expatriate companies got bigger while the small local companies got smaller.

Furthermore, the banks invested most of their profits in Britain, thereby compounding the problem of capital shortage for the development of local industries. The banks concentrated more on the acquisition of foreign assets than domestic assets. Table 2 below, shows the banks' domestic assets as a percentage of their external assets.

Between 1950 and 1957, the proportion of banks' domestic to foreign assets fluctuated between 25 and 88 per cent. They increased their external assets from 1951, when Nkrumah's party won the first election till 1957 when Ghana had full self-government. The establishment of the Ghana Commercial Bank in 1953 did not change this trend. Infact, that was the year when the banks held the greatest proportion of their assets in foreign instruments. Thus even though the banks in pre-independent Ghana greatly facilitated the monetization of the economy they, did not help much in the country's development because of their discriminating investment practices.

TALBE 2: RATIO OF BANKS DOMESTIC TO EXTERNAL ASSETS (1950-1957)

Year	1950	1951	1952	1953	1954	1955	1956	1957
Per cent	88	53	67	25	48	55	58	82

Source: Birmingham, Neustadt and Omaboe, *A Study of Contemporary Ghana*, Vol.1, p. 320.

THE STATE AND THE BANKS

1957 was a very fateful year for Ghana. For, not only did it gain independence; but in fact, three days prior to independence, Ghana got her own central bank. The advent of the Bank of Ghana ushered in a new phase of financial administration in the country. Independent Ghana then had in her own hands all the tools for carrying out its monetary policies.

The Bank of Ghana, as a central bank, has among its functions the authority to carry out such monetary policies as are necessary for shaping the economic development of independent Ghana. It is also responsible for supervising the operations of other banks operating in the country. For the latter reason, it is necessary to look at its activities in the development process too. Even though it is not directly involved in financial intermediation in the country, it nevertheless occupies a central position regarding the economic development of the country. It can contribute to the country's economic development by 'creating and nourishing the financial institutions needed for growth' and by advising the government on economic and financial matters related to the economy of Ghana so that, for example, there will not be 'too much money chasing too few goods' in the economy.

Soon after independence, the Nkrumah government launched a massive industrialization programme. The balance on the government's budget, which in 1954-55 had a surplus of £G35 million, was running a deficit of over £G50 million by 1963. To finance the deficit, the government resorted to short-term borrowing from both domestic and external sources. Domestically the issue of treasury bills increased from £G6 million at the end of 1960 to £G45.8 million at the end of September, 1964. The use of short-term domestic borrowing added to the total money demand in the country. But it was envisaged by the policy-makers, that if:

> local supplies of goods and services can be expanded to meet the increased demand, this form of deficit financing can be a stimulus to economic development.[9]

This claim turned out to be false in due course; for, as the policy-makers noted later:

> domestic supplies of goods, especially of food and housing, have not kept pace with the growth in demand. The method of financing budgetary deficits by treasury bills and ways and means advances has therefore tended to add to the inflationary pressures within the economy.[10]

Not only did the Nkrumah government's deficit financing policies set in motion an inflationary spiral; but it also led the country into balance of payments difficulties. This was because the expenditure of the domestic loans went on imported goods.

In all this, the central bank played a rather passive role. This is partly because the Bank of Ghana is not the independent institution that it ought to be. Instead, it is more or less controlled by the government. Ordinarily, the Bank of Ghana is expected to persue independent monetary policies which together with the government's fiscal policies will shape the country's economy. But, instead, various governments since independence, with the passive conivance of the Bank of Ghana, have dictated monetary policy. Furthermore, successive governments have borrowed heavily from the Bank of Ghana to finance their budget deficit. For instance, in 1977 government borrowed 639 million cedis to finance the deficit; by June 1982, government was borrowing 16,390 million cedis for the same purpose. Relate this to the total money supply of 2,386.4 million cedis and 17,032.5 million cedis for 1977 and June 1982 respectively. Heavy government borrowing from the banking system such as these 'crowds-out' the private sector.

We should remember that not only was government borrowing from the central bank but also it was borrowing heavily from the Social Security and National Insurance Trust (SSNIT). Table 3 shows the distribution of bank credit to government, public institutions and the private sector for selected years. As can be seen government borrowing fron the banking system far outstripped that of the private sector. For example, in 1975 bank credit to government was about four times what was given out to the private sector; in fact, the ratio gets higher if one adds the share of public institutions to that of the government. By 1981, credit to the public sector (government plus public institutions) had grown to about ten times that of the private sector. In fact, it was quite clear from the rate at which the public sector was expanding its credit from the banking system that the public sector would have totally 'crowded out' the private sector by 1982, but for the intervention of the PNDC.

This is not to say that private sector investment is preferable to

TABLE 3: DISTRIBUTION OF BANK CREDIT (Cedis million)

Year	1963	1965	1970	1975	1981	1982	1983	1984
Government*	70	192	340	1050	13488	16496	21036	25908
Public	—	—	94	190	591	708	1064	1808
Private**	114	167	126	298	1342	1557	2843	5970

Source: Bank of Ghana, *Quarterly Economic Bulletin* and *Annual Reports*, (various issues)
* Bank credit to government includes credit for cocoa financing.
** Bank credit data to private sector for 1963 and 1965 include data for public institutions.

state sector investment. However, it is noteworthy that most of government borrowing from the banks went into financing the recurrent expenditure rather than new investments. Therefore in terms of the country's development the benefit was zero. Moreover, much of the borrowing was from the central bank and hence added on to the money supply and thus fueled inflation in the country.

Loss of Confidence in the Banks

One of the biggest problems which has faced the authorities in post-colonial Ghana has been the high currency ratio over the years. The currency ratio, definitionally, is a behavioural assumption about the public holdings of cash. If the banking system is weak, then people will prefer to hold more money as cash. This means that little money will be held in the banks as savings which can be rechannelled into investments.

Low investment implies low growth. Hence, the currency ratio is inversely related to the economic development of the country. A high currency ratio weakens the efficacy of monetary policies.[11] The currency ratio, which prior to independence had been maintained at a constant ratio of about 50 per cent started to increase soon after independence (see Appendix B). This ratio, however, fell from a high of 64 per cent in 1960 to a low of 43 per cent in 1973 and remained at an average of about 50 per cent throughout the sixties and the seventies. In 1980, the currency ratio rose to 58 per cent. Since then it has maintained a consistently high average level of about 60 per cent.

This high ratio is the result of many factors. First, the high inflationary trends in the country, coupled with low saving rates, forced people to hoard cash rather than deposit it with the banks. In other words, most people prefered to invest their monies elsewhere to saving them with a bank. Secondly, it might be due to a lack of awareness of the useful role played by the banking system in mobilizing savings and rechanneling them into profitable ventures as investment; or in facilitating commercial transactions. For instance, even though banking had been in Ghana for more than three-quarters of a century, very few business concerns accept cheques for transactions. Most exchange transactions take place on cash basis only. This problem can be traced to a larger problem of loss of confidence in the banking system.

The major cause of this loss of confidence was persistent government interferance in the banking system. For example, in March 1979, the government of the Supreme Military Council headed by General Akuffo, decided to mop-up excess currency in the system by changing the cedi-notes. This exercise was aimed at only those with cash outside the banking system. People with amounts not exceeding 5,000 received back only 70 per cent of what they exchanged; whilst those with amounts exceeding 5,000 received back only 50 per cent. Ironically, this exercise did more harm than good: it affected more people in the lower strata than those in the top strata. There are two explanations for this. The 'big-shots' in the country got wind of the change and therefore deposited their monies with the banks before the exercise began. But of greater significance is the fact that generally, poor people keep a greater proportion of their income on hand as cash for everyday transactions. Accordingly, they lost more than the wealthy people.[12]

The greatest cause of the loss of confidence in the banking system, is however the vetting of people with accounts over 50,000 in their bank accounts when the PNDC came to power. In this instance, even though the rich and the dubious social elements were targeted, the exercise impugned the credibility of the banking system as a confidential institution. One cardinal principle in banking is secrecy concerning a client's transactions. The access to the banks' books which the government secured therefore undermined this principle and shook the public's confidence in the banking system. It will take a long time before that confidence is restored, because it will take more than a governmental pronouncement or high interest rates to induce people to develop confidence in the banking system.

Savings and Investment

The public's loss of confidence in the banking system did not augur well for the mobilization of savings. Even though in nominal terms, savings have been increasing, in real terms they have been falling because of the inflationary trends in the economy.

The country has one of the lowest domestic savings rates in Sub-Saharan Africa. For example, total savings as a percentage of GNP fell from about 17 per cent in 1960 to about 1 per cent in 1982. A corollary to this was that investment in the country also fell. From a level of 14.2 per cent of GDP in 1970, investment also dropped to about 1.3 per cent of GDP by 1982. Certainly, a country with such a record should not be surprised that a year later it would become bankrupt. No country consuming almost 100 per cent of its output should expect to survive for long. Therefore, what happened in Ghana in 1983, was not a natural disaster; it was something which was bound to happen sooner or later.

Whereas governmental policies have not done much to encourage savings by Ghanaians, the banks themselves have not done much by way of mobilizing funds. Rates of interest on savings which until 1987 were being fixed by the Bank of Ghana, have always been behind the rate of inflation. Throughout 1980-86 the real rates of interest on savings in Ghana remained negative.[13]

In 1987, as part of the IMF-instigated liberalization policies interest rates were allowed to be 'freely determined by the forces of demand and supply'. It is believed that this would promote competitive banking. Even though it is too soon to evaluate the success of this policy, the record so far has not been encouraging; for confidence in the banks is still low and the inflation rate is still high.

The 'susu' system of funds mobilization has not been properly studied. This is an indigenous system which seems to have its roots in the 'nnoboa' system of the traditional sectors. Under this system, a group of people collect monies and give them to one person in the group for use. A system of rotation is enforced whereby each member of the group takes turn in receiving the total collection. This kind of funds mobilization has helped a lot of small-scale businesses, such as fishmongers and petty traders, to set up their businesses. To operate efficiently, it needs the trust of every member of the group.

In an attempt to mobilize rural savings, the government, through the Bank of Ghana, set up rural banks. The central bank owns a substantial part of the initial capital with the rest being subscribed by members of the rural community where the bank is established. The first rural bank opened in the Central Region in 1976. By 1985, 105 rural banks have been established throughout the country.

The most attractive thing about the rural banks is that they facilitated the operation of the 'Akuafo Cheque' system. The 'Akuafo Cheque' requires that cocoa farmers should be paid by cheque through the banks. With rural banking, the farmers do not have to travel far to receive their payments. Another important aspect of rural banking is the fact that it affords the rural communities easier access to credit facilities which would aid the development of the rural areas.

Even though it is good in principle, the rural banking system has been beset with many problems. The main one has been the problem of qualified management staff. Most of the qualified staff do not want to go to the rural areas where these banks are situated. Another problem faced by the rural banks is the high loan default rate. This inhibits their ability to contribute fully to the development process.[14]

Loans and Advances

It is in the granting of loans that one fails to see much difference between banking in post-independent Ghana and that of the colonial times. Loans and advances granted by Ghanaian banks have always been biased towards trade. This is so probably because of the high and quick turn-over on credit to this sector. The Bank of Ghana, in its *Annual Report* of 1969, reported that there is:

> an imbalance in the pattern of growth with undue bias towards the trading sector of the economy at the expense of other vital sectors such as agriculture and the manufacturing industry.

Table 4 shows the allocation of commercial bank loans by end use in selected years.

Whereas agriculture contributes over 70 per cent to Ghana's GNP, in terms of beneficiaries of bank credit it has, up to 1982, always trailed behind several sectors. This could be interpreted to mean that the small scale farmers do not require heavy capital and hence do not need much of bank credit. However, government corrective measures have not succeeded in reversing this trend in any significant way. The exception was in 1983 when the situation improved. Out of a total bank credit of 6.25 billion cedis, 2.01 billion cedis went to agriculture.

The Bank of Ghana has been using selective and mandatory credit controls to make agriculture, manufaturing and export trade top priority areas for credit allocation. Agricultural credit was made to carry no ceiling; and loans to the agricultural sector initially carried selectively low interest rates. Today, credit to the agricultural sector still carries no ceiling. However, there is no more differential interest rate on agricultural credit. In spite of this favourable credit policy, agricultural credit has not increased to levels commensurate with its place in the economy.

In contrast, commerce has always taken a greater percentage of

TABLE 4: ANALYSIS OF COMMERCIAL BANKS LOANS AND ADVANCES BY END-USE (Cedis million)

	1962	1967	1972	1977	1982	1983***
Agriculture	2.5	3.1	16.0	65.3	688.6	2012.9
Mining and Quarrying	.5	1.2	1.9	35.9	233.0	416.2
Manufacturing	1.4	15.5	75.9	149.9	635.2	1366.6
Building & Constr.	4.5	12.5	23.9	90.9	511.1	796.9
Electricity & Water	8.2	.2	1.4	2.1	42.1	49.7
Commerce*	34.2	42.2	88.6	207.9	913.9	900.3
Transport & Comm.	.7	1.7	11.6	69.1	201.8	331.3
Services	1.1	14.6	30.2	48.3	175.0	250.8
Other	6.8	8.4	6.6	23.7	96.0	124.1
Total**	59.9	99.5	256.0	701.3	3191.7	6248.9

Source: Bank of Ghana, *Quarterly Economic Bulletin* and *Annual Report*, (various issues).
* Commerce includes import/export trade, cocoa marketing and others.
** Totals may not add-up due to rounding.
*** Data for 1982 and 1983 are totals for primary and secondary banks.

bank credit. In the early sixties commerce alone received over 45 per cent of total commercial bank credit; with agriculture averaging about 10 per cent over the years. The situation is even gloomier when one compares the share of the non-productive sectors — that is the sum of the shares of commerce, services, and others — to those of directly productive sectors such as agriculture and manufacturing. The manufacturing sector increased its share of bank credit from a meager 3 per cent in 1963 to about 20 per cent in the 70s and 80s.

Another problem of the banking system is the lack of adequate staff to appraise projects properly. Most people who emphasize the importance of the services of financial intermediaries in economic development base their argument on the quality and quantity of information that these intermediaries provide. According to Bernanke and others:

> The basic premise is that in the absence of intermediary institutions, informational problems cause financial markets to be incomplete. By specializing in gathering information about loan projects, and by permitting pooling and risk-sharing among depositors, financial intermediaries help reduce market imperfections and improve the allocation of resources.[15]

We have already mentioned (above) the problem of mismanagement in the rural banks. This problem permeates the entire banking system: they all lack the expertise to properly appraise projects. The following are some of the consequences:

a) The banks' inability to engage in venture capital.
b) High default rates for bank loans and
c) Widespread fraudulent practises in the banking system.

In effect these problems are also indications of the banks' inability to perform their intermediary role effectively and thereby contribute to the development of the country.

Development Banking

Ghana has three development banks. These banks were initially set up to see to some specific aspects of development. For example, The Agricultural Development Bank (ADB) was established by an Act of Parliament in 1965 and charged with the provision of credit facilities for the development and modernization of agriculture and allied industries, to grant loans to producers of food crops, industrial crops, to those engaged in livestock production and fishing, and agro-based industries.

The National Investment Bank (NIB) on the other hand was established earlier than the ADB — in 1963 also by an Act of Parliament. The NIB was expected to operate not only in the field of industry, but also to help agricultural, commercial and other enterprises. The functions of the bank are:

(a) to assist in the establishment, expansion and modernization of enterprises;
(b) to stimulate and facilitate domestic and foreign capital to participate in such enterprises;
(c) to counsel and encourage small Ghanaian business concerns and
(d) to bring together internal and external capital, investment opportunities and experienced management.

The third development bank, the Bank for Housing and Construction (BHC), was established in November 1972 under NRCD 135 to promote the housing and construction industry.

All these development banks operate an active commercial wing. The BHC, for example, obtains its short term funds from its commercial wing. Long term funds for these banks are acquired mainly through equity shares by Government and other state institutions. The biggest problem facing these banks is that they are seriously undercapitalised. This problem is due mainly to the high rate of inflation in the country.

In addition, they face serious financial problems due to the persistent devaluations of the cedi. All three banks, at one time or the other, obtained loans from overseas multilateral institutions at a time when the cedi was changing at a very low rate to the dollar. By the time these loans were due for repayment the cedi had depreciated substantially. For instance, in 1976 the ADB got a loan of $1 million from the African Development Bank. At that time the exchange rate was $1: 1.15. Now the ADB has to repay the loan at a time when the cedi has depreciated by more than 16,000 per cent. Again in 1980, the ADB got another loan from the African Development Fund at an exchange rate of $1: 2.75. The ADB has to repay this loan at a much higher rate. These developments have eroded the capital base of the bank and limited its lending ability. The Agricultural Development Bank is not the only victim of the exchange rate adjustment policies. Other development banks like the NIB and the BHC have also suffered from them.

Lack of collateral has been the major reason for bankers' refusal to grant loans to their customers. Governments have attempted to tackle the collateral problem in various ways — for example, through the Bank of Ghana's Credit Guarantee Scheme. This Scheme was set up in 1969 to step up commercial bank lending to small scale borrowers. It provides insurance credit for small scale borrowers undertaking viable agricultural and industrial projects. However, the Scheme has not been as active as it was intended to. One of the three primary banks which initially participated in the Scheme has now withdrawn.

The Stock Market

The absence of an established Capital Market in Ghana has also prevented businessmen from taking advantage of the full intermediation processes in the country. Most businesses in Ghana are established with either family funds or by bank credit. In most cases after the business is established it relies solely on bank credit for its growth. A stock market, which allows for sale of stocks and shares to the general public can contribute greatly to the capital base of most Ghanaian businesses. With the establishment of a stock exchange in Ghana, people could rechannel their savings from bank deposits to investment in industrial securities.

The establishment of a stock exchange will bring in many

advantages which cannot be realised under the present financial system of the country. The major advantages are:

> matching projects with funds, bringing flexibility to the portfolios of institutional and individual investors, spreading the benefits of ownwership of industries throughout the community, protecting the investor and enabling him to realise his investment quickly, and making the current value of every listed security known publicly.[16]

The idea of the establishment of a stock exchange in Ghana was first thought of in the early sixties. Two decades later, all that Ghana has is the National Trust Holding Company. This company partially performs the functions of a stock exchange. The government of the PNDC has recently established a Discount House as a forerunner to the Stock Exchange.

BANKING REFORMS UNDER THE ERP

On the 10th of December 1982, as part of its Economic Recovery Programme, the PNDC government announced a new banking policy for the country. The main aim of the new policy was to:

> Strengthen the banking system to enable the commercial, development and specialist banks to play a more dynamic and effective role in the (country's) reconstruction and development effort.[17]

The main banking policy measures contained in the programme were as follows:

1. the Banking Act of 1970 was to be amended to bar foreign-controlled banks from retail banking and to redirect them to specialist banking;
2. the state's shareholding in foreign-controlled banks — Barclays Bank of Ghana Limited and Standard Bank (Ghana) Limited — was to be increased from 40 per cent to 80 per cent with effect from January 31, 1983;
3. the National Investment Bank (NIB) would be required to specialise in long-term lending and equity participation in mining, manufacturing and transportation ventures.

4. the Bank for Housing and Construction (BHC) would be required to serve as the Government's main financial institution for the financial control of all construction projects in the entire public sector (including local authorities and state corporations). The BHC would thus take over the financial control hitherto exercised by certain ministries and government departments;
5. the Social Security Bank (SSB) would be required to shift its emphasis from hire-purchase financing of consumer goods and trade finance to long-term financing of the following: (a) irrigation projects; (b) plant pools or plant-hire companies; (c) agro-based industrial projects; and (d) rural development projects.[18]

Up to January 1988, most of these banking reforms have not been implemented. The policies regarding the operations of NIB and BHC were not really new. The original Acts establishing these banks provides for these services but they have not been properly exploited by these banks. It is doubtful whether the two foreign banks can be made to contribute more towards Ghana's development by taking majority shares in them; especially since there is no evidence to suggest that the 100 per cent state-owned Ghana Commercial Bank has contributed more towards national development.

Recently, the PNDC government commissioned a World Bank team to study the Ghana financial sector with the intent of restructuring this sector to make it more viable. This new banking reform study which was under the Structural Adjustment Programme (SAP), is ready and discussions have been held with the managers of the banks on it. However, the report has not been made public. One only hopes that some of the problems which, as discussed above, prevent the banks from contributing fully towards Ghana's development would be addressed.

CONCLUSION

Finance is the oil of growth. Financial intermediation is an essential service that involves the mobilization and rechanneling of resources from idle hands into productive sectors of the economy. Independent Ghana has seen over thirty years of financial intermediation and yet the activities of the intermediaries have not had much of an impact on the economic development of the country.

There has been too much interference by government in the banking system. This has led to the loss of confidence in the financial system as a whole with the consequent fall in savings. The banks on their part have not been aggressive in the mobilization of savings and rechanneling them into investible resources. These two factors, coupled with high interest rates, have caused investments to fall, and have led to low national output.

NOTES

1. *The World Bank, Toward Sustained Development in Sub-Saharan Africa — A Joint Program of Action*, The World Bank, Washington,D.C., 1984.
2. Refer, for example, Tony Killick's *Development Economics in Action*, (London, Heinemann, 1978), and N. Ahmad's *Deficit Financing, Inflation and Capital Formation*, (Munchen, Weltforum Nerlag, 1970), and J. M. Due's 'Development Without Growth — The Case of Ghana in the 1960s?' in *The Economic Bulletin of Ghana*, Vol. 3, No. 1. 1973, pp 3-15.
3. Bernanke, Ben and Mark Gertler (1986), '*Banking and Macro-economic Equilibrium*', SSRI Workshop Series, University of Wisconson, p. 1
4. See, for example, Gurley and Shaw's (1956) 'Financial Intermediaries and the Saving-Investment Process', *Journal of Finance*, pp 259-275., Patinkin (1961), 'Financial Intermediaries and the Logical Structure of Monetary Theory', *American Economic Review*, Vol. 51 , pp 95-116. and Brainard, W. and J. Tobin (1963), 'Financial Intermediation and the Effectiveness of Monetary Control', *American Economic Review*.
5. Ahmad, Naseem (1970), op. cit., p. 22
6. McPhee (1926) *Economic Revolution of West Africa*, quoted by J. C. de Graft-Johnson in 'Some Historical Observations on Money and the West African Currency Board' in *The Economic Bulletin of Ghana* Vol. XI, 1967, p. 3-19.
7. Money supply can be functionally related to some policy variables, including, high powered money, reserve ratio, interest rates, and the currency ratio. Of these variables, the currency ratio is the one which the central bank finds difficult to control. This is because the currency ratio, which is the proportion of money supply held by the public as cash, is based on a behavioural assumption which is difficult to control.
8. Hopkins, Anthony G.(1973), *An Economic History of West Africa*, London, Longman, p. 208.
9. Republic of Ghana, *Seven-Year Development Plan*, 1965, p.35
10. Ibid.
11. This is explained in footnote 7 above.
12. Another major cause of the loss of confidence in the banking system was the 50-cedi notes withdrawal exercise by the government of the Provisional National Defence Council (PNDC) in 1982. The Limann government which preceeded the PNDC had in recognition of the high turnover of the cedi, issued new 50-cedi notes in 1981. The 50-cedi notes which were withdrawn were not paid back to people until 1987. Even though the people got their monies with some interest payment, in real terms most people lost on this exercise. Again, in this episode, it was the poor worker/farmer who suffered most.
13. For example, the real rates of interest on deposits were −37% in 1980, −98% in 1981, −110% in 1983, and −24% in 1984.
14. See also Emmanuel Hansen's article in this book where the same subject is treated under the sub-title 'Agricultural Credit'.

15. Bernanke, Ben and Mar Gertler (1986), p. 1. See also Gurley and Shaw (1956), Patinkin (1956), and Tobin and Brainard (1963), op. cit.
16. Frimpong-Ansah, J. H., 'Stock Exchange in Ghana', *Quarterly Economic Bulletin*, Bank of Ghana, July-Sept. 1971.
17. Bank of Ghana, *Annual Report*, June 1983, pp. 15.
18. Ibid.

APPENDIX A

THE GHANAIAN FINANCIAL SYSTEM

Type	Name
1. Central Bank	— Bank of Ghana
2. Primary Commercial Banks	— Ghana Commercial Bank
	— Standard Chartered (Ghana)
	— Barclays Bank (Ghana)
3. Secondary Commercial Banks	— National Savings & Credit
	— Social Security Bank
4. Merchant Banks	— Merchant Bank (Ghana)
	— Bank for Credit & Commerce
5. Development Banks	— Bank for Housing & Constr.
	— National Investment Bank
	— Agricultural Dev. Bank
6. Co-operative Bank	— Ghana Co-operative Bank
7. Rural Banks	— Several
8. Informal Sector	— Several susu' collectors
	— Money lenders

APPENDIX B

SOME FINANCIAL INDICATORS

Year	Current GDP	Money Supply	Demand Deposit	Saving Deposit	Currency out of Banks	Currency Ratio	Interest Rates	CPI
1960	956	134	47	26	87	0.65	0.040	21.5
1961	1022	147	60	27	87	0.59	0.045	22.8
1962	1084	165	69	35	96	0.58	0.045	24.9
1963	1208	173	75	42	98	0.57	0.045	26.0
1964	1357	241	107	54	134	0.56	0.045	29.2
1965	1587	240	122	60	118	0.49	0.045	36.9
1966	1681	248	131	67	117	0.47	0.070	41.7
1967	1647	241	121	78	120	0.50	0.060	38.5
1968	1878	259	133	93	126	0.49	0.055	41.6
1969	2117	290	138	99	152	0.52	0.055	44.6
1970	2289	306	151	121	155	0.51	0.055	45.9
1971	2500	321	159	154	162	0.50	0.080	50.3
1972	2815	463	220	205	243	0.52	0.080	55.4
1973	3501	564	291	230	273	0.48	0.060	65.2
1974	4660	697	320	308	377	0.54	0.060	77.0
1975	5283	1009	495	378	514	0.51	0.080	100.0
1976	6526	1429	679	474	750	0.52	0.080	156.0
1977	11163	2393	1119	651	1274	0.53	0.080	337.8
1978	20986	4126	1787	1005	2339	0.57	0.135	584.8
1979	26230	4680	1873	1262	2807	0.60	0.135	903.0
1980	42832	6085	2090	1860	3995	0.66	0.135	1355.4
1981	72626	9413	3310	2620	6103	0.65	0.195	2934.4
1982	86450	11203	4048	3630	7155	0.64	0.105	3589.1
1983	184038	16717	5477	4090	11240	0.67	0.145	7998.2
1984	270560	26849	8778	5110	18071	0.67	0.180	11169.9
1985	334180	38308	13240	8410	25068	0.65	0.185	12321.9
1986		55156	17736	13960	37420	0.68	0.205	15348.6

Source: I.M.F. International Financial Statistics, *Yearbook*, 1987

Note: All values are in millions of cedis except the rates and ratios.

6. TRENDS IN GHANA'S FOREIGN POLICY AFTER NKRUMAH

Kwame Boafo-Arthur

INTRODUCTION

Ghana was the first nation south of the Sahara to attain independence. With an avowed commitment to fight for the eradication of the 'last vestiges' of colonialism, neo-colonialism and racism on the African continent Ghana pioneered black Africa's entry into international affairs.

At the same time these commitments became the cornerstone of Ghana's foreign policy, and were summed up in a dynamic and positive policy of non-alignment in the country's relations with the major power blocs. The person who did a great deal to fashion such a dynamic foreign policy for the country is Dr. Kwame Nkrumah, the first Prime Minister and later first President of the country. Even though Dr. Nkrumah in some instances adopted subversive, aggressive and hostile policy measures to attain his foreign policy objectives, it must be stressed that it was largely his progressive and militant foreign policy orientation centred essentially on African unity, decolonization and national development that constituted the moving force of Ghana's foreign policy.

Undoubtedly Ghana under Nkrumah's leadership accomplished a great deal in international affairs[1] and set the broad foreign policy parameters which have determined the choices made by his successors as well as influenced assessments of the performance of such successors.

Ever since the ousting of Nkrumah Ghana's external influence has waned and her foreign policy has in some cases (especially under the leadership of Dr. K.A. Busia) been marked by incoherence, ambiguities and confusion, especially on cardinal issues like the African liberation struggle and non-alignment. Worse still, the traditional militancy of the country's foreign policy has been lost; and policies have clearly lost the clarity they used to have to the extent that at times Ghanaians find it difficult to know where their country stands on matters of international concern.

The question then is: Why has Ghana lost its frontline role in Africa as well as its dynamism and militancy in international affairs? In other words, what major problems have prevented successive governments from pursuing an active foreign policy?

This chapter sets out to examine some trends in the foreign policy behaviour of successor regimes after Nkrumah, with special reference to policies on the African liberation struggle and non-alignment. The point is made that foreign policy issues have been haphazardly handled after Nkrumah to the extent that Ghana has lost her initial influence in international circles. The problem, it seems, lies in the weakness of the economy which makes her very vulnerable to severe crisis. Even though other variables like the political orientation of political leaders, the balance of social forces operating during the tenure of a regime, leadership style and national cohesion or stability help in explaining the apparent moderation in foreign policy behaviour of successor regimes, the central, overarching feature of the post-colonial phase of the Ghanaian political economy is 'one of recession; of economic impoverishment and of reduction on political capabilities'.[2]

So pervasive is the crisis that the substance and quality of post-colonial, post-Nkrumah foreign policies have been heavily affected. In what follows attention will be focused mainly on the governments of The National Liberation Council (NLC) 1966-69; The Progress Party (PP) 1969-72; the National Redemption Council/Supreme Military Council (NRC/SMC) 1972-79 and the Provisional National Defence Council (PNDC), the present government. However, we will give consideration to some aspects of the foreign policy behaviour of other governments like that of the People's National Party (PNP) where necessary. The analyses are preceded by a few remarks about what constitutes the determinants of foreign policy generally, but more especially that of a weak and small country like Ghana.

DETERMINANTS OF FOREIGN POLICY

The formulation of foreign policy is influenced by several variables. A nation's attributes, however, exert a preponderant influence on its international behaviour. These attributes include 'anything that describes the make-up of a nation, differentiating one state from another in terms of political, social, economic or as some might argue psychological characteristics'.[3] Rosenau, Sullivan and Kissinger[4] have all identified various domestic variables that tend to influence foreign policy decision-making. The size of the nation, level of economic or political development, type of governmental system, type of leadership structure, political or social unrest or strain, are common examples of domestic variables.

However, the economic wealth of a nation tends to exert the greatest influence on its level of participation in, and impact on international affairs than most other variables. A nation with great economic resources like the USA or Japan invariably has greater flexibility and influence in international affairs. It also enjoys greater security against external pressures (economic, military and diplomatic) than a nation with very meagre economic resources. On the other hand, a nation lacking economic resources, has very few resources or is faced with grave economic problems, like Ghana, is more vulnerable to external pressures and more likely to comply with the dictates of external powers or bodies.

The policies pursued by the NRC/SMC government after 1975, the undue influence external advisers had on the government of Dr. K. A. Busia and the marked shift in the original 'socialist inclinations' of the PNDC (as analysed below) amply demonstrate our point. In other words, the less endowed a nation is the more likely it is, when faced with severe economic problems, to succumb to the dictates of foreign powers in its international behaviour because it depends extensively on the munificence of such powers for its economic survival. Blau states the point as follows:

> By supplying services in demand to others, a person establishes power over them. If he regularly renders needed services they cannot readily obtain elsewhere, others become dependent on and obligated to him for these services, and unless they can furnish other benefits to him that produce interdependence by making him equally dependent on them, their unilateral dependence obligates them to comply with his request lest he cease to continue to meet their needs.[5]

Two other determinants of foreign policy are worth considering. These are (i) the political orientation of the ruling class and (ii) the external environment in which a country operates. It is true that changes do occur in the goals of the state with respect to strategies for national development, national objectives, selection of national priorities and ideological alignment, but these changes in almost all cases tend to reflect changes in the political leadership of the state which may have come about through changes in the state's principal social foundation.

That is, the state's domestic function of securing class domination combines effectively with its external function to promote the interest of the ruling class. As a result, the interest and motivations in foreign policy orientation are greatly affected by 'the changing personnel composition of the state and the principal sources of social legitimation of the state'.[6]

For example, the deposition of Dr. Kwame Nkrumah and subsequent composition of the liberal oriented pro-West military regime — the NLC — completely changed the basis of international relations from Nkrumah's pro-East to a pro-West stance. Similarly, the changes in the membership of the PNDC after 1982 paved the way for the close relationship that currently exists between the PNDC and capitalist international financial institutions like the International Monetary Fund (IMF) and the World Bank.

A crucial factor that complements the various internal factors shaping foreign policy behaviour is the external environment. This is more so because of the extensive economic interdependence of the contemporary world and the structural dependence of the post colonial state and society on the capitalist world economy. This system of interdependence and dependence has a greater impact on foreign policy behaviour than is normally realised. In fact, what happens in London or New York determines largely whether or not Ghana would obtain more for her agricultural products, or whether concessionary aid would be increased to accelerate national development.

Where a nation's productive activity and the structure of social relations are largely reflections of structures and processes located elsewhere in the international system, the impact of its foreign policies may be very slight. The simple fact is that the socio-economic bases of a dependent state like Ghana are heavily mediated. As Duval and Freeman have put it:

> The dependent state draws a great deal of support from and is strongly constrained by material and information from external actors in the world system. Its social foundations, its class basis of legitimation, for example, may be in an international capitalist class as much as any domestic group.[7]

The ever mounting debt of Third World Countries and the clamour for large doses of foreign aid to assist in national development effort have produced many instances of countries having to comply with the whims of their economic benefactors when they have had to deal with major international issues. In sum, the portents of success for a foreign policy option is diminished if superficial account is taken of 'what other states or groups have done, or are doing or are likely to do in the future'[8] in reaction to a given foreign policy option or other stimulus generated into the international system.

In the final analysis one must agree with Nwaogugu that the foreign policy of a state is 'the projection by whatever methods of state power, authority or influence beyond its national frontiers'.[9] However, a viable policy will evolve only when the various internal and external factors have been taken into account. Such a consideration must bear in mind the fundamental concerns of the state — especially, the post colonial state.

The fundamental concerns of all post colonial governments revolve around ensuring economic growth and development, higher living standard for the people, more equitable distribution of wealth and income, as well as the efficient harnessing and utilization of the human and material resources of the country. The way these goals have been pursued is invariably influenced by the ideological inclination of the political leaders and their class base as well as the economic well being of the country. While some political leaders and their class allies would depend on the state to mobilise internal resources for modernising the economy others would like the state to act as a kind of beachhead of international capital. Adherents of the latter viewpoint, on coming to power, use the state to win the support of international capital because for them it is with the support from international capitalist sources alone that the country can develop.

The ideological inclinations of successive political leaders after Nkrumah, coupled with the weak economic base of the state, has ensured that the latter tendency would prevail in foreign policy concerns. In fact the economic imperative has reinforced and legitimized the dominant ideological viewpoint of political leaders in pursuing foreign policy objectives.

Ideally foreign policy aims at the protection and enchancement of the interests of the state and its citizens. It must however be emphasised that the perceptions of policy-makers about the costs and benefits within the international system has usually formed the broad framework within which these national goals are pursued.

SEARCH FOR RECOGNITION

The NLC

Apart from a common commitment to the African Liberation struggle and to non-alignment, the pursuit of economic development objectives have dominated Ghana's foreign policy since the fall of Nkrumah.

The NLC, which overthrew the Nkrumah regime in 1966 however, had to contend with an initial problem of attaining international recognition if their basic foreign and domestic policy goals were to be achieved. As a result, the early part of the NLC's rule was devoted to legitimizing their rule and attaining international recognition.

The overwhelming popularity of the leader they had deposed on 24th February 1966 presented the NLC with initial problems in the international arena. Some African countries could not reconcile themselves with the change of government in Ghana and therefore opposed the regime at international meetings. This initial antipathy generated diplomatic tension at the sixth session of the OAU Council of Ministers in Addis Ababa in March 1966. Alex Quaison-Sackey's defection after being sent by Dr. Nkrumah to represent his government at the conference could not mollify some representatives. Countries like Tanzania, Egypt, Somalia and Guinea openly opposed the presence of the NLC delegation led by E.T.K. Seddoh; and the recognition that was eventually accorded to that delegation by the OAU secretariat prompted Mr. Ousmane Ba, the Foreign Minister of Mali, to resign as the First Deputy Chairman of the conference.[10]

External opposition to the deposition of Dr. Nkrumah was registered in several other ways. Zambia, apart from recalling her High Commissioner to Ghana soon after the coup, paid glowing tribute to Nkrumah's relentless fight for African Unity and liberation. In Simon Kapwepwe's words, Nkrumah's contributions to Africa's liberation struggles were 'unparalleled and unforgetable'.[11] Kenya not only looked down on Ghana's delegation to the OAU Council of Ministers' meeting but also withdrew its delegation in protest against the seating of the NLC representatives.

At the same time, the ousting of Nkrumah elicited enthusiastic support from the country's immediate neighbours — Côte d'Ivoire, Nigeria, Togo and Liberia for very good reasons. For Houphouet Boigny of Côte d'Ivoire, the coup could not have come at a more opportune time. Nkrumah openly referred to him as an accomplished 'neo-colonial puppet' and supported people opposed to Boigny's government. Both Togo and Nigeria had had uneasy relations with Dr. Nkrumah.[12]

The NLC's attempt at gaining international recognition was based on a strategy of reversing the militant, often aggressive, foreign policy posture of the Nkrumah government. Whilst in principle the NLC affirmed their commitment to the country's traditional foreign policy objectives, the style and strategies had of necessity to change. Quiet diplomacy was emphasised. Non-involvement in the internal affairs of other African countries and cooperation were preferred. African Unity was to be pursued not through hostile strategies like subversion but through economic co-operation and political understanding.

Relations with the country's neighbours and other African countries were therefore normalized. As a demonstration of their good intentions and friendly relations, the NLC's mission that was sent to Côte d'Ivoire soon after the coup handed over to the Ivoirian authorities Amon Ndouffou III, the secessionist Sanwi chief who had lived in exile in Ghana since 1959.

These strategies paid off because of the constant exposure of some negative acts of the Nkrumah regime. For instance, journalists and diplomats from several countries were taken on a visit to one of the camps which Nkrumah was alleged to have operated for training subversionists.[13] This was in addition to the release of numerous political detainees during the early months after the take over of power. Coupled with the early recognition, on 4th March 1966, by the US and Britain these developments immensely assuaged the fear and softened the moral basis of external antipathy toward the NLC.

External opposition mainly from some African countries and threats of subversion[14] from within remained the main challenges to the regime but these never prevented them from actively participating in African and other international affairs. Thus, for example, in accordance with UN Resolution the government imposed trade sanctions on Rhodesia even though by the time Nkrumah was overthrown, there was no trade with the Ian Smith regime. However, as a result of the NLC's concern for the economic problems facing the country, foreign policy issues of a political nature were relegated to the background while attention was paid more to renegotiations about debt rescheduling and new loan arrangements. The task of consolidating relations with the country's immediate neighbours and engaging more actively in both African and global affairs were left to the Progress Party government led by Dr. K.A. Busia.

Busia and Ghana's Relations with its Neighbours

The Progress Party government of Dr. Busia which took office in 1969 pursued the quiet diplomacy of the NLC and continued their policy of normalizing relations with the country's neighbours. Accordingly, Dr. K.A. Busia undertook a week long visit to Côte d'Ivoire. Similar visits to other neighbouring countries were undertaken by key members of the government.

However much the Busia government tried to achieve in the West African subregion, the passage and implementation of the Aliens Compliance Order in 1969/1970 severely undermined those efforts. Even though there was no official diplomatic rupture in relations with any of the country's neighbours the manner the 'quit order' was implemented and the time limit given to those affected generated a lot of ill-feeling in some West African countries. The country most affected was Nigeria. What nettled the Federal Government of Nigeria most was the refusal of the Progress Party government to consider all Nigerians in Ghana as refugees. Refugee status was conferred rather on Nigerians of Ibo extraction — the very elements constituting the secessionist Biafran government. It is this dimension to the Aliens Compliance Order[15] that compelled Alhaji Tanko Yakasi, Kano State commissioner for Information, to assert that the Aliens Compliance Order was a subtle means of recognizing the secessionist Biafran government.[16] And even more significantly he considered the order 'as a bad start for Ghana's new administration and for Nigeria-Ghana relation'.[17]

It must be emphasised that the passage of the Aliens Compliance Order was widely supported by Ghanaians. The Pan-Africanist aspirations of the Nkrumah regime had opened the nation's borders to all sorts of foreigners who openly flouted the immigration laws of the country. It was realised that citizens of other African countries as well as Syrians, Lebanese and Indians had completely taken over certain sectors of the nation's economy at the expense of Ghanaians. The PP government wanted the law abiding ones to regularise their stay. They at the same time wanted to ensure that enough job openings were created for Ghanaians.

But the ultimate aim was to ensure that Ghanaians controlled those sectors of the economy which aliens had monopolized. These were the main considerations which made the compliance order popular with Ghanaians. It was the Progress Party's policy on South Africa that rather elicited intense opposition from their own cabinet and from the country in general. It was also the policy that greatly affected Ghana's international image, at least on the African continent.

The Busia Government's Policy Towards South Africa

Successive regimes after Nkrumah did not change the substance of Ghana's foreign policy towards South Africa. All were opposed to racism, colonialism and apartheid and showed commitment to the liberation struggle in Southern Africa. For instance, the stand of the Progress Party government of Busia on foreign policy matters was summarised by Victor Owusu, the Foreign Minister, when he stated: 'We did not oppose Nkrumah's foreign policy but his domestic policy'.[18] This was an implicit commitment to a radical posture towards South Africa since Nkrumah's policy towards South Africa was radical.

In practice however, Busia's government demonstrated (quite contrary to Victor Owusu's assertion) that they were equally opposed to some aspects of Nkrumah's foreign policy and the methods for achieving total liberation, especially in South Africa. As a result, the approaches of the two governments to the burning issues of African liberation, and especially the eradication of apartheid, differed in many respects reflecting the differences in leadership style, outlook and perceptions concerning the urgency of the problem as well as the strategic instruments to be used to attain success.

Dr. Nkrumah was implacably opposed to racism and white minority rule in South Africa and staunchly supported the liberation movements. Surprisingly however, he did not fully pay up Ghana's dues to the Liberation Committee of the OAU. Instead he committed his government's resources to the training of nationalist fighters. Dr. Busia, on the other hand, paid Ghana's arrears in dues to the Liberation Committee from 1964 to 1968 which amounted to £53,875[19] thus indicating his preference to work within the framework of Pan-African institutions.

On the other hand Dr. Busia's foreign policy towards South Africa was a sharp departure from the traditional militant and active opposition to the apartheid regime. Busia preferred *dialogue* with the racist government to the armed struggle, thus prompting the question as to why his government decided to pursue such a policy towards South Africa against the current of African opinion. The question is: Why did Busia's government decide to pursue a policy of dialogue with South Africa against the current of African opinion?

Most probably the PP government felt that Africa did not have the resources to sustain the armed struggle against South Africa. Given the superiority of the South African military in the region, Africa's own military weakness and the poor state of the South African freedom fighters they must have felt persuaded about the futility and costly nature of an armed struggle. But in fact the government's policy must be understood in the context of Busia's own personality, and his liberal democratic inclinations. At home he was preaching a political doctrine of tolerance, of being each other's brother and keeper and the need for democratic discussion. Before he became Prime Minister he was the head of the country's Centre for Civic Education set up by the NLC to preach the virtues of democratic ethics and practice. Dialogue with the South African racist regime was therefore an extension of his own beliefs and his domestic policy.

Hence dialogue was perceived as a strategic, less costly and democratic weapon in the diplomatic armoury that would help in the eradication of apartheid. As he later informed parliament:

> My government is of the view that another weapon that could be effectively used is that of dialogue either with the government or with moderate forces black and white within South Africa.[20]

In fact he believed strongly that isolation of the South African Government would deprive concerned states of the chance of effective communication and the opportunity to influence Pretoria to abandon apartheid. He was nonetheless sure that apartheid is 'pernicious and dangerous and against world peace and ..... based on the wrong concept that the black man is not capable to be on his own'.[21]

These notwithstanding, the Progress Party's policy on South Africa has been criticised on several grounds. As Karikari bluntly put it, Busia's call for dialogue was 'the most serious blunder in the conduct of our foreign policy'[22] for many reasons. Firstly, the call for dialogue portrayed the government's ignorance of the South African problem and the events that led to the armed struggle against the racist regimes. Secondly, the OAU's Lusaka Manifesto gave the white minority regime a clear choice between dialogue and intensification of the armed struggle; but this was not heeded by the apartheid regime. It was therefore an act of betrayal for the Progress Party government to call for dialogue in contravention of the OAU's declared stand.

Thirdly, in the Afrikaneer mentality, the black man is less human, and is not fit to be treated as an equal of white people. And this had been admitted by the Prime Minister when he told parliament that apartheid is pernicious, dangerous and wrong. For the South African racist regime therefore to reject peace overtures from the OAU leaves the armed struggle — that is, force — as the only option in the situation. Besides Dr. Busia's fear that the blacks in South Africa could not triumph over the racist army in a guerrilla war has no historical basis. The FNLA in Algeria, MPLA in Angola, Frelimo in Mozambique, and ZANU in Zimbabwe have all succeeded under very trying conditions and against superior armies.

The dialogue policy advocated by the Busia government severely damaged Ghana's image of dynamism and militancy in African affairs and greatly affected the morale of the nationalist fighters who had looked up to Ghana for inspiration. Not even Ghana's own vote against the dialogue proposal at the 1970 OAU Summit Meeting could repair the damage that had been done.

As a correspondent of the Legon Observer noted, the Prime Minister never realised that white South Africa 'regard apartheid as an irreducible, unnegotiable principle' and therefore those who propose talks with them are merely ruining their country's prestige in Africa.[23] The arduous task of retrieving Ghana's sunken image at least in Africa was left to the National Redemption Council (NRC-SMC) government which overthrew the Progress Party in a military coup on 13 January 1972.

The NRC's African Policy

Any perceptive observer will note that 'Africa's freedom has been the central inspiration of Ghana's foreign policy'.[24] This follows from the early stand taken by Dr. Nkrumah who was of the view that 'the achievement of freedom, sovereignity and independence is the product of the matter and spirit of our people'.[25] The NRC government therefore reaffirmed Ghana's unyielding support for African Liberation movements and totally rejected the policy of dialogue with racist South Africa. Acheampong, the Chairman of the NRC stated on several occasions after seizing power that he and his colleagues in the army were bitterly opposed to the call for dialogue with South Africa first, as a matter of principle and in conformity with OAU's stand; and secondly, because of the dishonour that policy was doing to Ghana's image abroad.

Thus under Acheampong, Ghana regained her membership of the OAU Liberation Committee and for the first time played host to this Committee's meeting in January 1973.[26] To help in coordinating the affairs and progress of the liberation struggle, the government proposed to open a Liberation Information Centre in Accra in 1975. The proposed Centre was meant also to serve as the information and propaganda outfit for the nationalist fighters in Southern Africa. Commitment to the processes of decolonization in Africa was practically demonstrated when the government donated $50,000 to Guinea-Bissau in July 1974.

The stand taken by the NRC on African issues led to improvements in the country's relations with most African countries. In particular, relations with Libya, Algeria, Zaire and Zambia were consolidated. Special relations were established with President Idi Amin of Uganda. Trained personnel, mostly teachers were despatched to Uganda to fill vacancies created by the expulsion of Asian and British teachers by Idi Amin.

In comparison to that of their immediate predecessors, it should be noted that the foreign policy behaviour of the Acheampong government was militant. He succeeded to some extent in salvaging Ghana's sunken international image at least in Africa. It is appropriate to ask why Acheampong could achieve so much more in foreign policy than Busia.

Several internal and external factors help to explain the initial successes of the Acheampong government's foreign policy. It was a regime that had cross-sectional support right from the onset. This contrasts with the predominantly Akan-based Progress Party government of Busia. Furthermore, it pursued populist policies which helped in legitimizing its usurpation of power. For instance, the abolition of the development levy which would have led to the deduction of various sums of money from the monthly pay of all categories of workers for the purposes of national development though ill advised, was hailed especially by unionised labour. Students of the country's higher institutions readily gave their support when the new regime announced the abolition of the Students' Loan Scheme.

On the same populist grounds there was mass support for the government's 'Yentua' policy (i.e. repudiation of all debt suspected to be tainted by corruption and other improprieties which had been contracted by previous administrations).[27] However, the main spring of that government's success was the improvements in the economic fortunes of the state soon after the coup and also the relative political stability that the change brought to the nation. For instance, an excellent cocoa crop in 1971-72 and 1972-73[28] coupled with an equally unprecedented high world price which had jumped from a disastrously low level of £260 per ton in early 1972 to £900 per ton in 1973[29] greatly improved Ghana's foreign reserves. The higher cocoa price was supplemented by an equally remarkable increase in timber production in 1972. Exports of logs shot up from 325,000 tons in 1971 to 478,608 tons from January to August 1972.[30]

Moreover the NRC did bolster up Ghanaian economic and political nationalism through their policy of capturing the commanding heights of the economy. On grounds of economic nationalism the government took 55 per cent of the equity shares in foreign mining and timber enterprises. This was followed by the government's participation in the operation of various commercial and industrial enterprises through the acquisition of forty percent shares in foreign owned banking, insurance companies and a minimum of fifty per cent shares in the breweries. Direct participation and acquisition of majority shares in mining and timber enterprises, no doubt, increased the domestic resource base of the regime. For ordinary Ghanaian entrepreneurs, including even workers, the government's Investment Policy Decree of 1975 opened up infinite avenues for buying shares in foreign owned industries.

The NRC's bold measures on the debt issue compelled the western creditor countries to reach an agreement in March 1974 that would allow grace and repayment periods of five years and fifteen years respectively for short term loans. Payment of the principal of outstanding long-term debt was also stretched over twenty eight years with a grace of ten years at two and half percent interest.[31] These highly favourable debt repayment terms were possible because of the tremendous internal political support the new regime had managed to mobilize for its policies, both political and economic.

Ghana's militancy or active role in global and African politics has almost always been a reflection of her economic strength and internal stability. The Acheampong regime enjoyed these during the early part of their rule and could therefore participate actively in African affairs. Similarly, the state of the economy tends to dictate the sort of economic relation the country ought to develop with international financial institutions and governments. The weaker the economy the closer the relationship with international financial institutions; and the more dependent the country becomes on them. In the following section we appraise the nature of these relations under regimes since the fall of the Nkrumah government.

FOREIGN ECONOMIC RELATIONS

The poor economy has forced various regimes to court and strengthen relations with international financial institutions who according to Herb Addo, 'create developmental counterfinalities'.[32] Lt. General J.A. Ankrah, the Chairman of the NLC minced no words in outlining Ghana's relations with international economic/financial institutions when he stated: 'we shall make full use of the IMF and the World Bank and its associated institutions.'[33]

When the NLC took power in 1966 the economy was ailing. There was shortage of foreign exchange; economic growth was almost zero; shortages were pervasive and had affected every conceivable item of consumption; inflation was high and the cedi had lost its value; foreign investors had lost confidence in the economy; and the world market price of cocoa had virtually collapsed. There was therefore need for urgent measures to revitalize the economy and restore growth to it.

The immediate economic problem after the coup of 1966 was how to renegotiate repayment terms with western creditor nations and institutions. This had become urgent not only so the country could repay its debt without much strain on its slender resources, but there was also the need to attract external investment, which had almost dried up in reaction to the quasi-socialist policies of the Nkrumah government, as well as fresh loans for importing much needed consumer items and industrial raw materials, which were in short supply at the time of the coup. Close relationships with the IMF and the World Bank was to enable Ghana to obtain the needed financial help for development. Especially, a 'certificate of creditworthiness' from the

IMF was necessary to assure western creditors that the government was committed to the pursuit of sound monetary and fiscal policies. This would encourage the flow of interntational aid. Because of the government's conviction that its objective of ensuring the resumption of economic growth would be realized only with the financial assistance of western governments and financial agencies, close collaboration with western financial institutions and governments became an article of faith.

This close relation with western governments and financial institutions was maintained by the Busia government for basically the same reasons. Busia on the advise of the IMF and the Bank went further by inviting Harvard Development Advisory Service (DAS) economists to take control of the planning and economic policy-making departments of state.[34] As a result, major policy decisions (like devaluation), with far-reaching socio-economic and political implications, were taken in close consultation with, or on the recommendations of, such international economic advisers.

The disastrous impact of such relationships was reflected in Ghana's weak and, at times apologetic, foreign policy options — a typical example being the infamous policy of dialogue with South Africa. The NLC and Busia governments gave too much room to foreign economic advisors to the extent that local alternatives to our economic problems — like the policy of 'self-reliance' that was later pursued by Acheampong were either neglected or not considered at all. The fall of the Busia government in January 1972 underlines Libby's assertion that 'no government can continue for long if it formulates policies primarily to satisfy external constitutents'[35] unless that government resorts to extra-legal or dictatorial measures to survive.

The Acheampong government on the other hand, assisted by the upswing in cocoa, timber and food production, quickly revalued the currency which had been devalued by the Busia government. Even though the currency was not restored to its original value by the NRC and not all foreign debts were repudiated, the bold domestic measures taken by the government were far reaching enough 'to produce a wave of relief throughout Ghana'.[36]

Following the repudiation of some of the country's debt, Ghana's economic relations with western countries were strained. Britain refused to guarantee imports of goods to Ghana and the government was compelled to purchase items on 'spot cash basis'. Nevertheless, Ghana maintained a remarkably active foreign policy because the economy was gradually bouncing back; so there was no compelling need to rely so much on external handouts.

Adverse changes in Ghana's economy in particular and the global economy generally affected the quality of the NRC's policies after 1974-75. The economy was put under severe strain by increased oil prices. As a result, the import bill increased from forty million cedis in 1973 to 132 million in 1974.[37] This forced the government to remove subsidies thus inviting internal discontent. At the same time the country could no longer capitalize on improved world prices for cocoa partly because of smaller crop yields. Only 330,000 tons of cocoa, which was thirty per cent below the average production levels, was recorded in 1975-76.[38]

What this dismal economic performance meant in terms of the pursuit of foreign policy goals is that the government could not sustain its characteristic dynamism and independence made possible by positive changes in the economy at the start of its tenure in 1972. Coupled with the political instability that threatened the very survival of the regime especially from 1976 to 1978[39], the government had to devote greater time, effort and resources to containing the domestic situation.

Briefly, attempts at independent foreign policy and economic relations were undermined by the declining economy, balance of payments difficulties, large government budgetary deficits, and low production of the country's major export commodities during the NLC, PP and the latter part of the NRC administration. The government of the Provisional National Defence Council (PNDC) is contending with similar problems. In what follows we examine the impact of these similar economic problems on foreign policy since 1982.

The PNDC Era

When the PNDC government led by Flt. Lt. Jerry John Rawlings took over power through a coup d'etat on December 31 1981, their immediate concern was how to bring about populist structural reforms of the economic and social systems.[40] Accordingly, the regime initiated a series of reforms which in some instances brought it in direct confrontation with international capital, represented by multinational corporations operating in the country.

Attempts were made, in some instances, to place the management of companies and corporations in the hands of Committees for the Defence of the Revolution (CDRs). Foreign investors were stigmatized as exploiters who always siphoned off the country's hard earned foreign currency. Threats of nationalization were rife and the government stoutly defended the state's sovereignty by renegotiating the VALCO arrangement with Kaiser International.[41] Efforts were geared at excluding foreign capital from a wide variety of economic areas because of the realisation that the externally imposed structure of trade and production which has engendered dependence on the world capitalist system constituted the greatest bases of the country's economic vulnerability and backwardness. The PNDC initially sought to terminate such dependence. Consequently, diplomatic and commercial relations already established with the Soviet Union, the Peoples's Republic of China, Cuba and North Korea in various forms by previous regimes were strengthened.

With such initial realignment in the country's external political relations, the government of the PNDC adopted a 'radical' foreign policy whose dominant chord was the incessant attacks on western and especially, American imperialism. The policies which were adopted, however, failed to improve the economy because they severely 'reduced the incentives for production, savings, investment and increased productivity'.[42] Added to the difficulties confronting the PNDC was a disastrous decline in cocoa production especially during 1982-83. Cocoa production figures for instance had fallen from 450,000 tons in the early 1970s to 180,000 in 1982.[43] The production of timber and gold had declined by similar margins. A huge external debt of US$1,723 million by the end of 1982 compounded the problems of the government. In addition, industrial production capacity had fallen drastically: factories utilized around twenty percent of their installed capacity by the time of the coup.[44] And then came the disastrous drought and bushfires in 1982-83 that adversely affected food and cash crop production and compelled the PNDC government to solicit food aid mostly from western countries.

As a result of the dismal state of the economy and the failure of initial government policies to arrest the situation, the need was felt for policy changes. The government in consultation with the IMF and the World Bank drew up the Economic Recovery Programme (ERP) which they launched in April 1983. The launching of the ERP meant a change in the government's foreign political and economic relations since foreign capital (mostly from the West) was needed to ensure the success of the programme. With the background of initial anti-western propaganda by the government, political leaders in their speeches had to emphasise the importance of western aid in their endeavour to resuscitate the economy. Thus contrary to the previous assertions about the injurious nature of relations with western capital, governments and multinational corporations, the government made it quite clear that 'without wider and adequate international support in the form of long term concessional loans and credits the broad aims of the programme will be difficult to achieve.'[45]

The launching of the ERP was followed by the devaluation of the cedi in October 1983 by 9.91 per cent from 3.70 cedis to 30 cedis to the US dollar. By the end of September 1987 the cedi had been effectively devalued by 5,780 per cent with the foreign exchange auction rate standing at 175 cedis to one US dollar. The spate of devaluations marked yet another landmark in the government's policy change from its initial claim that 'currency devaluation was an invidious tool of the IMF to open up the Third World countries for international capitalist exploitation'.[46]

Later in 1983 a conference was organised in the United States for foreign oil companies in an attempt to sell geological data on Ghana's oil deposits. The spirit of the change and the new form of international economic relations the government was pursuing came out vividly in a statement issued in may 1984 by the Secretary for Finance and Economic Planning Dr. Kwesi Botchwey. He said:

> Ghana will actively encourage direct foreign investment and ensure that while safeguarding the interest of the economy and honour of the people, investors will not be frustrated when the time comes to transfer their profits and dividends to their shareholders overseas...[47]

By the end of 1983 it was quite clear that the political orientation of the government as well as their perception of the international environment had changed. Vigorous efforts were therefore made to bring radical supporters under firm control. In that year for example Rawlings, the leader of the Revolution, cautioned against revolutionary rhetoric. He declared:

> We can no longer postpone the time for halting the populist nonsense... We must not get into the way of thinking that revolutionary activities are substitutes for productive work.[48]

Two years later (in January 1985) Justice D.F. Annan, the Deputy Chairman of the PNDC explained why there was the need to abandon the revolutionary rhetoric. According to him, the flirtation with Marxism in the early months of the revolution:

> did us a certain amount of harm, in that it sought a short cut to modern government on the basis of the experience of Europe which was not quite germane.[49]

He noted further that there is now a clearer perception of what the 'revolution' is about because there has been a shift from the 'blood and thunder' politics of the earlier years. As a result, the tendency in the beginning to give it a Marxist or Socialist outlook has now been found to be inappropriate.[50]

The PNDC's record thus gives credence to Crawford Young's assertion that 'the pursuit of socialist orientation by given regimes is not necessarily irreversible'. He attributes such unexpected ideological changes to 'the strong economic positions and ideological influence over which imperialism continues to dispose'.[51] The PNDC's change of policy orientation had become inevitable because of the difficult economic conditions at the time they came to power. And of course the hostile external environment coupled with the government's own changing political orientation and appreciation of the power of this external environment contributed to make the change possible and complete.

It is clear from the foregoing that the state's weak economic base has undermined attempts at pursuing an independent foreign policy: successive governments have been compelled to seek aid from sources whose interests and aspirations in the world arena are incompatible with ours.

In the process governments have either been coerced or persuaded to change the country's development priorities to suit the donor countries. As Maurice East put it, the government of a poor state 'because of the relative lack of resources available for foreign affairs will seek methods and strategies of international interactions that are more economical'.[52]

The situation might logically call for ideological compromises and complete shifts in some cases as it has been demonstrated by the PNDC government during their five years in office. The country's non-aligned position in world affairs has also been affected by the same factors, the most important among which is the backwardness of the economy. In the section that follows we explore trends in Ghana's non-alignment position since the fall of the Nkrumah government.

NON-ALIGNMENT

In theory, non-alignment is the guiding principle of Ghana's external relations. The almost religious and, at times, ritualistic re-affirmation of commitment to this policy by successive regimes has historical origins.

With its emergence in the late fifties as a counterbalance to the bi-polarization of the world by the Cold War politics of the world's super powers, non-alignment was embraced by the Nkrumah government as the most rational option for the emergent nations. Thus, even though Ghana was still under colonial rule, the government attended the

Bandung conference of 1955. By the end of the conference the new nations that had met had reached agreement about the main principles of the policy of non-alignment.

Briefly, non-alignment as a policy came to mean non-commitment to the world's dominant ideological blocs, and the preservation of the right and freedom to judge world issues on their own merit. In effect, it was to ensure an autonomous course of action with regard to the conduct of relations with the power blocs. Translating these into Ghana's foreign policy Nkrumah declared:

> Ghana does not intend to follow a neutralist policy in its foreign relations, but does intend to preserve its independence to act as it sees best at any particular time.... In pursuing its independent policy the Government of Ghana will have regard, first and foremost, for the interest of the people of Ghana; in particular, their continued economic and social progress.[53]

African liberation and unity and 'the maintenance of world peace through a policy of ... non-alignment', according to Nkrumah were to constitute the pillars on which the country's foreign policy was to be built.[54]

However, the principles and practice of non-alignment in Ghana have more often than not clashed, especially when the realities and dictates of economic development lure various leaders, including Nkrumah himself, into some form of alignment with one power bloc or the other. In effect, the country's external relations, especially with the big powers have been determined not so much by a commitment to the pious declarations of non-alignment but by domestic economic exigencies and the dictates of international finance capital.

Dr. Nkrumah succeeded in maintaining a balance in his government's relations with the ideological blocs during the first part of his rule. His later attempts to align ideologically with the East and maintain a diversified trade pattern evinced sharp reactions from the West. Attempts were made to employ the power of international finance capital to enforce compliance and therefore abort such flirtations with the East. Credit terms for loans were tightened and loans which were granted carried high interest rates.[55]

In the final analysis the west won because of the poor state of the economy and the urgent need for international (mostly Western) finance capital: the fall of the Nkrumah regime paved the way for a reversal in the country's pro-Eastern foreign policy.

Even though the NLC was bent on reversing most of the Nkrumah policies, the underlying principles of the policy of non-alignment were maintained. In a reaction to accusations of a pro-west foreign policy, Lt. General J.A. Ankrah then Chairman of the NLC, said that their foreign policy was to restore proper balance and 'abolish that brand of non-alignment which in practice had all the attributes of alignment'. He further stated:

> Our policy of non-alignment and absolute neutrality must now regain its genuine character guided and inspired by the highest interest of the state. It must reflect itself in all our national policies affecting our interests both at home and abroad.[56]

Balance in the quest for technical assistance, objectivity in economic co-operation and genuine search for friendship with all countries were supposed to be the 'guiding principles and abiding characteristics of NLC's foreign policy'. Nkrumah's close relations with the East had affected the flow of western aid to Ghana and at the same time provided the basis for the immediate support and recognition accorded the NLC by Britain, the US and other major Western countries.

The western press heaped praises on the NLC and the new government responded quickly by restoring relations with Britain which had been broken by Nkrumah in repraisal for the British government's stand on Ian Smith's Unilateral Declaration of Independence (UDI) in Rhodesia (Zimbabwe) in 1965.

Almost immediately various forms of aid which had been frozen during the Nkrumah government's latter days began pouring into Ghana. The United States Agency for International Development (USAID) announced a $680,000 Food for Peace corn allocation in December 1966 claiming it was to relieve an acute grain shortage.[57] In addition, the UN Development Project approved a $356,000 loan to ease the country's balance of payments difficulties. Other forms of aid came from Britain, Canada and West Germany.

Whilst relations with the capitalist West were strengthened by the NLC regime, those with China and the Soviet Union were frozen. Some 620 Soviet technicians and teachers and a large number of military advisers who were then working in the country were sent packing.[58] Furthermore, the Soviet embassy was ordered to reduce its staff from sixty-seven to eighteen and all Aeroflot flights to Ghana were cancelled. Revelations by Mr. J.W.K Harley, the Vice Chairman of the NLC that China, Cuba and the Soviet Union were aiding subversive activities against the government led to further deterioration in the relations between Ghana and the eastern bloc.[59] The antagonism that the NLC showed toward the Eastern bloc accounted for their 'unreasonable abstention from voting on the question of admitting Peking China into the UN'.[60]

The Progress Party government that succeeded the NLC could not restore Ghana-Eastern bloc relations. With serious balance of payment problems, galloping inflation, mass unemployment and a huge foreign debt, Busia's government needed all the goodwill from the western world if it was to be able to cope with the economic crisis. Therefore a policy of close collaboration with the west was conspicuously pursued inspite of the avowed commitment to the policy of non-alignment. The Progress Party government, led by Busia, refused to re-establish diplomatic relations with China for fear of a western backlash. That government pursued pro-west non-alignment policy to such an extent that by the time of its fall, they could be described as 'Western puppet' *par excellence*.

It was the government of the NRC which balanced the equation in Ghana's relations with the two power blocs. Relations with Peking which had remained frozen since 1966 were fully restored. Thereafter Chinese assistance in the construction of the Dawhenya canal and other irrigation projects were secured. Chinese technical team researched into the lime stone deposit at Nauli. Chinese imports from Ghana also increased from 2.4 million in 1972 to 7.3 million in 1973 while Chinese exports to Ghana rose from 4.7 million to 9.3 million during the same period.[61]

It is arguable that the NRC government, having antagonised western creditors by repudiating some of the country's debt, had no option but to court the East. But we must not ignore the fact that the favourable changes in the Ghana economy at the beginning of NRC's rule assisted the government to chart a truly independent foreign policy, especially with regard to the big powers. Nothing demonstrated this new found balance in foreign relations more than the US government's decision to grant the regime a long term loan of $19 million in 1974 and the continued support they enjoyed from the World Bank.

Notwithstanding the PNDC's commitment to the policy of non-alignment[62] even the most casual observers are not deceived as to the bias in the government's foreign relations during the heady days of the revolution on the one hand, and their current inclination after the massive aid that has poured in from the West since April 1983 to sustain the Economic Recovery Programmeon the other. Nonetheless there is no doubt about the conscious efforts to maintain a modicum of balance in relations between the East and West. According to Dr. Obed Asamoah, Secretary for Foreign Affairs, Ghana maintains relations with East and West Germany, North and South Korea and also with other countries of the East and West. This shows how few ideological considerations influence Ghana's foreign policy.

The trend however, seems to be the strengthening of ties with selected Eastern countries for security purposes and with the West for economic ends. This is indicative of how the interest of the ruling group and, for that matter, the state in terms of national security and capital assistance respectively are being catered for by the ruling PNDC. However, a dive has already been made for western support in the form of aid for the country's economic survival. Indeed, realignment with the West, after the initial hostility towards it, has the potential of being total. This is clearly portrayed by the cautious manner government functionaries now attack 'western imperialism' in contrast with what prevailed 1981 in 1982-1983. This sharp cooling-off in the anti-imperialist rhetoric, according to Jonah, is 'in order not to risk the loss of US support necessary for an IMF stand by credit'.[63] Thus foreign firms which were threatened with nationalization or outright confiscation are now courted and promised generous terms for the repatriation of their profits.

CONCLUSION

The state of ambivalence, ambiguities, inconsistencies and at times unpardonable confusion that has been a feature of Ghana's foreign policy of late are partly attributable to the frequent regime change. This does not augur well for stability in foreign policy behaviour. The poor state of the economy has compounded the problem. All the post-1966 regimes have affirmed commitment to the cardinal policies of 'African liberation struggle and non-alignment'. However, the intensity and quality of the commitment has been determined by the interplay of several variables with the state of the economy being an independent variable and exercising considerable influence.

The state of the economy seems to be the pillar around which all other considerations revolve. The viability of the ideology of political leaders even seems to have been shaped or modified by the state of the economy. For it is clear that citizens will not hesitate to question the intrinsic values of a particular ideological focus if hardships persist beyond an intolerable limit; and the moment the economy stagnated, all sorts of political problems would crop up, for instance, the frequent regime changes appear to be closely related to the nation's economic fortunes, among other factors. This is why after the initial success in pursuing a dynamic policy of positive non-alignment the NRC regime turned increasingly to the West for aid, especially food.

Like the NRC government and others before them the PNDC have had to take into account the weak economic base they inherited by abandoning the initial militancy in international affairs for a calculated pro-west foreign policy, despite the activist role it appears to be playing in African liberation struggles.

In sum, the economy has proved to be the linch pin around which all other factors revolve. So long as the country's economy remains backward the compulsion to depend on others for economic survival will also persist. Charting an independent foreign policy will then continue to elude government and the commitment to even key foreign policy goals like Africa's Liberation and unity and non-alignment will suffer on the same grounds. For the moment, moderation and subservience instead of militancy and independence have become enduring characteristics of the country's foreign policy.

NOTES

1. Thompson, W.W., *Ghana's Foreign Policy 1951-1966 Diplomacy, Ideology and the New State*. (New Jersey: Princeton University Press, 1969), p.414.
2. Chazan, N. *An Anatomy of Ghanaian Politics, Managing Political Recession 1969-82*. (Boulder Colorado Westview Press, 1983) p.4
3. Sullivan, M.P. *International Relations: Theories and Evidence*. N.J. Prentice Hall, 1976, P. 103.
4. Rosenau, J.N. 'Pre-Theories and Theories of Foreign Policy' in *Approaches to Comparative and International Politics*, R. Barry Farrel, ed. (Evanston: North — Western University Press,1966.) p. 43. See also Sullivan, op.cit. p.117 and Kissenger, H. 'Domestic Structure and Foreign Policy', in *International Politics and Foreign Policy: A Reader in Research and Theory*' edited by J.N. Rosenau, New York: Free Press, 1969 p.267 ff.
5. Cited by Armstrong, Adrienne. 'The Political Consequences of Economic Dependence', *Journal of Conflict Resolution* Vol. 25 No.3 1981 p.405.
6. Duval, R.D. & J.R. Freeman, 'The State and Dependent Capitalism', *International Studies Quarterly* Vol. 25. 1 1981 p. 115.
7. Duval and Freeman, op. cit p. 109.
8. Reynolds, P.A. *An Introduction to International Relations* 2nd ed. (London, Longman 1970)p.97.
9. Nwaogugu, A.C. *Nigeria's Foreign Policy: Need for a Reappraisal* in Selected Seminar Papers (University of Port Harcourt, 1983) p. 185.
10. *Africa Digest*, March 1966.
11. Safo, Y. 'What has changed in Ghana — Ivoiren Relations' *Legon Observer*, 1968 pp. 4-7.
12. For detailed discussion on this see Aluko Olajide, Ghana and Nigeria, 1957-70. *A Study in International Discord*. (London, Rex Collins 1976).Also, Thompson op. cit.
13. Peasah, J.A., 'The NLC Regime (2)', *Legon Observer*, 1969, 24, (10), p.4.
14. *Africa Dairy*, 1967, p. 3324.
15. The Alien's Compliance Order was passed at the height of the Nigerian Civil War.
16. *West Africa*, 3 January, 1970, p.25.
17. Ibid
18. Karikari, K.A. 'The New Administration and Foreign Policy' *Legon Observer* 1970 2:(1:)pp.12-14. Victor Owusu later became the Attorney General and Minister of Justice. It is widely held that the change in portfolio was the result of his disagreement with the Prime Minister over the dialogue issue.
19. Wiredu, J.E., 'Dialogue as a Problem', *Legon Observer*, 1971, 14:(1) p.23.

20. Parliamentary Debate, 10 December, 1970
21. Ibid
22. Karikari, K.A., 'Ghana's Foreign Policy', *Legon Observer*, 1970, 5.20 p.18.
23. *Legon Observer*, 3 December, 1971, p.14.
24. Felli, Roger. *Fundamentals and Topical Problems of African Foreign Policy*. Institute of International Relations Federal Republic of Germany, 1977.
25. Quoted by Felli, Ibid.
26. *African Contemporary Records* (ACR), 1971-72, pp.606-607.
27. For details of the NRC government's stand see Hutchful, E. 'International Debt Negotiations: Ghana's Experience' *Africa Development* Vol.9, no.2 1984.
28. ACR., 1972-73, p.610
29. Libby, R.L. 'External Co-optation of a Less Developed country's Policy Making: The Case of Ghana 1969-1972', *World Politics* 1:10 1976 p.68.
30. ACR, 1972-73, p.654.
31. ACR, 1974-75, p.654
32. See Herb Addo, *Illustrating the Underdeveloping Role of International Economic Institutions: The Case of IMF* Unpublished Paper. Institute of International Relations University of West Indies St. Augustine, Trinidad, West Indies, 1985 p. 2.
33. *West Africa*, 12 March, 1966, p.30.
34. For an interesting account of how Dr. K.A. Busia's Finance Ministry was discredited and put firmly under the control of DAS, see Libby op. cit.
35. Libby, op.cit., p.89.
36. ACR, 1972-73, p.596.
37. ACR, 1974-75, p.B.651.
38. ACR, 1975-76, p.B.584.
39. It included a series of coup attempts and mounting civilian dissatisfaction with the conduct of the government and its methods of rule. See ACR 1977-78 B 640.
40. These included instigated takeovers of the management of certain companies by CDRS, and threats of nationalization of foreign companies. See Yao Graham's work included in this volume for typical examples of worker-management conflicts.
41. For inside views about those negotiations see Tsikata, *Fui Essays From the Ghana — Valco Renegotiations*, 1982-85 Accra: Ghana Publishing Corporation, 1986).
42. See also Ahiakpor James C.W. 'The Success and Failure of 'Dependency Theory' — The Experience of Ghana' in *International Organization* 39, 3, Summer 1985 pp. 534-552.
43. *Economic Recovery Programme*, (Ministry of Information Ghana, 1986) p. 12.
44. *Ghana Economic Survey*, 1977-80, p.94.
45. ERP Report, op.cit., p.2.
46. Ahiakpor, James, C.W., op.cit., p.547.
47. *West Africa*, 4 June, 1984, p.1155.
48. *West Africa*, 12 September, 1983, pp.21-23.
49. *West Africa*, 28 January, 1985, p.1987.
50. Ibid.
51. Crawford Young, 'Africa's Relations with the Major Powers' in *African Independence: The First Twenty Five Years*. ed. G.M. Carter and P. O'meara, (Indiana, Indiana University Press, 1986) p. 227.
52. East, Maurice. 'Size and Foreign Policy Behaviour: A Test of Two Models', *World Politics*, 4, 1973 p. 556.
53. Nkrumah, K. *I Speak of Freedom: A Statement of African Ideology* (London, Heineman, 1961) p. 151.
54. Ibid.
55. Pellow, D. and Chazan, *N. Ghana: Coping with Uncertainty* (Westview Press Inc., 1986) p. 192.

56. *Ghanaian Times*, February, 1966
57. *African Report*, Vol.12, 1967.
58. Legvold, R. *Soviet Policy in West Africa*. (Harvard University Press, 1970) p. 263.
59. *Africa Report*, Vol.12, 1967.
60. Peasah, op.cit. p.4.
61. ACR, 1974-75, p.B.651
62. *Daily Graphic*, 6 January, 1986.
63. Jonah, K. '*The Rawlings Revolution and the Libyan Connection: Analysis and Evaluation*', Unpublished Seminar Paper, Department of Political Science, University of Ghana, Legon, 1987. p. 19.

REFERENCES

Addo, Herb, 1985, *Illustrating the Underdeveloping Role of International Economic Institutions: The Case of IMF*, Unpublished Paper. Institute of International Relations University of the West Indies, St. Augustine, Trinidad, West Indies.

Armstrong Adrienne, 'The Political Consequences of Economic Dependence' *Journal of Conflict Resolution* Vol.25 No.3.

Ahiakpor James C.W., 'The Success and Failure of Dependency Theory; the experience of Ghana', *International Organization*, 39, 3, Summer. 1986.

Aluko, Olajide, 1976, *Ghana and Nigeria, 1957-70: A Study in Inter-Discord*. London: Rex Collins.

Armstrong A., 1981, 'The Political consequences of Economic Dependence' *Journal of Conflict Resolution* Vol. 25 No. 3 (401-428).

Duval and Freeman, 1981, 'The State and Dependent Capitalism,' *International Studies Quarterly*, Vol. 25, 199-118.

East, Maurice, 1973 'Size and Foreign Policy Behaviour: A Test of Two Models', *World Politics* 4: 556-576.

Felli, Roger, 1977, *Fundamentals and Topical Problems of African Foreign Policy*. Institute of International Relations, Rederal Republic of Germany.

Karikari, K.A., 1970a., 'The New Administration and Foreign Policy', *Legon Observer* 2: 1:12-14.

Karikari, K.A., 1970b 'The New Administration and Foreign Policy' *Legon Observer* 5: 20: 13-18.

Jonah, K., 1987, *The Rawlings Revolution and the Libyan Connection: Analysis and Evaluation*, Unpublished Seminar Paper, Dept. of Political Science University of Ghana, Legon.

Kelman, H.C., 1977, 'The Role of the Individual in Decision-Making', In *The Theory and Practice of International Relations*, edited by D. Mclellan, W.C. Olson and F.A. Sondermann, 167-71. New Delhi: Prentice Hall of India.

Kissinger, H., 1969, 'Domestic Structure and Foreign Policy', *In International Politics and Foreign Policy: A Reader in Research and Theory*, edited by James N. Rosenau 267 ff. New York: The Free Press.

Legvold, R., 1970, *Soviet Policy in West Africa*. Harvard: University Press.

Libby, R.L. 1976 'External Co-optation of a Less Developed Country's Policy Making: The Case of Ghana 1969-1972'. *World Politics*. 1:10; 67:89.

Ninsin, K.A., 1987, '*Capital-Labour Relations under the C.P.P. and PNDC Regimes*'.

Nkrumah, K., 1961-'*I Speak of Freedom: A Statement of African Ideology*'. London: Heineman.

Nwaogugu, A.C., 1984, '*Nigeria's Foreign Policy: Need for a Reappraisal*' in Selected

Seminar Papers (1981-85) 183-199, University of Port Harcourt.

Nyerere, J.K., 1970, *Non-Alignment in the 70s*. Address delivered on 13 April 1970, Dar-es-Salaam, Tanzania.

Peasah, J.A., 1969, 'The NLC Regime (2)' *Legon Observer* 24:10:3-6.

Pellow, D. and Chazan, N., 1986, '*Ghana: Coping With Uncertainty*'. Westview Press Inc.

Reynolds, P.A., 1970, *An Introduction to International Relations* 2 ed. London: Longman.

Rosenau, J.N., 1966, 'Pre-Theories and Theories of Foreign Policy', In *Approaches to Comparative and International Politics*, ed. R. Barry Farrel Evanston: Northwestern University Press.

Safo, Y., 1968, 'What has Changed in Ghana — Ivorian Relations', *Legon Observer*. 4-7.

Sullivan, M.P., 1976, *International Relations: Theories and Evidence*. New Jersey: Prentice — Hall.

Thompson, W.S., 1969, *Ghana's Foreign Policy 1957-1966: Diplomacy, Ideology and the New State*. New Jersey: Princeton University Press.

Wiredu, J.E., 1971, 'Dialogue as a Problem', *Legon Observer*. 14:1 23-29.

SECTION II

AGRARIAN AND SOCIAL ISSUES

7. THE LAND QUESTION SINCE THE 1950s

Kwame A. Ninsin

INTRODUCTION

Customary land law recognises the usufructuary right of the member of the communal group which is either the family or kingship group. In fact, customary land law affirms this right as the highest form of individual ownership which is further reinforced by the principle that the 'expenditure of labour creates right ... ... and operates to vest in the person who is first to clear the land of virgin forest permanent right of exclusive occupation over the area so cleared'.[1] Once the right of occupancy has been established the usufruct becomes heritable. But this right remains essentially usufructuary and NOT proprietary; for it terminates with the extinction of the original owner's family. Secondly, the various communal land tenure systems are closely bound up with the unity, sovereignty and religious underpinnings of the traditional polity; and so the usufructuary right in the lands of the communal group is restricted to its members: it is not transferable to non-members of the group[2]. Reversionary rights in all communal lands thus belong to the traditional authority in perpetuity. In other words, the right of the member of the communal group in the group's lands does not confer on him freehold title. The right of the traditional authority, which is fiduciary is superior to that of the subjects.

It is these limitations of customary land law which made it possible for traditional authorities to infringe on the right of the subject in communal lands when land acquired exchange value from the very beginning of colonial rule, but more especially since the gold rush and the cocoa revolution of the 1870-1920 period. It is these same limitations which have placed the peasantry at the gravest disadvantage in terms of access to land as well as security of title in communal lands. The term communal lands is used interchangeably with stool lands to refer to all land tenure systems other than public lands and private lands.

This chapter argues that the development of capitalist production relations has undermined the stability and viability of communal land tenure systems, particularly since independence. During this period the growing need for food and for agro-based industrial raw materials, the booming of small scale diamond and gold mining industry during the last decade, and the expanding urban real estate industry have increased the need for freehold title in land as a means to secure the heavy investments in these sectors. However, the continued political relevance and influence of chiefs in the political economy of the country as well as the ease with which the ruling classes are able to secure lands under communal land tenure have effectively restrained successive regimes from initiating wholesale land reforms that would meet the needs of the peasantry. At the same time, members of the ruling classes have employed state power, using legal, constitutional and often blatant political means to secure proprietory rights in land so that they could invest profitably in agriculture, mining, the timber industry and the urban real estate industry. Peasant farmers as a whole — but more especially the so called 'stranger' farmers, have been the main losers in this pressure being brought to bear on communal lands by the ruling classes.

The chapter is divided into four parts. The first part examines the rule of the lower fraction of the petty bourgeoisie and the attempts made to assert the power of the state over communal lands as a means of ensuring that the state and members of this class have ample access to such lands. The second analyses the efforts by the moderate fraction of the petty-bourgeoisie, whose representatives assumed power from 1966, to lay the basis for capitalist agriculture and strengthen the development of freehold interest in land. Part three deals with the development of large scale farming by state capital, and by foreign and Ghanaian private capitals while communal land tenure was being strengthened. The fourth part focuses on the intensification of efforts by the ruling classes and the state to introduce and/or strengthen commercial production, by medium scale capitalists, in food and cash crop agriculture, and in timber and mining industries. It also examines the measure of progress that all of these capitalist developments on the land have produced in the form of land title registration.

The Radicals and Land

The victory of the Convention People's Party in the 1951 and subsequent elections marked the accession to political and economic power of the militant wing of the petty-bourgeoisie. These were the small property owners based in agriculture, commerce and the professions;

namely, the small and medium scale cocoa farmers, timber merchants and traders as well as teachers and white collar workers.[3] They dominated the leadership of the CPP. The control they won over state power gave them the political means for advancing their economic position. For in contrast with their moderate counterparts, the radicals had been excluded from the mainstream of colonial politics up to as late as 1949[4]. They also bore serious economic grievances against the European banking and mercantile interests who monopolised much of the commercial activity in the country — from bulk imports to distribution; and against chiefs. Among their grievances against the chiefs were the arbitrary manner in which chiefs managed stool lands and appropriated the revenue accruing from it. The conduct of chiefs concerning stool land management and revenue interfered severely with the drive of this group for wealth; and they expressed their indignation in the form of anti-chief agitations.[5] There was also the multitude of small cocoa farmers who were equally aggrieved by the demand of what they considered as extortionate land rents by chiefs as well as usurous interest rates by money lenders. They constituted one of the main pillars of the CPP's rise to power.[6] Thus the economic interests of both the upper and lower strata of the party were strong enough to compel the CPP government to initiate measures against chiefs and to regulate their management of stool land.

But there was another reason which was equally compelling for the CPP government to attack the economic base of chiefs. This was the fact that chiefs were among the staunches political opposition that confronted the CPP during the 1950s. As one CPP parliamentarian summarised it during the debate on the *Local Government Ordinance of 1951*, chiefs had become the symbol of power and privilege; and they had 'stolen our lands. It is our duty therefore to see that these Stool Lands are maintained in the interest of the common people ...'

The CPP's land and anti-chief policies may be divided into two. The first was aimed simply at weakening the economic base of the politically most powerful chiefs while the second sought to assert the state's supreme dominium over all the lands of the nation-state. None of these two streams of policies transformed the basic structure of communal land ownership: both accepted communal land tenure as the point of departure.

From 1951 to 1957 the CPP government took measures that would consolidate its position as the ruling party. The measures included the enactment of the *Local Government Ordinance of 1951*, the *State Council Ordinances of 1952*[7] and the *Municipal Ordinances of 1953*. Even though these laws were, in the main, designed to reform local government in the country they nonetheless also provided for the control and management of stool lands and stool revenue by bodies other than the chief's court: the new local councils were made 'estate agents for the whole of the revenue accruing to the Stools'[8]. The allordial rights of chiefs in communal lands however remained intact. But the subversive thrust of these laws were quite clear. Above all, they contributed to the electoral success of the party in the local council and national elections which were held during the 1950s.

By 1958 the government was strong enough to move first against the most powerful chiefs, and later on chiefs in general. It did so by undermining the independent economic base of these chiefdoms. Between 1958 and 1962 the following laws were enacted: *The Akim Abuakwa (Stool Revenue) Act, 1958 (Act 8), The Ashanti Stool Act, 1958 (Act 28), The Stool Lands Control Act, 1960 (Act 79)* and *The Administration of Lands Act, 1962 (Act 123)*. These laws, in various ways, gave the state power over stool and other lands; power to authorise the acquisition and use of such lands for either private or public purposes; and to regulate the collection and use of stool revenue. In the end it succeeded in deepening the dependency of chiefs on, and their subordination to, the state.

The second phase of the government's land and anti-chiefs policies coincided with the period when the regime had declared its determination to modernise agriculture and increase productivity through large scale farming systems that would be directly under the control of the state. This approach symbolised the government's conviction that the modernisation of agriculture and increase in productivity could not be achieved through the small scale farms and primitive farming methods of the peasantry. The government could appropriate large tracts of land for large scale farming under Acts 79 and 123. In spite of this successful intervention in agriculture, there was the concrete fact that the peasantry continued to account for the bulk of cocoa and food production. Accordingly their interest could not be ignored. There was also the political consideration of the CPP's own dependence on them — a point that I have already mentioned. Accordingly, the government, in addition to promoting state enterprises in agriculture also attempted to respond to some of the grievances of the peasantry through the *Farm Lands (Protection) Act, 1962 (Act 107)* and the *Rents (Stabilisation) Act, 1962 (Act 109)* and related instruments.[9] The purpose of Act 107, as stated in the preamble, was '... to protect farmers whose titles to land are found to be defective'. The obvious aim was to protect peasant farmers against their rampant harassment and ejection by chiefs and other landlords. But owing to widespread illiteracy and the constraints inherent in customary land law it was only those 'farmers who acquired their defective title for valuable consideration...'[10] who could enjoy the protection offered by this law. The majority of farmers were left defenceless.[11]

It was, rather, Act 109 which seems to have had the greatest impact on the relationship between peasant settler farmers and their landlords. This law was designed to redress the situation of extortionate rents being charged by landlords; and so it regulated such rents by fixing ground rent at five shillings per acre. Given the general insecurity of the peasant's rights in land it was apparent that the success of that law would rather fuel the spate of ejections by landlords.[12] In any case landlords remained resentful of that law until it was repealed in 1967 by NLCD 34.[13]

Despite the political need to respond to some of the problems of the CCP's large peasant base, the law's social objectives remained quite limited because by 1962 the CPP itself was rapidly degenerating into a corrupt machine for political opportinists[14]; the nation was moving toward a single party regime; and so the masses in general were in the process of depoliticisation[15]. Therefore, the party could afford to ignore the fundamental question about land tenure in so far as the peasantry's interest was concerned; viz, access to land and security of right in, and of title to, land.

In contrast, the budding group of Ghanaian entrepreneurs who were based in the CPP received considerable support in their effort to advance economically. Members of this group had been agitating for the government's support in wrestling especially the timber industry and internal commerce from foreign domination.[16] Through the Ghana Timber Marketing Board (GTMB) which had been set up in the 1950s, the CPP government granted and/or reallocated timber concessions to party supporters. In one case that affected Messrs Gliksten (West Africa) Ltd., for example, timber concessions were reallocated to Messrs Kataban Timber Company and eighteen others.[17] Following the establishment of a 2,000,000 cedis fund in 1962 for the promotion of indigenous entrepreneurship in the timber industry, the number of Ghanaian timber merchants shot up from 121 to about 621 overnight[18a].

The Blay Commission which investigated the timber industry in 1967-68 made the popular mistake of suggesting that the sudden increase in the number of Ghanaian timber merchants was due to political corruption[18b]. While there may be a measure of truth in this allegation, it must be recognised that the prevailing political economy made it imperative for the government to act in the way it did. There was the need not only to secure land for the state farms but also for distribution to the emerging class of entrepreneurs who needed land for a wide range of industrial and commercial purposes. To achieve these goals the government had to effectively take control of stool lands in the country. Hence the enactment of the *Administration of Lands Act, 1962* (Act123) and the *Concessions Act, 1962* (Act 124) which replaced judicial control over the granting of concessions with exectutive control. Sections 7 and 10 of Act 123, for example, gave the state power to vest in the president, in trust, any stool lands as well as authorise the use of any such lands for purposes which are in the public interest. Act 124 (Section 4) on the other hand gave the state power to intervene in the award of concessions if the government considered such intervention to be in the public interest.

The demand for land for agricultural purposes and for timber extraction was paralleled by a similar demand for urban lands for real estate development. Within the framework of customary land law the country's economic and political leaders had acquired considerable interest in urban lands. In a large number of cases the legality of title was often the subject of protracted litigation. Once more, the government felt obliged to intervene simply to ensure that such acquisitions would be insured, even where illegality was proved, without interfering with the land tenure systems which produced such irregularities. The government enacted the *Land Development (Protection of Purchasers) Act, 1962 (Act 2)*. During the second reading of that law it became clear that its purpose was to protect the title of the new class of urban landlords. And significantly enough, the subtitle of that law states that it was intended 'to protect purchasers of land and their successors whose titles are found to be defective after a building has been erected on the land'. There is no doubt, as Bentsi-Enchill[19] points out, that this law encouraged piracy on the land market. What he could not grasp however is that in an open market situation it is the economically powerful who tend to prevail. On the land market the economically powerful had the additional advantage of having state power on their side. And so it was logical for the government to transmute injustices into justice; and that called for measures of extraordinary character, as correctly understood by Ollennu[20], even if it meant undermining fundamental principles of indigenous law. Act 2 of 1962 achieved precisely this effect. The determination of the government to uphold the right of this minority is evident also from the fact that later in that year Act 123 gave it power to grant persons owing allegiance to the Asantehene 'one lease at a nominal rent of one shilling per annum, of one vacant plot of land for residential purposes only in any area within the boundaries of the Kumasi town lands'. (Section 5).

By 1966 the petty-bourgeois elements within the party had succeeded in employing state power to ensure that the petty bourgeoisie as a whole would be able to acquire freehold interest in agricultural and urban lands[21]. But the land tenure system remained fundamentally the same as before. The peasantry had been left to contend with chiefs and other trustees of communal lands. It meant that the peasantry would remain the largest producer of cocoa and other cash and food crops without security of title to land. Even the right of access remained subject to invasion or to benign indifference by the more powerful social groups.

THE MODERATES AND COMMUNAL LANDS

The 1966 coup d'etat brought the political representatives of the moderate wing of the petty bourgeoisie to power. It ensured that this group would also have the political means to translate their values into policies. This group was distinguished from the radical fraction by its advocacy of liberal democratic principles and institutions, including traditional institutions like chieftaincy and therefore communal lands. For them communal property like land, has the intrinsic value and status of private property and should therefore be accorded the same sanctity. Accordingly much of their political effort was directed at insuring communal lands against violations of the type that characterised the tenure of the CPP government.

The most significant achievement in this regard was the constitutional safeguards secured for stool lands under the 1969 constitution. Article 164:1 of that Constitution provided that:

> All stool lands in Ghana shall vest in the appropriate Stool on behalf of, and in trust for, the subjects of the Stool.
>
> Subsequent sections of this article provided for the establishment of a Stool Lands Account such as would protect the interests of chiefs against encroachment by the state. However, the importance which the new regime of the ruling classes attached to communal lands stands out more clearly when Article 164:1 is read together with Article 18:1 which stated that
>
> No property of any description shall be compulsorily taken possession of, and no interest in or right over property of any description shall be compulsorily acquired by the State.....

The ideological reasons for according communal property the same value, status and protection as private property was clearly stated in the 1969 Constituent Assembly during the debate on Chapter 18 of the Constitution. The controversy centred on whether stool lands which had been leased to aliens should, upon the expiry of that lease, revert to the State or to the Stool which had granted the lease. In the opinion of Justice Azu Crabbe and Nene Azu Mate-Kole[22] the right to property was the fundamental question before the house because stool lands formed the very basis of Ghanaian society and embodied the rights of the citizen. They therefore urged caution in deciding the matter so that the foundation of society and the rights of its citizens would not be undermined. When the issue was decided in favour of the State some members of the Assembly described the decision as confiscatory[23]. Earlier on the Constitutional Commission[24] had deplored the way and manner in which the CPP government had acquired 'Properties ... ostensibly ... in the public interest ... and handed (them) over to favoured personalities...'. It considered all such acts as an 'invasion of private property... (and) a trespass...' which ought to be punishable under law.

While this fraction of the petty bourgeoisie sought frantically to protect stool lands, developments in the agricultural sector also opened up profitable opportunities for them to advance their interest as capitalist farmers. The post-1966 policy of transforming Ghanaian agriculture through private enterprise enjoyed considerable push from the State — in the form of soft loans, tax holidays, subsidised inputs like fertiliser, and improved seeds as well as subsidised support services.[25] By 1972 businessmen, politicians, serving and retired bureaucrats, and top military and police personnel had taken advantage of such liberal state support and established themselves as private farmers in the northern savanah lands. While the State encouraged them to go into the production of grains through capital-intensive methods, the peasants were urged to concentrate on labour-intensive crops like groundnuts, yam and cotton. The former group of farmers were to form the pioneers of capitalist rice farming in the northern sector of the country.[26] But for the peasantry the communal land tenure systems would not hold any promise for land security. Developments in agriculture during the following two decades exposed the fragile nature of the peasantry's right under communal land law. Concurrently these developments affirmed the facilities available to the ruling classes to transform their political and economic power into freehold interest in land.

CAPITALIST FARMING

The economic and political conditions of the 1970s and 80s have been most conducive to the development of capitalist farming. By 1972 the country was experiencing a severe food deficit; and food imports as a percentage of total imports, was growing — for example, 16.0%

in 1969 and 15.6% in 1971.[27] At the same time the government of the Supreme Military Council (SMC) — formerly the National Redemption Council, which seized power in January 1972, made large scale intervention in agriculture by both private and state capital its primary strategy for solving the food problem in the country. For them the alliance between these two capitals was the key to the problems of low productivity and stagnation in agriculture. To overcome the food deficit the government launched a special action programme called Operation Feed Yourself (OFY) which effectively lasted from 1972 to 1974. Accordingly the budgetary allocations to agriculture was stepped up during the period. From the 1972/73 allocation of approximately 40 million cedis, it increased to 65 million cedis during the 1978/79 financial year — the year in which the S.M.C. government was overthrown. The rate of increase was about 62.5% in those six years. In addition to direct government budgetary support for agriculture, the country's major development banks — Ghana Commercial Bank (GCB), the Agricultural Developement Bank (ADB), and the National Investment Bank (NIB) were directed to liberalise and increase their lending to the agricultural sector. Even foreign banking, commercial, and manufacturing concerns were urged to get involved in the government's programme to increase the production of food (and later raw materials.)[28]

The three local lending institutions came to play a crucial role in this exercise as they served a much wider circle of clientele from all the social groups. The lending of the ADB, for instance, increased from 8,622,441.00 cedis in 1971 to 28,468,713.00 cedis in 1972. The NIB's lending activities also showed a similar trend — with an increase of 83% in 1972 over the previous year's. It is equally important in this regard to note that government had committed itself to major irrigation works like the Tano Irrigation Project in the North for which 15.5 million cedis was voted. And there was also the 63 million cedis Upper Region Agricultural Development Programme (URADEP) project. The impact of these policy changes on agricultural production was considerable; and the volume of grains which public boards and corporations purchased reached unprecedented levels.[29]

This dramatic increase in agricultural production showed that investment in land would yield enormous profit. Therefore, Ghanaian entrepreneurs who were in a position to take advantage of the enormous opportunities opening up in agriculture, did not hesitate to do so. Rice production in the Northern Savanah zone offers a remarkable example of how the wealthy and influential members of society acquired agricultural lands and transformed themselves into capitalist rice farmers.[30]

The banking institutions gave them enormous support in the form of credit facilities. For instance as much as 56.3% of all of the loans which were approved by the ADB in 1974 went to the 3.5% of its total applicants who could apply for a minimum of 20,000 cedis. Similarly, the NIB gave out loans to only those clients who could absorb a minimum of 10,000 cedis.

Such abundance of liberal agricultural credit on the money market was sufficient to encourage members of the ruling classes to intensify their acquisition of lands throughout the country for both agricultural and speculative purposes. By 1977 considerable expanses of arable land had therefore been cultivated to produce grains and cash crops. The Northern and Upper Regions — the hub of the government's agricultural programme — led the entire country with 423,144 and 305,564 hectres, respectively, of cropped land. They were followed by the Brong Ahafo and Ashanti Regions with 291,258 and 256,543 hectres, respectively.[31]

The rush for farm lands involved the state as well as foreign private capital. Under the government's *Special Scheme for Participation in Agriculture* which was outdoored in 1974, foreign companies were encouraged to invest in agriculture part of their profits and dividends awaiting repatriation as a gesture of support for government efforts to boost production to meet the country's food and raw material needs. The outcome of this policy was the penetration of agricultural production by multinational capital. Among the agro-companies that emerged from this period are the Benso Oil Palm Project which is jointly owned by the state and United Africa Company (UAC); SCOA Farms, Nasia Rice Company, Ghana Livestock Limited, Glamour Farms, Ejura Farms and Ghana Industrial Farms.

This unprecedented level of intervention in agriculture by big capital from outside the agricultural sector itself implied large scale land acquisitions and therefore massive ejection of the peasantry from their farm lands. A very good example of how these interventions deprived the peasantry of their land and, in many cases turned them into actual or partial wage earners is provided by the impact of the following state sponsored large scale agricultural projects on the peasantry: the Twifo (Hemang) Oil Palm Project, (in the Central Region); Kwae Oil Palm Plantation (Eastern Region); Benso Oil Palm Project (Western Region); and Cocoa Marketing Board Coffee Plantations at Kwantakese (Ashanti Region). There are many more of such acquisitions which involved private companies. In all such cases the affected farmers were lucky if they got fully compensated, or if they received plots of land to cultivate as outgrowers for the main plantations.

During the 1960-65 period the development of state farms by the CPP government did not create landlessness among the peasantry.

State farms rather went a long way in ameliorating the unemployment problem by putting a large number of unemployed youth back to work on the land. The growth of capitalist agriculture since then has,on the other hand, been depriving peasants fully or partially of their land and forced a large number of those affected to become wage earners. The victims of this new scourge have been settler farmers as well as 'subject' farmers.

It is clear from the foregoing analysis that, from the point of view of the country's ruling groups, the land question has nothing to do with the communal land tenure systems which might be said to restrict access to land. On the contrary, they provide ample opportunity for those who are willing to take up agriculture to acquire land for development. The problem is rather one of insecurity of title. The government of the SMC's response must be seen in the enactment of the *Limitations Decree 1972 NRCD 54*, the *Conveyancing Decree, 1973 NRCD 175* and the steps that culminated in the entrenched clauses of the 1979 Constitution that protected all communal lands. The NRCD 54 was an attempt to curtail the protracted and costly litigations which are the benchmark of the land market and also impose a final settlement on such contests. The NRCD 175 on the other hand provided for a systematic method for transfering interest in land. In particular, it provided that thenceforth all oral grants, as practiced under customary law, would be valid only if they were specifically recorded. In a predominantly illiterate society like Ghana the advantages provided by these two laws could benefit only those who are enlightened enough to appreciate their import, namely members of the ruling classes.

If communal land tenure systems do not impede the development of the country in any respect, then all communal lands without exception, should be vested in the appropriate traditional authority and protected. Even though the 1969 Constitution had vested all stool lands in the appropriate stools, the communal lands of the north were not affected because of an old colonial law which had vested those lands in the state.[32] The considerable appreciation of the values of Northern lands during this period, following the development of capitalist rice farming, revived interest in the need to secure a reversion of those lands to the appropriate traditional authorities of the North. Accordingly the 'Chiefs and Peoples' of the northern regions appealed to the SMC to repeal the 1931 law so that the stool lands would revert to their original owners.[33] The government responded by appointing the Alhassan Committee to enquire into the ownership of those lands as well as the position of tenant farmers in these areas. It is remarkable that this Committee's Report dwelt mainly on proving the allordial rights of traditional authorities in those lands. It explained that establishing those rights would ensure that present and future users of lands there would be able to deal directly with such authorities, as well as pay the appropriate rents to them.[34]

Essentially the Alhassan Committee's position favoured the restoration of the communal lands in the North to those authorities through whom the leading classes could more easily appropriate communal lands for private commercial purposes. Meanwhile, The Proposals of the Constitutional Commission for a Constitution for the Establishment of a Transitional (Interim) National Government for Ghana[35] had, in accordance with these interests of the leadership groups of the Northern regions, recommended the revesting of all northern lands in the appropriate traditional authorities. To give legal form to these strong socio-economic pressures, the 1979 Constitution (Article 188:3) audaciously reversed two score and eight years of 'confiscation' of northern lands in the following pugnacious terms:

> For the avoidance of doubt it is hereby declared that all lands in the Northern and Upper Regions of Ghana which immediately before the coming into force of this Constitution were vested in the Government of Ghana are not public lands...

The significance of this preference for communal lands should be further underscored. Since the 1960s when the state assumed powers to appropriate communal lands for public purposes public lands have become a major source of much of the private lands acquired by the ruling classes for non-agricultural purposes. This advantage was further strengthedned by Article 189 of the 1979 constitution which assured Ghanaians the right to acquire freehold interest in land — including lands which were held by aliens before the constitution came into force. Meanwhile, members of the ruling classes had indulged themselves excessively in a scramble for public lands so much that by the close of the 1970s it was clear that a minority within this strata was acquiring more lands than was socially acceptable. The SMC had therefore been compelled to intervene to impose some order on that expanding anarchy; *the Lands Commission (Amendment) Decree 1973 NRCD 192* was enacted to limit to one the number of plots of public land any single person could aquire for residential purposes. It would therefore appear that the development of capitalist farming lay behind the frantic attempts since the late 1960s to revest communal lands in the appropriate traditional authorities and conserve them. First, the protection of communal lands would continue to assure the ruling class freedom from bureaucratic delays and corruption as well as political controls. And second, it would greatly enchance their prospects for capital accumulation in the agricultural sector.

To this end the 1979 constitution consolidated the security of the communal land tenure systems against dejure disintegration by guaranteeing the institution of chieftaincy (Article 177:1) and giving chiefs representation on the Lands Commission (Article 189:1) and on the proposed district councils. (Article 183:1b) Both of the latter bodies had been given power under the 1979 Constitution to manage lands in the country. Therefore it was not only the institution of chieftaincy that was safeguarded by that Constitution but also the economic basis of chieftaincy — land; and that was done for the benefit of the leading classes of society — the very groups whose representatives drew up the constitution.

Economic Recovery and Land Security

Part of the agricultural development programme of the SMC government had been devoted to the production of agro-industrial raw materials for both domestic consumption and export. One of the industrial crops that received the greatest support of the state is oil palm. The object was not just to revive interest in the production of a crop that had been eclipsed by cocoa. The primary goal was rather to make the country self-sufficient in palm oil (the principal product) for both domestic use and industrial consumption. By the close of the last decade therefore the state had succeeded in attracting many Ghanaian entrepreneurs — retired civil servants, ex-police and military officers, small and big businessmen and so on into the oil palm industry. All such people acquired large tracts of land — mostly from traditional authorities, with all the limitations of security associated with such land transactions.

During the 1980s this second wave of top public servants into capitalist agriculture had been reinforced by a third wave of prospective Ghanaian capitalists attracted by the revival of the timber industry and small scale mining operations in the diamond and gold industry. Under the Economic Recovery Programme (ERP) of the the Provisional National Defence Council (PNDC) Government considerable financial and technical support together with a package of incentives have been made available to the timber and mining industries. These industries are considered among the key sectors of the economy. They are therefore being given financial and technical support as part of the strategy of economic revival through export sector rehabilitation. The impact so far has been overwhelming: there has been a big increase in economic activity in the mining and timber industries. Estimates based on an incomplete series of the *Land Concessions Bulletin* published by the Ministry of Lands and Mineral Resources show that during the 1980-82 period the following applications were filed: Application for Timber Leases and Licences: 83; Applications for Diamond Digging Licences: 32; and Applications for Prospecting Licences: 15. During the 1983-85 period the number of such applications rose significantly — to 249; 74; and 92 respectively. Based on these estimates it is apparent that another land scramble has been occurring in the country. Naturally people with investments or who are prospective investors in agriculture and other land based industries like mining would show grave concern about the future of their investments if insecurity of land title is widespread.

During the 1870-1910 period the anxieties expressed by foreign companies over the rampant litigations on the land market were defused by passing the Concessions Ordinance of 1900. During the 1958-65 period the CPP government met the problem of access to communal lands by both the the state and the petty bourgoisise through the corpus of laws which gave the state power to control and authorise the use of communal lands as well as the Land Registry Act 1962 (Act 122). After 1966 the land question has come to centre increasingly on security of title to lands acquired from traditional authorities, especially those which have been acquired for commercial farming and other economic activities. The solution provided by the 1969 and 1979 Constitutions as well as the Limitations and Conveyancing Decrees of the SMC government seem to have proved unsatisfactory for the proprietary dispositions of the country's rising bourgeois class. The PNDC's response to this growing need for land title security is the *Land Title Registration Law 1986 PNDCL 152*.

In a memorandum accompanying this law the government stated the point very clearly. This statement is worth quoting extensively.

> The object of this law is to provide a machinery for the registration of title to land and interests in land.
> 2. Systematic land tenure research in Ghana has revealed radical weaknesses in the present system of registration of instruments affecting land under the Land Registry Act, 1962 (Act 122). The chief among them is litigation, the common sources of which are the absence of documentary proof that a man in occupation of land has certain rights in respect of it; the absence of maps, and plans of scientific accuracy to enable identification of parcels and ascertainment of boundaries; and lack of prescribed forms to be followed in case of dealings affecting land or interests in land.

In an article published in one of the country's newspapers, the *Weekly Spectator* of August 16 1986, the Chief Registrar of Lands dilated on the practical reasons behind the PNDCL 152. He explained that under previous legislation — the Land Registry Act, 1962 Act 122 — the person who purchased a parcel of land could register only the instrument covering the transaction and not his or her title to the land. 'Consequently, if the title is defective, mere registration of the instrument cannot be pleaded in any court of law as an answer to an action for the recovery of the land.' This and other inadequacies of the Land Registry Act, which have been recognised over the past decades, include the fact that 'purchasers and mortgages of land are not protected against any liability should the title of the land be affected by fraud or mistake'. 'These and other defects and the increasing confusion and insecurity of title have led the PNDC to introduce this new law in order to give certainty to land titles and to facilitate the proof thereof and also to render the dealing with land more simple and economical'.

The problem of land title insecurity does not affect only the members of the leading classes some of whom are trooping into commercial farming. It also affects peasant farmers even more severely.[36] The land right problems of the peasantry have included (i) being chased away from the lands they have been cultivating for decades as shown by the case of the 1,000 peasants resettled by the Volta River Authority who were forced to flee by Krobos of Akokoma-Sisi near Asesewa in the Eastern Region;[37] (ii) the payment of exhorbitant ground rents to landlords;[38] (iii) ejections, brutal assaults, illegal arrests and other forms of intimidation by landlords as have been the experience of tenant farmers in the Sefwi Wiawso and Wasa Amenfi Traditional areas of the Western Region;[39] (iv)bloody confrontations between contending parties as shown by the recurring conflict between the Konkomba and Nanumba poeples; or (v) protracted and costly litigations which are often interspersed with bloody conflicts. The pertinant question is whether the PNDCL 152 provides remedy for this multitude of disadvantaged citizens of the country who derive their livelihood from the land.

Both the government and the Chief Registrar of Lands suggest that the peasantry would secure protection from the law. In the words of the Chief Registrar of Lands 'Complete protection will be given to persons who have limited rights over land such as those operating under the *abunu* or *abusa* or other share-cropping tenancies or arrangements'. But if we would recall that the bulk of the peasantry are illiterate and above all ignorant of such avenues for redress; that they are too poor to afford the services of a defence lawyer; and that the procedure for consumating such title registration is such as would appeal more to the literate and enlightened, then the chances that the mass of the peasantry would benefit from this law are indeed doubtful. In fine, the prevailing balance of class forces in the country and the concerted drive by the ruling classes to promote their interest in the agricultural sector as well should make it quite clear that the purpose of PNDCL 152 is to enable the dominant classes to realise their class goals in the framework of the existing communal land tenure systems.

CONCLUSION

The capitalist economy is the motive force behind the far-reaching changes occurring in the communal land tenure system of the country. The changes have been in the direction of private or freehold interest in land; and they have has gathered momentum with the rapid pace at which capitalist organisation of production has penetrated agriculture. This process is being spearheaded by the ruling classes who are increasingly turning to investment in agriculture and other land-based industries as attractive theatres of capital accummulation. For them the land question is primarily one of title insecurity. Over the years they have sought to obtain security of the freehold interests they have acquired from traditional authorities. In this regard they have received the active support of the state which has been providing, on a continous basis, legal and constitutional as well as financial and technical support or protection, as the case may be.

The peasantry on the other hand have been the main losers in this 'silent revolution' that is occurring on the land. Their rights in the lands they till still remain tenuous and may continue to be violated for as long as they are unable to meet the food and agro-industrial raw material needs of the country. This situation has over the years attracted the ruling classes who find it necessary to move into agriculture and other land-based economic activities with the aim of producing to fill the deficit. At the same time, the prospects for the peasantry to transform agricultural practices and raise productivity are not getting any brighter; because the policies of successive governments show that state power would always be used to promote the accumulation needs of members of the ruling classes in all branches of the economy. The support which the peasantry require to enable them to modernise agriculture is therefore not going to be available to them. Even the old support services being provided by the state may be withdrawn as has happened under the PNDC's ERP.

NOTES

1. Bentsi-Enchil, K., *Ghana Land Law* Lagos: African University Press, 1964) p. 109.
2. *Ibid.* See also Asante, S.K.B., *Property Law and Social Goals in Ghana*, 1844-1966 (Accra: Ghana Universities Press 1975) and Ollennu,N.
3. The development of a class of small property owners and small producers in various sectors of the economy was evident long before Britain colonised the country; but the process intensified particulary after 1900. For a discussion of aspects of this development see Reynolds, E., *Trade and Economic Change on the Gold Coast, 1897-1874* (London: Longmans, 1974), Kimble, D., *A Political History of Ghana, 1850-1928*. (Oxford; Clarendon Press, 1963), Cardinall, A.W., *The Gold Coast, 1931* (Accra: Government Printer.), and Hill, P., *The Gold Coast Cocoa Farmer* (London: Oxford University Press, 1958) and *The Migrant Cocoa Farmer of Southern Ghana* (Cambridge: Cambridge University Press, 1963).
4. For an instance of this refer to the composition of the *Committee on Constitutional Reform*. (Chairman: J.H. Coussey) appointed in 1949 to make recommendations for constitutional reforms following the 1948 political unrest in the country.
5. A discussion of the question of mismanagement of stool lands and stool revenue by chiefs as well as the anti-chief political agitations they produced will be found in Danquah, J.B., *Akan Laws and Customs* (London: Routledge, 1928), Busia, K.A., *The Position of the Chief in Modern Political System of Ashanti* (London: Oxford University Press, 1951), and Kimble, *op cit*.
6. There is an excellent case study of the part played by peassant indebtedness and other financial problems in mobilising peasant cocoa farmers behind the CPP in Owusu, Maxwell, *Uses and Abuses of Political Power* (Chicago: Chicago University Press, 1970).
7. The State Council Ordinances under reference are *The State Council (Ashanti) Ordinance, No. 4, 1952*; *State Councils (Northern Territories) Ordinance, No. 5, 1952*; and the *State Councils (Colony and Southern Togoland) Ordinance*, No. 8. 1952.
8. As recommended by the *Coussey Committee. op. cit.*
9. A number of instruments were issued in pursuance of the *Rents (Stabilisation) Act, 1962 Act 109*. They are: the *Rent (Cocoa Farms) Regulations, 1962* L.I. 186; and the *Rents (Cocoa Farms (Amendment) Regulations, 1965 (L.I. 382)* The principal act was repealed 1967 in NLCD 34.
10. For a discussion of the basis of the rights of individual members of the primordial group, and the limitations imposed on such rights by customary law, see, Bentsi-Enchill, *Op cit.*, Ollenu, *Op. cit.* and Asante, *Op cit*; also his 'Interests in Land in the Customary Law of Ghana: A New Appraisal' *Yale Law Review*, 74, 1965.
11. And so ejection and other forms of harassment of peasant cocoa farmers became widespread. For a discussion of aspects of this problem see Kom, E.B. 'Land Tenure Reform' in S.B.A Missah (ed). *Title-Registration, Land Resource Management and Land Use Policy* (Kumasi: LARC, UST, 1980.)
12. *IIbid.*
13. Much of the ideological justification for repealing Act 109 was provided by the *Report of the Committee of Enquiry into the Local Purchasing of Cocoa*. (Chairman: J.C. de Graft Johnson) (Accra: Ministry of information, 1967)
14. Ryan, Selwyn, 'The Theory and Practice of African One-Partyism, The Case of the CPP Re-Examined' *Canadian Journal of African Studies*, 4(1), 1970
15. *Ibid.*
16. See Ghana, *National Assembly Debates*. Vol 8, 1957 pp 449-502; and vol. 9, 1958 p. 307.

17. Refer to Ghana, *Report of the Commission Appointed to Enquire into the Affairs of the Timber Marketing Board and The Timber Cooperative Union*. (The Blay Commission) (Accra. Ministry of Information, 1968.) for detailed information on this case and several others.
18(a). *Ibid.*
18(b). *Ibid.* Paragraph 127.
19. Bentsi-Enchil, *Op cit.*, p. 272.
20. Reported in Mensah-Brown, A.K. 'Statutory Control of Land Development in Ghana: The Land Development (Protection of Purchaser's Act), 1960 (Act 2) — Summary of Judicial Interpretation' *Land Administration Journal*, Vol. 2, 1979.
21. Refer to the reports of the committees appointed after 1966 to enquire into the assets of Kwame Nkrumah and his key party and government lieutenants. See also Ghana. *The Proposals of the Constitutional Commission for a Constitution for Ghana* (*The Akuffo-Addo commission*) (Accra: Ministry of Information, 1968.)
22. Reported in Ghana. *Constituent Assembly Debates, 1968/69*. pp. 2137-38.
23. The speaker was R.R. Amponsah who defected from the CPP to become one of the leading members of the moderate members of the petty-bourgeoisie. It is significant that in 1931 when the *Lands and Native Rights (Northern Territories) Ordinance* was passed by the colonial legislature Casely Hayford (formerly of the Aborigines Rights Protection Society, and later on founder and leader of the National Congress of British West Africa) is reported to have protested that that law was 'confiscatory'.
24. Report of The Akuffo-Addo Commission, *Op cit.*
25. The range of policies which were implemented to support the growth of Ghanaian private commercial farms are examined by Shepherd, A.W., *The Development of Capitalist Rice Farming in Northern Ghana* (Ph.D Thesis, University of Cambridge, 1979.)
26. See *Ibid.*
27. See Hansen's contribution to this collection — Chapter 8 for a discussion of the food question in general.
28. This component of the government's agricultural policies was implemented under the *Special Scheme for Participation in Agriculture* which is discussed in the following paragraphs. See also Hansen in this volume.
29. For data on grains production for the period refer to the speech delivered by Col. F.G. Bernasco, Commissioner for Agriculture, at the 1974 New Year School of the Institute of Adult Education. Published in *Food and Population* (Legon: University of Ghana, 1974.)
30. See *Shepherd*, Op cit.
31. These developments and others related to it are analysed in: Ghana. *Report of the Land Use Planning Committee*. (Unpublished) (Accra: Ministry of Lands, Natural Resources, Fuel and Power, 1979.)
32. *The Lands and Native Rights (Northern Territories) Ordinance, 1931.*
33. The background to the appointment of the Alhassan committee is recounted in this committee's report. Infra.
34. Ghana.*Report of the Committee on Ownership of Lands and the Position of Tenants in the Northern and Upper Regions*. (The Alhassan Committee). (Unpublished) (Accra: Ministry of Lands Natural Resources, Fuel and Power, 1978.)
35. The Constitutional Commission that produced this report was also appointed by the government of the SMC.

36. *Kom*, Op cit.
37. *Ghanaian Times*, November 10 1983, p.8
38. *The Voice*, December 6-12 1982, *Ghanaian Times*, November 26 1983 and *People's Daily Graphic*, December 28 1983.
39. *Ghanaian Times*, July 18 1987.

8. THE STATE AND FOOD AGRICULTURE

Emmanuel Hansen(*)

INTRODUCTION

It is now easily conceded even by the most optimistic observer that Africa is in the midst of a severe crisis. This crisis has been going on for more than a decade now. Robert Macnamara, former President of the World Bank captured the essence of this crisis when he declared:

> The harsh truth is that sub-Saharan Africa today faces a crisis of unprecedented proportions. The physical environment is deteriorating. Per capita production of food grains is falling. Population growth rates are the highest in the world and rising. National economies are in disarray. And international assistance in real terms is moving downward'.[1]

Not surprisingly, the World Bank itself expresses a similar position:

> ...for most African countries, and for a majority of the African population, the record is grim, and it is no exaggeration to talk of crisis. Slow overall economic growth, sluggish agricultural performance coupled with rapid rates of population increase, and balance-of-payments and fiscal crises-these are dramatic indicators of economic trouble.[2]

Africa's political leaders share the same prognosis. At the nineteenth session of the Meeting of African Ministers of Economic Development and Planning of the ECA, held in Addis Ababa in May 1984, considerable alarm was expressed about the economic and social crisis on the continent:

> We the African Ministers responsible for Economic Development and Planning...have reviewed once again the economic and social crisis which has engulfed virtually the whole of Africa since the eighteenth session of the Commission... We are most greatly concerned by the very alarming and significant deterioration in the economic and social conditions of the African countries, and in particular, by the effects of the drought which now affects thirty four of our member States; and the devastating impact of the global economic recession which is gripping the African countries with its attendant collapse in commodity prices, the unprecedented high level of interest rates, sharp exchange rate fluctuations, increased protectionism, balance of payments difficulties, mounting external debt and the decline in real terms of official development assistance.[3]

Nor do the continent's intellectuals disagree with the above perception of the current reality. Thus Peter Anyang Nyong'o writes:

> Looking at all the indicators of development performance of African countries during the last two decades, it would be difficult to deny that this continent is now faced with a major crisis of social reproduction.[4]

It is not only the peasant or agro-based economies which are facing this problem. Even the mineral-based economies are in no better position. For oil importers, per capita output fell by 0.9 per cent in 1981 and 1.7 per cent in 1982; but in 1983, the year of recovery in Europe, per capita output fell by a further 2 percent. The oil exporting countries also experienced their own version of the crisis. Their per capita output fell by about 11 percent in 1981-2 and by a further 7 per cent in 1983. For Africa as a whole, per capita output in 1983 was 11 per cent below the 1980 average level, thus offseting all the modest gains of the 1970s.[5]

This means that the continent is facing a threat of survival and security. But unlike the industrialised countries of the North where the threat to man's security comes from his control over nature and the environment through his mastery of science and technology, in Africa it is the very lack of control over nature and the environment which poses the problem.

It is true that when one looks at the continent it is not difficult to see major conflicts in every sub-region some of which have endured for a long time and have taken many lives. But it must also be said that famine in one year perhaps takes more lives than a whole decade of armed conflict. This is not to suggest that wars should be tolerated. It is merely to call attention to the fact that for us the question of security calls first and foremost for action to deal with the food and nutritional needs of the mass of the people. For it is precisely in this area — i.e, the field of agriculture that the current crisis manifests itself in its most virulent form. Agriculture as a whole is in a poor situation: food agriculture in particular is in a more serious crisis.

The 1972-1974 food crisis brought the problem dramatically to the attention of the world. A decade later Africa faced another food crisis of major proportions. The international community responded to it, as if it were an emergency, with international conferences and emergency assistance of one sort or the other. In Europe for example, assistance was mobilised in the form of Band Aid, Live Aid and Sport Aid. Although the effort was commendable the form it took tended to give the impression, also freely disseminated by the mass media, that the crisis was just a fleeting one that had been caused by the prolonged drought.

Although the drought did indeed exacerbate the situation the trends towards a crisis were already apparent for almost a decade before it actually broke out. The World Bank Report of 1981, for example, noted that:

> Total food production rose by 1.5 per cent per year in the 1970s, down from 2 per cent in the previous decade. But since population was rising rapidly — by an annual average of 2.5 per cent in the 1960s and 2.7 per cent in the 1970s — food production per person was stagnant in the first decade and actually declined in the next. Imports of food grains (wheat, rice and maize) soared — by 9 per cent per year since the early 1960s — reinforcing food dependency. Food aid also increased substantially. Since 70 to 90 per cent of the population earns its income from agriculture, the drop in production in this sector spelled a real income loss for many of the poorest.[6]

By 1980 food self-sufficiency ratios had dropped from 98 per cent in the 1960s to around 86 per cent, which means that each African has on the average 12 per cent less home grown food in 1980 than 20 years ago. Production of cereals increased by a mere 1.2 per cent annually over the two decades reaching only 58.4 million tons in 1980.

And while overall food production has tended to stagnate for more than a decade, growth in food demand has increased with population growth. To meet the deficit the continent has had recourse to more food imports. Between 1970 and 1980 the volume of total food imports increased by an average annual rate of 8.4 per cent. This increasing reliance on food imports, even if it can be sustained, creates other problems of structural dependence on other foods like wheat in particular, which cannot be so easily grown in the region. And worse of all, such large food imports as well as food aid still leaves a large number of people under-nourished since such food items do not often reach the urban and rural poor.[7]

Although the situation has improved from the desperate situation of the last two years the continent is by no means out of the woods. The 1985 crop was reportedly encouraging and the FAO's estimates for this year indicated an increase in cereals to the tune of 55.7 million tons, an increase of 21 per cent above the average for the last 5 years.[7] However, as many as 40 African countires which suffer food deficits will in the 1986/87 year need as much food assistance as 3.2 million tons. It is when viewed against this background that one sees the magnitude of the problem. It means that the continent is far from achieving any measure of food self-sufficiency, let alone food security. But it is recognised that food security is the basis of social reproduction and therefore of all social development.

Thus Europe may consider nuclear weapons as the immediate threat to its survival, but in Africa, it is not overstretching the case to argue that the acute food deficit constitutes the immediate threat to the survival of its people. Adequate food and nutritional provision for the mass of the population is the critical minimum for social reproduction without which no development can take place. We shall now examine the specific case of Ghana, to illustrate the point that the recurring food crisis is neither an accidental situation nor an emergency created by an occasional failure of the weather.

THE CASE OF GHANA

Ghana provides an interesting and rewarding case study of the problem of food self-sufficiency and security in Africa. In the first place, it would appear that there are no ecological, or even social, reasons why it should experience food problems of the kind it has experienced in the last two and a half decades. Second, it would appear that it is the one country which demonstrates how, in the eyes of the World Bank and the IMF, an African country can achieve recovery through the ruthless appplication of the neo-classical prescriptions of the Fund.

Now let us look at the crisis of Ghanaian food agriculture and the policy responses to it and see to what extent there has been a recovery. It would be wrong to look at the crisis of Ghanaian food agriculture outside the framework of the crisis in the economy in general. In a peasant-based economy like Ghana, a crisis in the economy is, essentially a crisis of agriculture. It is therefore important to describe the main features of the agricultural economy of the country.

Unlike other African countries, it would seem that there are no ecological or social reasons why Ghana should have the kind of endemic food problems which it has been experiencing for the last two and a half decades. In the first place, Ghana is not in the arid or semi-arid zone. Nor is it in the Sahel region like Niger, Burkina Faso, Mali, large parts of Ethiopia, Mauritania or parts of Senegal or Somalia. And neither does it have large tracts of land which cannot be used because they are in the desert or in swampy conditions. It is, however, estimated that cultivatable land constitutes only about 15-20 per cent of the entire land area.

Futhermore, although aspirant commercial farmers sometimes speak of their frustration at the complex land tenure system, this does not constitute a real obstacle to land acquisition and therefore to agricultural production. Moreover the state often intervenes in cases where it is convinced of the genuine need for it to procure land for big commercial farmers. Although one can talk of land pressure, particularly in certain cocoa growing areas of the Eastern Region, this has been occasioned more by customary land use practices than land shortage as such. There is really no land problem as such in Ghana.

It is also true that soil fertility is not particularly high; but with efficient soil management, it is good enough to support crop production and animal husbandary. There is relatively dependable rainfall, not evenly distributed in the Northern and Upper Regions, but well enough to sustain rain-fed agriculture. There are two huge dam projects in the country. The agricultural cycle has not been interrupted by such natural disasters as floods, rampaging locusts and other widespread insect infestations. Nor have there been long and extensive periods of drought as has been the case in the Sahel, although there was drought in the cereal growing areas of Northern and Upper Regions in 1975-6.

Of course, the country had its share of the drought which ravaged the whole of the West African sub-region in 1982-3. During the same period there were also man-made disasters like forest fires which reportedly destroyed large acres of cropland. However, these could only explain temporary interruptions in the country's normal weather cycle. They cannot be used to account for the seemingly intractable food problem of the last two and a half decades. To supplement these ideal ecological conditions the social situation has remained stable: no widespread social disruptions have occurred to inhibit production: there have been no civil disturbances like the wars which have afflicted

Ethiopia, Mozambique, Angola, Uganda, Chad or the Sudan and interfered with the cycle of food production. It could be argued, however, that the long period of political instability did create a certain element of uncertainty which discouraged investment in projects with long gestation periods like farming.

A look at the social character of the agricultural economy also does not reveal any specific reasons why Ghana should have any food problems. Ghana's agricultural economy is based on the 'peasant model'. Over 90 per cent of food production is in the hands of small farmers. Unlike Algeria, Kenya or Zimbabwe, Ghana did not experience a history of settler agriculture. Nor did it experience plantation agriculture as countries like the Cameroun, Liberia or Mauritius did. So there could be no question of plantation-type cash crop production competing with peasant food production for labour and other resources. Multinational involvement in agriculture, and food agriculture in particular, is of very recent origin and its impact on agricultural output is negligible. The small-scale grower could, it is argued, inter-crop export with food crops and thereby meet his food needs as well as his need for consumer goods. There are no huge agricultural estates with powerful connections at local and international levels, making claims on the state for substantial subsidies.

The prevalence of the 'peasant model' means that there was no ruthless alienation of land from the peasant as happened in the areas of white settler agriculture. Since the 1970s there have been some displacements in the Northern and Upper Regions where capitalist rice farming has been taking place on extensive scale; but this is not enough to introduce significant distortions in the agricultural economy.

Agricultural labour cannot be regarded as a severe problem either. The rate of proletarianisation of the labour force has been slow. And although Ghana's mining industry had at some earlier date tended to compete with cocoa production for labour, at the moment its labour requirements do not compete seriously with the labour requirements for either cocoa or food production. It does not, however, mean that the country has no problem of agricultural labour. The argument here is that the source of the problem of agricultural labour should be sought somewhere else. It would seem from this that there should be no reason why the peasant who has traditionally supported food agriculture more or less successfully should now have problems in meeting the country's food requirements.

In addition to these Ghana has been credited with having a good social infrastrature to support food production. The country has had a good network of roads. However, from the late 1970s to the early 1980s, these had fallen into a state of serious disrepair. Even so by the standards of other African countries, the situation was not too bad; and even though it certainly could be better the poor state of the roads did not seem to constitute the main obstacle to increased food production. The country also has a fairly developed marketing system although sometimes its operation can be frustratingly inefficient. To manage all these resources there is a relatively good corps of trained manpower although a good many of them have been migrating recently because of the deteriorating social and economic conditions.

There has also been a relatively good system of health and educational institutions; but like the others this has also, in recent times, been in need of some urgent improvement. It would seem from the foregoing therefore that there are really no reasons why the country should not be able to feed itself and leave some for security and for export. If there are problems then they should be sought at the level of policy. And it is to this that we shall soon address. What have been the national policies pursued by the state to satisfy the food and nutrition needs of the country and guarantee a minimum of food security so that social reproduction can take place? Before we tackle this there are two other questions which we would like to examine. One is the importance of food in the national economy; and the other is the problem of food availability.

FOOD AND DEVELOPMENT

There are three main areas in which we can talk of the significance of food in national development. In the first place it seems banal to state that unless there is adequate food to meet the nutritional needs of the people they will not be able to reproduce themselves in order to undertake the urgent task of development. Development implies not only the ability to satisfy basic material needs but also a certain degree of psychic well being. The later implies the achievement of a minimum level of security, freedom from anxiety and from any experience of self degradation. A critical minimum for the attainment of such a condition is the provision of adequate food needs of the growing population.

Another reason for the importance of food in national development is that it lays the basis for security. As we have already noted, in the industralised countries of the North the threat to man's existence comes from the products of his own ability to control nature, i.e. from the products of science and technology, and in this particular case from nuclear weapons. In Ghana, and the developing world generally, this danger comes more from our inability to control the environment. Peace researchers have traditionally paid a great deal of attention to conflict as a way of promoting security. In Europe this is as it should be; but in Africa, it is not so much war which poses the threat to our existence as the ordinary things of life — like lack of adequate and nourishing food, and diseases. One famine year could probably wipe out more people than a whole decade of war, although it has to be conceded that conflict is often responsible for the decline in productivity as it interferes with the agricultural cycle. This is graphically illustrated by the case of Mozambique and the Sudan. At any rate, what makes security in the country so urgent is the threat the recurring food deficit poses to the dignity of its people and the sovereignty of the nation.

Third, food security is a right and should be defended and fought for like other rights such as the right to life, freedom, liberty etc. The right of access to and enjoyment of adequate provision of food is at the very basis of human survival and dignity. Indeed, the United Nations Declaration of Human Rights adopted by the General Assembly in December 1948 recognises this:

> Everyone has the right to a standard of living adequate for the health and well-being of himself and of his family, including food, clothing, housing and medical care and necessary social services, and the right to security in the event of unemployment, sickness, disability, widowhood, old age or the lack of livelihood in circumstances beyond his control.

From this it is clear that food is a human right which should above all, be guaranteed. There are therefore ethical as well as developmental reasons for having a food policy which would ensure for the mass of the people their adequate food needs.

Lastly, the ability to satisfy food needs locally means that the vital foreign exchange resources used to finance food imports could be saved for domestic development. It is for these reasons that in most countries food agriculture is regarded as a strategic industry and justifies state intervention. This is so even in countries where the free market ideology reigns supreme. The question therefore is not whether there should be state intervention or not. It is what kind of intervention will make it possible to achieve self-sufficiency in food and guarantee food security for the people. It is this which makes the consideration of state policies towards food production paramount. But what does food security mean, and what is the nature of Ghana's food problem?

Food Security

There have been many discussions on the concept of food security. One can identify three main ways in which food security has been conceptualised — namely, as availability, accessibility and adequacy. For the purposes of this paper, I would merely regard it first, as the provision of food and nutrition needs at affordable prices to the mass of the people; and second, as the capacity to produce enough surplus for storage so that in the event of crop failure or some other national emergency the mass of the people could draw upon it thus 'securing' them against the scourge of famine which has often resulted from such a development. In this way the basic subsistence needs of the people would be guaranteed.

THE FOOD PROBLEM

What evidence is there that Ghana has a food problem? Over a decade Ghana has experienced a food deficit. The situation reached crisis proportions in the period 1977-1983, and although the situation has now improved from what it was during the 1982-3 period, it is by no means over. The improvement has been quite marginal. The food problem manifests itself several ways: first at the level of shortage of staple foods like yams, cassava, maize, rice etc.

Second, there is an even more serious shortage of high protein foods like pulses, meat, fish, eggs etc. For a large number of people, meat, fish and eggs have virtually disappeared from the daily diet. During the 1982-1983 'hungry season' food was unavailable. Today, it is available but unaffordable. An important characteristic of the current food problem is that it is not a temporary shortfall in an otherwise stable supply situation. It is not the result of a temporary deficit caused by natural disasters like drought (although the country has had this too), or the periodic supply problem during the 'lean season' — the period of about three months before the next harvest when supplies are virtually exhausted due to a combination of factors like low productivity, lack of surpluses and inadequate storage facilities. It has been with the country in different degrees for almost two decades now.

A third feature of the current food problem is that although there was a severe drought in the Northern and Upper Regions of the country in 1977-78, in general the food problem is not confined to a specific geographical location where ecological conditions are more harsh; or where communication problems make the movement of food more difficult. There have been local or regional variations in the severity of the problem. But one important fact is that it is a national, not a local, problem. It is not confined to the urban or rural areas; nor is it a symption of changing consumer tastes, although it has to be said that like any other African country, there has been a movement away from tubers to cereals owing to increased urbanisation and wage employment. It is also true to say that in the midst of the general crisis certain classes of people have greater access to food than others. This however does not invalidate the fact of a food crisis. What then is the problem?

There used to be the claim that the country's level of food production was adequate and the problem was with marketing and distribution.[9] It is true that Ghana's system of food distribution leaves a lot to be desired. One can also not underemphasise the link between production and distribution, including the unreliability of agricultural statistics especially when assessing the extent of the food problem. However, it is difficult to avoid the conclusion that there have been serious production problems. The crux of the matter is that with a population growth rate of about 2.6 per cent per annum food production has hardly been able to keep pace, let alone outstrip it. The 5-Year Development Plan, 1975-1980 concludes:

> Except in the case of a few of them, production of most of these crops (cereals, starchy staples, pulses, vegetables, fruits) in the past years, especially between 1970-1974 had not increased significantly in response to domestic demand for these basic staples.

This was before the difficult years of 1977-83. It has been estimated that output in the food sector as a whole either declined or stagnated between 1970-and 1981. 'According to the data available, food production per head of population declined by about 30 per cent during the 1970s.'[10] Acreages for the main food crops such as cereals, starchy staples, pulses and nuts and vegetables showed a steady decline from the peak years of 1973 and 1974 to the disastrous levels they hit in 1982 and 1983.[11]

Nothing demonstrates the food problem more than the price system. It is true that Ghana's system of tortuous food distribution distorts the pricing system. But that alone cannot explain the spiraling food prices. Nor could the prices be accounted for in terms of the difference between farm gate prices and retail prices. Since the 1950s the prices of food stuffs have been going up. The retail price for local food has risen faster than any other item of consumption. It has been estimated that between March 1963 and September 1965 the prices of locally produced food increased throughout the country by 82.3 per cent. Over the same period the prices of imported food went up by 30 per cent.[12] Apart from this trend, Kodwo Ewusi[13] has also estimated that foodstuffs have been responsible for the overall price rise at the national, rural and urban levels. He contends that price indices showed that local foods became the most expensive commodity in the rural and urban areas between 1964 and 1969; and further that 90 per cent of the increase in the overall price levels can be traced to the rise in food prices.

The price situation in recent times has been even more severe. If we take 1963 as the base year (1963=100), by 1970 the total national consumer price index (CPI) was 188.5. For imported food the CPI was 150.1 and for locally produced food it was 210.0. By 1977 the figures were 759.9 for imported food; 2,033.9 for locally produced food; and 1,382.55 for all commodities. Again if we took

TABLE 1: MARKET PRICES OF SELECTED FOOD ITEMS IN ACCRA

			Average prices (cima)	
Item	Unit	January 1982	January 1983	April 1983
Maize	bag(50kg)	500	1,000	4,000
Maize	American tin(3kg)	30	80	200
Kenkey	ball	1	4	10
Cassava	tuber	10	15	25
Gari	American tin	15	65	190
Yam	tuber	45	80	160
Rice	bag(50kg)	600	900	1,200
Rice	American tin	80	200	200
Plantain	bunch (100)	160	250	1,000
Plantain	one	4	5	20
Tomatoes	three	4	10	40
Meat (beef)	1b	20	30	60
Bushmeat	grasscutter	250	450	600
Chicken	21b	45	75	180
Eggs	crate(30)	80	90	180
Eggs	one	3	4	6
Sugar	American tin	70	150	300
Sugar	cigarette tin	5	15	25
Bread	loaf	4	Disappeared	Disappeared

Note: ..2.75 $1.00
Source: J.A. Dadson, *Food and the Nation* West Africa July 1983 P. 1597.

the year when food prices went up steeply, 1977 as the base year (1977=100), by 1980 the food price index was 393.5; but by April

1983 it had reached 2,755, and 2,367 for all commodities. It has further been estimated that between 1979 and 1982 the prices of wholesale maize and millet increased by 500 per cent while that of yams increased by 1,500 per cent in the same period. The table by Dadson[14] demonstrates even more clearly the eratic movement of consumer prices: 1983 was a particularly severe year.

Another feature of Ghana's food problem is its tendency to become an important import commodity. Even before the food problem reached crisis proportions in the mid 1970s culminating in the extremely severe years of 1982-3, food already constituted a high proportion of total imports. Total food imports as a percentage of total import earnings for 1962-1973 are as follows:[15]

1962 — 65	= 19.3%
1967	= 19.3%
1969	= 16.0%
1971	= 15.5%
1973	= 12.4%

It has to be noted that the figures for food imports do not indicate actual demand. Rather, they reflect the availability of resources to fund such imports. Thus, as the foreign exchange situation became very severe, although the food situation was much worse, it could not be revealed in the corresponding import figures.

For a country where agriculture employs 57 per cent of the labour force and which, in 1974, accounted for 35 per cent of GDP the volume of food imports is a clear sign that something is seriously wrong somewhere. When one takes into consideration the fact that Ghanaian agriculture is peasant-based, then the situation is grave indeed. Joseph Bogner, the Hungarian economist recognised the problem about two decades ago. In 1962 he wrote:

> Food imports amounted to 19.18 per cent of all imports in Ghana in 1960. It is obvious that such continued high levels of food imports could not be tolerated; assuming unchanged structure, imports in 1970 would amount to £129.6 million in 1960. Such a volume of imports cannot be balanced by exports... It is necessary to act very quickly to increase agricultural production by 1965 by between 40 to 50 per cent to avoid an increase in food imports.[16]

It is clear, as will be seen in subsequent sections of this paper, that this advice was not heeded; or if it was heeded the government was unable to achieve the recommended level of output. The result is that by 1977 the country would experience a severe food problem.

In the past the country had been able to finance food imports through the sale of primary products like cocoa and timber which together accounted for 75 per cent of export receipts; but with the dwindling of export revenue because of declining output and falling world prices, the country lost its capacity to import food. Hence the food crisis which hit the country in the late seventies and eighties. Therefore the food crisis has to be looked at not in narrow terms but as part of the general crisis of capital accumulation which is manifested in its most dramatic form in declining agricultural output.

It has often been claimed that food imports were more a function of changes in consumption habits than lapses in domestic production. This may have had some element of truth particularly in the late fifties and possibly in the early sixties. But the growing volume of imports in the latter period could not establish anything but serious problems with domestic production especially when it is recalled that during 1961-65 the government had instituted foreign exchange and import control which ought normally to have affected the imports of food as well.

It is when one looks at the problem at the individual level and in relation to the workers' purchasing power that one grasps the full significance of the food crisis. This is graphically illustrated by the gap between food prices and the price of labour. At a minimum wage of 35.0 cedis per day in 1984, it took the average worker more than a week to buy an American tin of rice (3kg); more than a day to buy 3kgs of maize; ten days to buy a tuber of yam; over a day to buy a bottle of edible oil; and more than a day to buy an American tin (3kg) of gari (cassava grains). One finger of plantain costs more than the value of half a day's labour. The situation was worse than these cold figures indicate because many workers did not even get the minimum wage. Some would be lucky if they got a fraction of it while others went unemployed.

In addition to the astronomical food prices, one has also to consider the hassle and humiliating experience which workers had to undergo in order to secure these commodities. The situation was further made worse by the corrupt and inefficient system of distribution. The net effect of all these was widespread dispair among the population as the poor food situation in the country began to affect public health as well. Rawlings was not far from wrong when he declared after his second year of coming to power:

> The hard and bitter truth is that in several years of national effort, the government and people of our country have failed to work together to implement policies and programmes necessary for the achievement of reasonable standards in our living conditions. Basic needs for food, health, transport, shelter and recreation remain largely unfulfilled and out of the reach of the majority of our people. There is evidence of mounting despair, deepening apathy and growing withdrawal and rejection of national responsibility on the part of ordinary people.[17]

This was in reference to the situation in 1983 when the food problem was at a crisis point. Since 1984 the government has been talking of improvements in the economy. The World Bank and the IMF have been particularly lavish in their praise of the policies of the government. There have been optimistic statements about the state of agricultural production, particularly food. Figures indicate that production particularly of food went up in 1984 only to drop again in 1985. Even so, the national consumer price index for food rose to 3,304.2 in 1984 compared to 2,357.4 in 1983; and yet 1984 was a good harvest year. Food prices have continued to rise since then. In 1985, the CPI for food alone was 3,647.2 (Base Year = 1977).

Obviously this is the kind of situation which no government will find comfortable. Quite apart from the fact that it is unethical, it also has serious consequences for the developmental initiatives of the state. It undermines the legitimacy of the state and its leading institutions. This is even more serious for military regimes which have no source of legitimacy other than their political and economic performance. The question then to consider next is what specific policies have been embarked upon by governments to alleviate this situation; provide for the food and nutritional needs of the mass of the people; and guarantee food security.

FOOD POLICIES

The Colonial Background

Since the present problem has some basis in the past, it is useful to take a look at past policies and see how they have helped to shape present policies. Two main views have guided food policy in Ghana since the end of World War II. One view is that there was no problem of actual food production in the country. The problem was rather with distribution and marketing. If there was to be state intervention, then it should be at the level of distribution and marketing. The question then became: what sort of state intervention was necessary to ensure effective distribution of the product? The other position was that the problem had to do with production: productivity is far too low to support demand and the reason for this was the specific form of peasant production. It was asserted that the peasant farmer had been unable to keep pace with demand in a period of growing population, urbanisation and wage employment. This view first originated among colonial officials soon after the war, but was to get the full endorsement of the African nationalist government that took over at independence. This position was summed up by the last of the colonial administrations as follows:

> It is now becoming apparent that the peasant had used methods in cultivating and preparing crops which will have to give way to mechanisation if the country is to continue to progress rapidly.[18]

Government leaders were to make similar statements in the post-independence period and even before. In 1976 a statement attributed to the Commissioner for Works states:

> The small farms must give way to plantation type of farms. Seasonal crops designed to depend on the rainy seasons must give way to all-year cropping assured by irrigation.[19]

It has to be stressed that the two contrasting positions do not merely reflect technical approaches to the problem of Ghana's food agriculture. They also reflect class interests and contrasting ideological positions that have prevailed within, or were in control of, the state apparatus at any point in time. For example, British colonial interest in Ghanaian agriculture arose out of demands for export crops to feed metropolitan industries. Historically three main methods have been employed to achieve this: plantation agriculture, settler agriculture and peasant agriculture.

In Ghana due to ecological factors, internal social structural factors, and the division of labour that was imposed on colonies in the Empire, the peasant model was preferred. This set the pattern for the development of the agricultural economy of the country, its pattern of capital accumulation, the structure of the class system which was to evolve later and the country's structure of politics. Above all it also conditioned its food policy as the colonial state encouraged export crop production and left food production to be determined by the force of its own momentum. Except for the brief period of the war years when the colonial state intervened both at the level of production and of the market to ensure adequate supply of locally produced food in order to feed the large European population whose food needs could not be satisfied through imports because of the exigencies of the war, this policy continued into independence.[20]

Food Policy Under the First Republic 1957-1966

It was during the time of the First Republic that anything resembling food policy was initiated. At this time the state initiated a policy of active intervention in agriculture generally in a purposeful way. This policy should be seen within the context of the CPP's policy of active intervention in the economy. What was strikingly innovative about this was the plan to intervene at the level of production. This was based on the understanding of the Nkrumah government that small-scale production was a hindrance to progress and had to give way to large-scale agriculture. It was also in line with development thinking at the time which saw social progress as a movement from tradition to modernity. Consequently, state production units were established. These were the State Farms Corporation, the Workers Brigade, The United Ghana Farmers' Co-operative Council (UGFCC) and the Young Farmers League.

The idea was to change the form of production from the small-scale peasant-based production units to large-scale mechanised schemes organised and run by the state. The transformation was to come not through a change within the peasant mode of production, but through a change of the peasant mode of production. This was in line with the ideological thinking as well as the economic thinking of the party at that time.

The CPP's policy of transforming Ghanaian agriculture through the establishment of co-operative and collective farms could be judged only on the results. If the cocoa output of 1965 which was the highest Ghana has ever attained was the result, then it did have some success. However, in the area of food production the policy did not achieve much, partly because of corruption, and mismanagement; and partly because it was not the government's priority. Besides it has been demonstrated that tree crops are more amenable to plantation type of agriculture which was undertaken by the state and co-operative farms.[21] An examination of the production records of the State Farms Corporation also confirms that food production was not their priority. Only 40 per cent of total acreage cultivated was devoted to what could be called food crops; and of this only rice and maize received any attention at all. In 1963, in response to the deteriorating food situation in the country the State Farms were instructed to turn their attention to food crops only, to be then instructed almost immediately to revert to industrial crops to feed local industries. The sudden reversal of policy had become imperative as a result of the import substitution industrialisation strategy of development initiated by the CPP government. Thus it could be argued that government tended to look at food production more as an emergency measure than a purposeful attempt to respond to the food problem in the country. Thus even under the CPP government, food policy matters showed a measure of continuity with the past.

In the colonial period because of the demographic balance of society such a casual approach to the food problem did not pose severe problems. However, the changes in the rate of urbanisation following the war years; the increase in wage employment, the building boom and increases in urban food demand following the political changes brought about by the movement towards independence, all rendered that approach irrelevant and dangerous for the future of the country.

The next question is why the CPP embarked on this particular slant of development policy? The pursuit of large-scale mechanized agriculture under the aegis of the state was consistent with the CPP's political strategy of establishing the class hegemony of the petty-bourgeoisie throughout society. In this particular case the rural sector was the target: it satisfied the class and ideological position of that fraction of the petty bourgeoisie which controlled power through the party. Unlike the opposition United Party, the CPP leaders did not have close ties with the ruling elements in the rural class structure. Expanding the public sector into agriculture was therefore like building political bridges. That policy extended the political basis of their power and influence, which they tried to use to control and direct the pattern of politics in the rural areas, particularly through the Workers Brigade, the Young Farmers League and the UGFCC.

Food Policy Under the Second Republic 1966-1971

After the overthrow of Nkrumah in 1966, the National Liberation Council (NLC) and the Progress Party (PP) governments which succeeded it embarked on a policy of disengaging the state from the economy in general, and agriculture particular. The ideological position of the petty bourgeois fraction which achieved control of the state was different from that which controlled the state at the time of the CPP. These were people with strong ties to the power structure in the cocoa growing areas of Ashanti, Eastern and Brong Ahafo regions. Their ideological perspectives on the nature of Ghana's problems and solutions to them were consequently shaped by their particular class position and that of their class allies. This orientation coincided with political views held by powerful outside forces, particularly the United States and Britain which saw the political demise of Nkrumah as the opportunity to bring Ghana back firmly under Western political and economic influence.

This convergence of political and ideological positions made it possible for the Harvard Advisory Group to virtually take over and determine the economic policy of the country during the 1966-71 period. The policies of the NLC and PP were consequently shaped by these. The PP's 1969 election manifesto for example states at page 9 as follows:

> The Progress Party affirms its support for and confidence in private enterprise. Our Government will constantly search for and advance other schemes to promote, assist, reward and encourage private risk taking.

Consequently, the two governments tried to dismantle the state organisations concerned with agriculture. The Ministry of Agriculture was reorganised. The Young Farmers League and the UGFCC were abolished. The Workers Brigade was reorganised into the Food Distribution Corporation (FDC) and its scale of operations reduced. It was no longer to engage in direct production but to intervene at the level of the market to buy food in bulk, store and release it on to the market during the 'lean season', when prices tend to be very high, in order to stabilize the prices of food. Due to lack of capitalisation the achievements of the FDC in this area was very minimal. The state farms were reduced in number from 105 in 1966 to 62 in 1967, and to 33 by 1971.[22]

Although the PP government always posited its policies as the opposite of those of the CPP in the case of its attitude towards agriculture, it would seem that there was continuity between it and the CPP regimes in one respect. The PP also held the belief that the future of Ghanaian agriculture lay with large-scale mechanised farming. The only difference between them was that unlike the CPP, the PP government held the view that agricultural modernisation had to be in the hands of private capitalists. The policy of the state was not to invest in the small-scale producer in order to increase his turnover and turn him into an expanding capitalist but to encourage and capitalise the petty-bourgeoisie in the bureaucracy, commerce and industry and in the liberal professions to go into agriculture.

That policy was clearly a vote of no confidence in the peasant producer who had almost single handedly shouldered the burden of Ghana's agriculture, producing both export and food crops. In practical terms, the state created opportunities for generous credit facilities, the provision of high yeilding seeds, inputs like fertilizers, tractor for hiring and so on. It was particularly in the Northern and Upper Regions where upland rice farming provided the opportunity for large-scale commercial agriculture that attempts were made to put this policy into practice in any determined way. To ensure the success of the policy in this region the PP government initiated the 'focus and concentrate' programme by which the state provided 50 per cent subsidy for fertilizer, high yeilding seeds and land clearance for so-called modern farmers.[23]

Following the policy of disengaging the state from the economy that was pursued in 1966-72, public expenditure on agriculture as a percentage of the total budget declined markedly. The following table emphasises the point:

TABLE 2: PUBLIC EXPENDITURE ON AGRICULTURE

1965	10.8%
1966	10.1%
1967	8.1%
1968	7.1%
1969	6.9%
1970	6.5%
1970-1	6.5%
1971-2	6.3%
1972-3	6.8%

It must be emphasised that both the CPP's method of seeking to transform Ghana's agriculture through large scale mechanised agriculture ran by the state, and the Progress Party's policy of doing the same through the promotion of private enterprise did bypass the peasantry who produce the bulk of the food in the country. Perhaps this is why none of these measures had much impact on domestic food supply. But unlike the CPP, the PP government did not even make the most perfunctory response to the labour problem. It believed that this could be left entirely to normal market conditions.

On the contrary, its policy of promoting Ghanaianisation of industry by expelling aliens without resident permits deprived the agricultural sector of considerable labour and resulted in serious consequences on agricultural production. By the time the PP government was overthrown in 1972, urban food prices had become one of the main political issues in the country.

FOOD SCHEMES

Operation Feed Yourself

It was against this background that Operation Feed Yourself (OFY) was launched by the new military government which overthrew the PP government. The National Redemption Council (NRC) (or the Supreme Military Council (SMC) as it later came to be called) sought to build legitimacy on the basis of a coalition of all the important petty bourgeois fractions in the country under the hegemony of the petty bourgeoisie located in the military. The political expression of this coalition was the corporate state. It was supported by the critical social groups in society, with the working class and the peasantry as junior partners in the grand coalition that was constructed. The exact political form it finally assumed was the abortive quest for 'Union Government'.

Considering the contradictions which are inherent in such a class base, the regime's ideological stance was not surprisingly centrist. Whereas the Nkrumah government had sought to use the state as the main vehicle of capital accumulation, and the Busia government had tried to rely on private capitalists, the Acheampong government sought to use both state and private entrepreneurs as a means of resolving the problem of accumulation. The policies of that government reflected this centrist perspective. It was in the area of food production that this centrist policy was applied quite forcefully; and it was in this area that we also see how that coalition of petty bourgeois class interests which had dominated Ghanaian politics since independence was able to maintain its dominant position. It is to that regime's agricultural initiatives that we shall now turn.

The OFY was the most ambitious programme ever lauched in the country to respond to the food problem. It was a crash programme aimed at increasing food production and thereby make the nation self-reliant. Projected as a populist measure to meet the food problem, it initially enjoyed a great deal of popular support as students from the country's universities and youth organisations responded to the call from the new military leaders to contribute free labour in harvesting sugar cane, vegetables and rice on state farms.

Three significant features of the OFY may be noted. For the first time, it set definite production targets to be achieved in agriculture although as it turned out the targets were very unrealistic. It also, for the first time turned attention to staple crops like plantain, cassava, tomato, yams, etc and not just rice and maize, as has been the case in the past. However, in the actual implementation of the plans, the latter staples still attracted predominant attention. Finally, it set up a definite machinery for the realisation of set targets.

OFY was divided into three phases. Phase one was to be devoted to increased food production for the domestic market; phase two was for the production of agricultural raw materials for local industry, and the final phase was for the production of agricultural products for export. It is a sad commentary on the fate of OFY that it hardly achieved the first objective let alone the subsequent ones.

The state created a military style organisation for the implementation of the programme. At the head of the structure was the Commissioner of Agriculture. Below him was the National Operations Committee of which he was Chairman, and which was the instrument for implementing the OFY programme nation-wide. The Committee brought together representatives from various government agencies connected with food production and distribution. Departments which were represented were those of Agricultural Economy and of Fisheries, the Seed Multiplication Unit, the Crop Production Unit and the Agricultural Mechanisation Unit. The same structure was replicated at the regional level, where the Regional Commissioner occupied the position of Chairman of the Regional Agricultural Committee. This was responsible for carrying out the policies and plans formulated by the National Operations Committee.

In addition to its hierarchical structure there were some institutions which became associated with it in order to enchance its operations. They included the State Farms Corporation, the Food Distribution Corporation, the Grains and Legumes Development Board, State Fishing Corporation and the Pomadze Poultry Enterprises.

The Regional Development Corporations which had been set up as centres of regional economic development were to laise closely with the OFY effort. They were expected to organise agricultural programmes for the production of food, and industrial raw material to feed local industries. Of these the most important from the point of view of agriculture was the Upper Regional Agricultural Development Project (URADEP). This was an 'integrated' rural development project funded by the World Bank, the United Kingdom government and the government of Ghana. It was meant to increase food production so as to increase rural incomes, provide amenities and raise the general standard of living and the quality of life of the rural people. Depending on its success similar projects were to be set up in other regions.

Like other agricultural undertakings of its kind the project was badly planned and, even worse, badly managed. The peasants, on whose shoulders the burden of agricultural production in the country lay, were left out of all aspects of it. There was no place for peasant participation either in its conception, planning or implementation. And so it was perhaps inevitable that it would not have much support from them. The scheme failed also because of a series of inter-departmental wranglings, bad management and bureaucratic corruption.[24] One of the most serious problems of Ghanaian agriculture bequeathed by the PP government has been that of labour. It was partly to meet this problem that the Acheampong government established the Ghana National Reconstruction Corps to involve the youth in agriculture. This body was to concentrate mainly on food agriculture as part of the national programme for food self-sufficiency. In its operations, it was basically a youth settlement farm for large scale agriculture in the food growing areas. Like other projects of this type it did not achieve much. It became a breeding ground for political faithfuls more than a serious agricultural scheme; and like its predecessor the Workers Brigade, it finally became an instrument for fighting the regime's opponents especially during the campaign for the Union Government system.

Next the government attempted to overcome the problems of labour and organisation in peasant agriculture through the use of traditional ideas of self help whereby peasants of a particular community came together to help each other on a collective basis. The Nnoboa system, as it was called, was useful for harnessing labour to clear and prepare the land for planting and to harvest. However the government's intention to institutionalise it as the basis for co-operative agriculture did not materialise. Although it attracted an unspecified amount of capital investment from the financial institutions its actual impact on agriculture, and food production in particular, was negligible. It also became a scheme for securing political support from the rural community.

Even though the OFY had certain positive features which, as I have already indicated, distinguished it from other policies, it nonetheless had certain problems. In the first place the programme was rigidly bureaucratic. As we have seen, there was no input into the decision making apparatus or its implementation machinery from the peasant community. In the process there was not much support from the peasants, which justified the bureaucrats in their thinking that the peasantry are far too primitive or backward to realise what is good for them.

There were other problems which were the unintended outcome of certain policy decisions. Among them three may be mentioned. Import duty on agricultural machinery was removed. On the surface of it, that policy would be helpful to growers. But if it is recognised that it was the big growers who, most of the time, did not and still do not, grow food crops except grains like rice and maize, would use such facilities, it would then mean in real terms that the state would be subsidizing the big growers at the expense of peasant producers. Furthermore, there were improved seeds, fertilizers and other inputs available to the peasantry at subsidised prices. In actual fact however the canker of widespread bribery and corruption which has plagued the system of distribution ensured that only the big growers could get hold of these inputs most of the time. Some did not even use them after securing control over them. Rather they passed them on to smaller growers at speculative prices.

Lastly, while tractors, combined harvesters etc were made easily available together with attractive provisions for their purchase or hire, the basic instrument of agricultural production in the country which was used by the mass of the peasantry — the hoe and cutlass, were almost unavailable and could only be obtained at speculative prices.

Agricultural Credit

One mechanism by which the state sought to promote and encourage food production was in the provision of agricultural credit. The lack of adequate credit for food producers has been a perenial problem in Ghanaian agriculture for more than two decades. Its recognition by the Nkrumah government led to the establishment of the Cocoa Purchasing Company (CPC), but as the name implies it was to provide credit for cocoa growers. Such rural credit as existed therefore often bypassed the food grower; and he had to obtain credit at usurious rates. Hence the initiative of the state in this area was particularly significant.

The state worked out schemes to provide credit to civil servants, army officers and members of the petty bourgeosie in industry, commerce and the distributive sector of the economy as well as in the liberal professions so that they could go into agriculture. In addition, the state encouraged commercial banks to adopt more flexible lending policies and provide credit to aspirant entrepreneurs in agriculture. Of all the financial institutions providing credit, the most liberal has been the Agricultural Development Bank (ADB). But the peasant farmer who is usually the food producer did not fare too well. For sometime, before a grower could qualify for credit from the ADB, he was expected to have cleared at least six acreas of cultivatable land and to have an acceptable collateral security. Considering that the average holding in the country was only 3.5 acres and for food crop growers it was and still is even smaller, it meant that the bulk of the peasantry would not qualify for institutional credit. They had to continue to depend on informal sources of credit from local agents at usurious rates.

This situation continued till 1969 when the ADB introduced what it called the Credit Commodity Scheme or Group Loans Scheme by which a number of growers, usually of food crops such as maize, rice, cassava and sometime ginger could get together to constitute a group on the basis of a common crop. The minimum membership of a group was to be ten in order to qualify for credit. In this way the ADB could extend credit to a corporate group rather than an individual. The group would have an executive body that would guarantee the loan and be responsible for repayment.

Between 1969 and 1976 the ADB disbursed loans totalling about 52 million cedis to 241,009 farmers cultivating such crops as maize, cassava, yam, rice and tomato[25]. This, however, was only a drop in the ocean compared with the credit requirements of the small farmer. Moreover, most of the loans continued to go to large scale farmers. One reason which has been given for the reluctance of the financial institutions to meet the credit needs of the small scale food producer is that of fear of default. A study of the ADB Credit Commodity Scheme, however, revealed that between 1971 and 1977 the recovery rate among small scale producers was between 23-26 per cent with a mean of 43. On the other hand among large-scale producers the recovery rate was only 23 per cent[26] during the same period.

In 1976 the Ghana Commercial Bank also initiated a Group Lending Scheme similar to that of the ADB's Credit Commodity Scheme. Farmers were advised to form Farmers Associations and encouraged to grow food crops. Members of the Association could continue to cultivate their own individual farms but in addition they had to cultivate a group farm on co-operative basis. In return the bank advanced credit for agricultural machinery and other inputs. Just as in the case of the ADB scheme, the group's leaders had to guarantee the loans and all loans must be paid before new ones are contracted. Membership was limited to a maximum of 50 and a minimum of five. Each member was expected to cultivate between 4 and 25 acres.

As these forms of institutional lending proved inadequate a supplementary institution was created to cater specifically for the financial needs of the small creditor. This is the rural banking scheme which was also started in 1976. One of the ideas which guided the establishment of the rural banks was that it would replace the private money lender who is well known for his usurious interest rates, and thereby help to capitalise the small farmer among other small producers. In short, it was hoped that the rural banking scheme would become an instrument of rural development. The scheme became very popular among the rural communities soon after the first rural bank was opened at Nyakrom in the Central Region. By 1978 five rural banks had been established and by 1985 the number of rural banks had reached 105. These were very impressive by any standard.

From its inception the focus was on the small scale producers most of whom were in food crop production. The central bank's definition of 'small scale farmer' turned out to mean anyone holding not more than 100 acres. In 1984 the Bank reported that a large proportion of rural bank credit went to small-scale agricultural farmers – mainly food crop, livestock and fish farmers. The credit accruing to them increased by 77.1 per cent. In 1985 however, the increase was just 1.1 per cent. At any rate, the bank's rather flexible definition of small scale farmer would mean that practically every Ghanaian farmer could qualify. In the scramble that this flexibility is likely to generate the peasant farmer may again get trampled upon by the big ones.

The banks investment practices further contradict their peasant or rural orientation. For example in 1978 they were able to purchase 1.2 million cedis of central government bonds. By 1985 they were able to invest 210.83 million cedis in government stocks and treasury bills.[27] It would seem from these lending and investment trends that the rural banks have become a conduit through which capital is transferred from the rural areas to the urban centres for the latter's development rather than a mechanism for mobilising savings for the development of the rural communities.

It is clear from what has been said so far that the various credit schemes have not helped to stimulate food production. They also seem to be biased to assist the petty bourgeoisie to go into agriculture and engage in speculative practices. This was bound to happen so long as the peasantry have no control of, or influence in, state policy formulation.

Marketing and Distribution

The state has intervened also at the level of marketing and distribution since the 1960s. A number of state agencies have been established to assist in marketing and distribution. The best known of these are the Cattle Development Board (later to be more appropriately called the Meat Marketing Board), the Food Distribution Corporation (FDC) and the State Fishing Corporation (SFC). For our present purpose we will concentrate on the role of the FDC. During the 1970s the FDC became a production as well as distribution unit. In the mind of the public, however, its activities in the field of distribution were much more prominent. Its main tasks were to buy food in bulk from the rural areas and retail them at designated prices through its retail outlets either directly to the consumer or through middlemen who would then retail them to the public. This was to help to stabilise prices especially during the 'lean season'. The assumption underlying this strategy when the FDC was set up during the past 1966 was that inefficient distribution and marketing was at the heart of the food problem and the state had to tackle this itself. It was also defended on grounds of equity.

Whatever merits such a scheme might have had were rendered ineffective by three main weaknesses in the system: problems of transportation, inadequate storage facilities, state control over the pricing of the food items it sold, and inadequate capital for its operations. For example, the corporation did not have enough road-worthy vehicles to cart food from the rural areas to the cities. Because of this problem it was unable to either increase dramatically the amount of marketable food or compete effectively with its main rivals, the market women who act as intermediaries between the producer and the urban consumer, and do so at a great loss to peasant producers. The second problem was storage. The FDC's inadequate storage facilities led to a high rate of spoilage. Sometimes it had to sell food even below its purchase price in order to avoid such spoilage.

But in spite of all this perhaps the most important weakness which completely undermined whatever influence the organisation might have in alleviating the problem of inadequate food supply in the urban areas was its pricing policy. These took two forms: first, the prices at which it offered to buy food from the peasants; and second, the prices at which it sold its produce on the market.

The FDC offered prices lower than what the peasants could get from the market women. Hence in the competition to puchase their produce the peasants were at a disadvantage if they sold to the FDC instead of the market mammies. To realise a margin of price advantage they often opted for the latter. Secondly, because of the transportation problems, the visits of the FDC were more infrequent and unreliable. Sometimes peasants had to carry their produce all the way from the farms to wait almost all day for the FDC vehicles to appear. Sometimes they had to carry them back when the trucks did not show up. Considering the fact that peasants have limited storage facilities this was a great inconvenience.

There was also the problem that sometimes the FDC was unable to make prompt payments to the peasants due to either its own problem of inadequate capital or to bureaucratic corruption. On the other hand the market women paid promptly and even some capitalised the peasants by advancing them money or buying a whole farm's harvest in advance. This was very convenient to the small peasant farmers who dominated this kind of trade because it gave them financial security — a service which the FDC was unable to provide. In these circumstances, and particularly after 1977 when the economic situation was so bad that it was difficult to secure consumer goods of any kind in the country, the temptation was very strong especially for peasants in border areas to transport their produce across the frontiers where they could obtain a more rewarding price for them.

The second problem associated with pricing was the price at which the FDC sold its products on the market. The differential between the open market price and the prices at which the FDC sold its goods were so huge that the same market women found it lucrative to purchase the corporation's stocks and sell them at a substantial profit to themselves. This created a conducive situation for enormous corruption on the part of its managerial staff. Because of the growing incentive to be corrupt during the late 1970s it became difficult for ordinary people to gain access to the FDC's food stocks. One had to be high and mighty in order to purchase food at the controlled price from the FDC. Thus in the end the establishment which was meant to stabilise urban food prices and help the poor also became another weapon of petty bourgeois accumulation on the one hand, and on the other a means whereby poor peasant producers subsidized the food needs of this class and their hangers-on.[28]

The Special Scheme for Participation in Agriculture

We should now briefly examine a programme that distinguished the NRC/SMC government of Acheampong from all previous regimes. This was in the attempt to get multi-national companies (MNCs) to be involved in the production of industrial raw materials and food. We have seen that in the Second Republic the PP government tried to enlist the support of the local petty bourgeoisie in food and cash crop production. The fact that now it was the multinational corporations which the state turned to was an indication that the earlier scheme had failed.

One has to appreciate that this NRC/SMC policy marked a complete departure from the policies of both the colonial and the earlier post-colonial governments. Unlike the situation in Eastern and Southern Africa where MNC involvement in agriculture is very strong, in Ghana until recently they were hardly known in agriculture, especially in food production. However, with the emergence in government circles of the idea that only foreign capital could transform agricultural production and thereby solve the food problem it was not long before the conviction that the answer lay in the operations of the MNC's would come to the fore. A number of developments made this inevitable:

i) The intervention of both state and private capital had

failed to resolve the problem of low food output.

ii) By the mid-1970s the economic crisis had become acute, and very evident especially in agriculture. It therefore became necessary to look around for alternative solutions.

In these circumstances, some leading members of the petty bourgeoisie began to turn to the experience of the Ivory Coast and Kenya with admiration. They saw those two countries as a model of success in agricultural production. They attributed the success of these countries to large capital investments in agriculture by the MNCs. Other developments in the economy made this option quite attractive. By this period because of foreign exchange control regulations, many MNCs had piled up huge profits waiting for repatriation overseas. As the state had no foreign exchange to effect the necessary transfers, this huge money lay idle in the country. Meanwhile the government was implementing a policy of partnership with foreign capital in industry for the mutual benefit of MNCs and the state. Therefore it was regarded as complementary if a similar partnership would be promoted in the agricultural sector using the unrepatriated profits of MNC subsidiaries operating in the country.

What became known as the Special Scheme for Participation in Agriculture was to encourage the MNCs to go into agriculture to produce food crops for the local market, raw materials for domestic industries and export crops. It was the highest stage of the OFY policy. The specific food crops that they were to produce included cereals like rice and maize while the export and industrial crops were cotton, palm oil, coconut and kenaf. The production of fruits like pineapples and bananas as well as non-traditional crops like ginger with export potential was also to be encouraged. Also included were livestock and poultry production.

The projects were to be financed by the MNCs accumulated profits and dividends awaiting repatriation. State participation in the scheme included equity shares, land acquisition and site selection and the provision of social infrastructure like roads, electricity, etc. In addition the state also provided among other things, guaranteed minimum prices, exemption from duty and levy on imported machinery and other inputs, and a five year tax holiday. In spite of these attractive conditions, the response was not particularly enthusiastic. By 1979 only eight companies were participating in the scheme.

What was the impact of the scheme on the production of food and other crops? Quite apart from the fact that the scheme did not significantly improve food production in the country, it has had some deleterious effects on her agriculture and the economic situation in general. For example Kwesi Jonah has, in an excellent study demonstrated how the operation of the scheme resulted in de-indigenising Ghanaian capital and the displacement of some 3,000 peasant producers in the Western Region.[29]

The government policies, however, show indications of qualified success. The first two years of the OFY scheme did show some modest success. Cultivated acreage of maize went up from 997,000 acres in 1970 to 1,050,000 in 1974. Production also went up from 378,000 to 478,000 long tons within the same period. The production of rice registered a similar increase: production went up from 48,000 to 72,000 long tons between 1970 and 1974.[30] This was reflected in import figures. In 1974, that is for the first time in over two decades Ghana did not import any rice. Government leaders were enthusiastic, and proudly announced that the country had achieved self-sufficiency in rice.

That proclamation however turned out to be premature. Although one could not deny the initial success, it had to be pointed out that, like the success of the Green Revolution in other parts of the world notably India, the shortlived success in rice and maize production was obtained at the expense of other 'traditional' food crops like yams, millet and guinea corn. This was particularly the case in the Northern and Upper Regions of the country where capitalist rice farming on a large-scale was initiated mostly by members of the petty bourgeoisie, mainly from the south. After 1975 production started to decline and in the following years the situation became so desperate that the country had to request emergency food aid. Admittedly part of the problem was due to drought; but this was confined to the north-eastern part of the country.[31]

Thus the programme which was meant to respond to the food needs of the country with the miracle capital of MNCs also failed. One reason for the failure was that in spite of public declarations to the contrary, emphasis was still on export and industrial crops. We have already seen how in the area of capitalisation, extension and research a disproportionate attention was given to export and industrial crops. The second reason was the old tendency to treat the food question as an emergency measure. The whole national fever which was invoked in support of OFY did have the atmosphere of emergency about it. Although this had the advantage of bringing public awareness to the problem and soliciting as well as mobilising enough manpower, it eroded the social basis of a permanent policy response.

Even on the part of the government this was clear. For barely two years after its inauguration, when rice production reached a scale that was marginally close to national self-sufficiency the government declared the programme a success and went on to launch the second phase: 'Operation Feed Your Industries'. That decision diverted attention to the production of industrial and export crops; and the concern for food took a back seat. In the long run the country was unable to feed either her people or her industries.

The policy of seeking to replace the peasantry did not succeed because neither the bureaucracy nor MNC capital was in a position to make it succeed. In the short-run, the scheme merely satisfied the accumulation needs of the upper stratum of the petty bourgeosie. There was no attempt to advance particular assistance to women who formed a substantial section of the labour force engaged in food production, distribution and processing. On the contrary, much public effort went into harassing them in the distributive sectors of food and other marketable commodities, because they were said to be making excessive profit.[32]

THE PNDC AND FOOD AGRICULTURE

The two years of the People's National Party (PNP) under Dr Limann's constitutional rule were uneventful: no major new programmes for food production were started. Its investment policy indicated a continued preference for increasing MNC involvement in the agricultural economy. On the one hand its two year reign was too short to register any notable results. On the other hand the period saw the continued decline of the economy in general, and agriculture in particular. By the time the regime was overthrown in December 1981 the country's economy had reached crisis proportions with massive shortages in all sectors.

The initial months of the PNDC's rule indicated a return to some of the interventionist policies of the Acheampong regime, especially during the 1972-74 period. These were mostly attempts to intervene at the level of the market. They included seizure and compulsory sale of goods seized, particularly from traders accused of hoarding, and more stringent efforts to enforce the existing price control legislation. In all of that, it was particularly about food that urban workers were most vigilant. There were attempts to limit the role of the market women in the distribution and marketing of food. It must be recalled that this same concern with food availability and prices for urban workers lay at the heart of the initiatives of the Armed Forces Revolutionary Council (AFRC) period when Rawlings first came to power in June 1979 and ruled the country for about three months before handing over to the constitutionally elected government of Dr. Limann. On both occasions there were no specific policy measures particularly at the institutional level, except the ad hoc attempts to keep prices at a level which would be within the means of the urban masses.

However, in April 1983 the PNDC introduced the World Bank/IMF programme of rehabilitation and restructuring of the economy called *Economic Recovery Programme* (ERP). The programme provided for a one year period of reconstruction and consolidation. The purpose was to create the requisite economic, social and political conditions for the three year medium term development plan to come into effect in 1984.The objectives of the plan as stated in the *Economic Recovery Programme* included the adoption of measures to increase the production of food and industrial raw material to planned levels in the context of the Three Year Medium Term Plan.

Just as the policies of the Nkrumah period came under the influence of the dominant economic thought of the period which was Keynesianism, so have the postulates underlying the ERP been determined by the prevailing economic thinking in the world economy; namely, monetarism. The ERP policy measures have entailed specific actions of which the most important has been the devaluation of the local currency. In December 1981 when the coup was staged the value of the cedi was 2.75 to US$1.00. By March 6 1988 it had declined to 183.0 to US$1.00. The government accepted the IMF argument that of all the obstacles which undermined growth in the economy, the major one was the over-valued currency in relation to the major international currencies. Over-valuation of the currency, it was argued, discouraged exports, particularly from cocoa and the mining sectors. It made it difficult for the Cocoa Marketing Board, now Cocoa Board, to pay a realistic price to producers in order to encourage production with the result that peasants either shifted to the production of other crops or smuggled cocoa out of the country.

The second policy measure is the phased removal of price controls which had been one of the essential features of previous attempts to regulate urban consumer prices even though efforts to enforce price controls had, in the main, proved illusory. By July 1985 the list of essential commodities subject to statutory price control had been reduced from 23 to only 8; and by 1987 price controls had been virtually abandoned. Interest rates have also been raised. Towards the end of 1984 government policy moved in the direction of flexible interest rates. The twelve month deposit rate was 9.0 per cent up to October 1983. By May 1987 it had reached 22.5 per cent.

Similarly, the maximum lending rate for all categories of industry, except agriculture, had gone up from 14.0 per cent to 26.0 per cent within the same period. For agriculture it had reached 23.5 per cent. Subsidies have also been removed from a wide range of services, particularly health and education, under a cost recovery policy. And to reduce public expenditure and control inflation, employment in the civil and public services is being cut back while a tight control has been put on wages. At the same time, there are moves to divest the state of a wide range of enterprises. And to cap it all a new investment law, The Investment Code (1985 PNDCL 116) was issued to lay a new and more attractive legal framework for foreign investment. These policies have raised considerable controversy in the country and pitched the government against, labour, radical and student organisations all of whom have been extremely critical.[33]

The PNDC's food policies should be examined in the context of these major policy initiatives. In February 1984 the government issued a Medium Term Agricultural Programme in which it stated its policies regarding food production for the period 1984-86. In this document the government set the following targets:[34]

i) to meet 80.0 per cent of the country's maize requirements; 60.0 per cent of her rice requirements and be self-sufficient in cassava production.
ii) meet 50.0 per cent of the country's fish needs and 60.0 per cent of her meat requirements; and
iii) maintain reasonable levels of domestic production of other starchy staples, pulses, nuts, oil-seeds, fruits, vegetables and industrial crops.

In pursuit of these targets, the PNDC's position on appropriate strategy, as well as the assumptions behind it, seem quite close to those held by the Acheampong government. In line with the thinking behind the ERP, the government's food policy seems to be based on the belief that private capital — both foreign and local — is the best agent through which the country could raise the level of food production. The 1985 Investment Code gave ample credence to this commitment: it made agriculture one of the priority sectors of the economy requiring foreign participation. Accordingly, it stipulates certain types of facilities that the state should provide for foreign investors who would go into food production. It also guarantees state intervention in securing farm-land for the establishment of such agricultural projects.

In addition to all these the state is committed to providing the following:

a) the requisite permission for importing essential plant, machinery, equipment and accessories required for the enterprise;
b) exemption from the payment of customs and duties on plant, machinery, equipment and accessories imported

especially and exclusively to establish the enterprise once approved;

c) corporate income tax rate of forty-five per cent with allowance and deductions.

In all its essentials the PNDC's food policies are close to the Acheampong government's Special Agricultural Scheme. Especially, the idea of block farming which refers to a system of getting farmers from neighbouring villages to undertake farming activities collectively brings the two approaches closer to each other in both their expected mode of financing and organisation of production. The Block Farming System is said to have the advantage of permitting each producer to benefit from the infrastructure for large-scale farming while at the same time permitting each individual or farming household to operate its own farm. It is also regarded as an improvement on the traditional farming practise of scattered farming households.[35]

Furthermore it will help in bringing the following within easy reach: access to credit, mechanised services, input delivery services and storage and marketing facilities. Added to these are the Farm Service Centres which are being established in various farming districts throughout the country. They are meant to provide farm inputs, mechanisation services, workshops, agricultural information, and training services to farmers.[36] Farmers who come within the jurisdiction of each of the centres will be registered and made to buy shares in the operating capital of the centre.

In one respect it would seem that some attention is being paid to women and their role in the food industry. A Home Extension Unit is being planned to deal almost exclusively with women farmers by supplying them with information on improved farming practices as well as seeds in order to improve food production, processing and preservation. But essentially the programme for improving the role of women in food production is seen more as part of a social welfare and community development programme rather than economic. Thus in one respect where women in the food industry desperately need assistance — namely, easy access to capital, the scheme is silent.

Furthermore the government has taken the problem of security of title a step nearer to solution: it has made a law providing for land title registration.[37] For sometime now the petty bourgeoisie in agriculture have been complaining that the lack of land title security has militated against investment in agriculture. However, the enactment of this law means that once more it will be possible to eject considerable numbers of peasant producers from the land — this time by national capitalist farmers. It would mean that small under-capitalised peasant holdings will probably have to give way gradually to large-scale farming.

In the short run this could boost the production of export crops, maize and rice. It is however doubtful whether it can be considered as the final solution to the food problem. In the first place most of the big growers who feel handicapped by the land tenure system are not in food cultivation — except rice and maize farming. Secondly, although they may end up ejecting some peasants from their farms, large scale food farmers may not be able to step up food production in such a way as to replace production by peasant food farmers. On the other hand, if the partial reason behind this strategy is to resolve the problem of labour shortage by creating a class of landless peasants then one might wonder whether the current high cost of agricultural labour would make the project feasible. It might then mean that only an extreme authoritarian regime would be able to ensure the expected supply of cheap labour; but that might also affect the legitimacy of the regime and completely erode its already fragile support base.

The problem of farm labour and of evolving a more efficient form of organizing food production are being tackled from another angle, through the establishment of Mobisquads and the National Mobilisation Programme. These two bodies are responsible for harnessing manpower principally in the rural communities to respond to these problems. However, they have their origin in the emergency created by the expulsion of over one million Ghanaians from Nigeria in 1983.

Initially, the main idea was to establish an organisation that would organise the resettlement of those Ghanaians who were affected by the Nigerian Government's expulsion order and also distribute food and other materials which had been donated. Currently, however, the National Mobilisation Programme in particular is increasingly assuming a very high profile in the government's programme of redeploying into agriculture some of the workers who are being retrenched from the civil and public services. What seems to be evolving therefore is a collection of projects, programmes and organisations all of which are related to the goals of achieving adequate food production levels which nonetheless lack coherence.

What have been the results of these policy measures? The food situation has obviously improved from what it was during the critical years of 1982-83. Agricultural output in 1985 expanded by 2.8 per cent in real terms. The following table shows the performance of the major food crops.

Government leaders, the IMF and the World Bank have all been very encouraged by these figures and have attributed the upturn to the success of their policies. However, the statement from J.S. Addo, former Governer of the Bank of Ghana, is more to the point. He said: 'Several factors accounted for this turnabout. Perhaps the most significant was the return to normal climatic conditions. Adequate rainfall

TABLE 3: PERFORMANCE OF MAJOR FOOD CROPS

CEREALS	1970	1980	1981	1982	1983	1984	1985
Maize	435	382	378	346	172	574	411
Rice	64	78	97	36	40	66	90
others	177	213	250	162	96	140	155
Cassava	1618	322	2063	2470	1729	4083	3076

Source: The PNDC Budget Statement and Economic Policy, 1986, p.7)

in 1984 played a major part in restoring agricultural production after three catastrophic years of drought'.[38] Here it is important to note that the modest increase in production is in line with the situation in many parts of Africa. The FAO's Food Outlook (February 1986) states that aggregate production of cereals in some 45 countries is provisionally estimated at 21 per cent above the average for the last five years. What has this marginal improvement in food output meant to the mass of the people? Although wages have gone up substantially for the urban wage earners one still has to work for more than half a day to earn the cost of a simple meal.

It would seem clear that in two specific areas the present policies are a continuation of policies which have failed in the past: the disproportionate attention being given to export crops in spite of the rhetoric about the need to step up food production; and the belief that Ghanaian agriculture could be redeemed through the efforts of the petty bourgeoisie located in the bureaucracy, the military, trade and commerce.

CONCLUSION

If agriculture is to be transformed and productivity raised, it could only come about through the class currently based in agriculture. It is becoming increasingly clear that price incentives is not the answer to the problem of low productivity in food agriculture. The futility of the PNDC government's policies on this score is evidence of this. It is not being suggested that an attractive price system is not important. Certainly not. Unfortunately the evidence suggests that high prices alone have not stimulated production of food crops. And even the World Bank has been compelled occasionally to admit this:

> That adequate incentives are a necessary but not a sufficient condition for a production response is nowhere more

> clearly demonstrated than in the case of predominantly rainfed food production such as in Ghana. Even before the drought years of 1982 and 1983, the available data show that the production of almost all food crops (including the most important one, viz. maize) was stagnant or declining between 1970 and 1983, despite a fairly substantial increase in real food prices at the wholesale and consumer level.[38]

It would then seem that a combination of measures, including prices, is necessary to raise the level of food output. The most central requirement for a successful food policy is that the measures should be directed to the most socially relevant group that is currently engaged in food production. In the Ghanaian case it is the small scale producer.

Secondly, any such policies should address specifically the problem of women who dominate food production, distribution and processing. These two groups, as we have seen, constitute the most strategically placed in the food industry; and it means that until food policy takes their interest, needs, and aspirations into close account all efforts will be futile and the goals of food self-sufficiency and food security will forever elude the country, its people and their political leaders.

NOTES

* This chapter was in a draft form when the author's tragic death occurred. The editorial work by the co-editor was done bearing in mind the need to maintain the author's orginal style, as well as the tone and basic structure of the essay. An earlier version of this paper had been submitted for publication in T. Mkandawire and N. Bourenane (eds.) *The State and Agricultural Development in Africa* (CODESRIA Book Series, 1987).

1. In the *Sir John Crawford Memorial Lecture* (Washington, D.C. 1985)
2. The World Bank, *Accelerated Development in Sub-Saharan Africa: An Agenda for Action*. (Washington, D.C. 1981.) (Alias the Berg Report p.2.).
3. *Special Memorandum by the ECA Conference of Ministers on Africa's Economic and Social Crisis*. Adopted by the 19th session of the Commission held in Addis Ababa from May 24-38, 1984. P.1
4. Anyang' Nyong'o, Peter. *In Eastern Africa Social Science Research* Vol. 1, No. 2, June 1985. P.1
5. World Bank. *Toward Sustained Development in Sub-Saharan Africa*. (Washington D.C. 1984) P.10.
6. ibid., p.3.
7. The foregoing data on trends in food production and imports were taken from *The Berg Report*.
8. F.A.O. *Monthly Report on the Food Situation in Selected Countries* (Rome 1986).
9. See S. La Anyane *The Role of Marketing in Present Day Ghanaian Agriculture*

USAID/Ghana 8th Annual Agriculture Conference. (Accra. 1976).

10. World Bank. *Ghana: Towards Structural Adjustment, Report* No. 5854-GH Vol. 1 The Main Report (Washington DC. 1985) p.50.
11. Ibid. Vol. 11: Statistical Appendix. Table 7.07
12. Reported in Jones, Trevar. *Ghana's First Republic*, 1960-1966. (London: Metheum Books, 1967.) p. 245.
13. Ewusi, K. 'Road Transport Facilities and their Effects on Local Food Prices in the Sixties' *Economic Bulletin of Ghana* (2nd Series) Vol 1, No. 3 1971. pp...
14. 'Food and Nation' *West Africa* July 11 1983 pp. 1596-1597.
15. F.A.O.: *Trade Yearbook* 1968 and 1974. cited in Norman Nicholson and John D. Esseks, 'The Politics of Food Scarcities in Developing Counties' *International Organisation*, Vol. 32 No. 3 Summer 1978.
16. Quoted in George Benneh, 'Some Policy issues in the Quest for Food Self-Sufficiency in Ghana'. Paper Presented at the ISSER Conference on Food Self-Sufficiency in West AFrica. University of Ghana, Legon. May 1-3, 1984. p.5.
17. Reported in the *People's Daily Graphic*, March 8, 1984
18. Gold coast (Ghana) *Department of Agriculture Annual Report 1947-8*. (Accra: Government printer, 1948) p. 1.
19. Reported in *Africa Contemporary Record*, 1976
20. For a detailed discussion of food policies of this period see Emmanuel Hansen, 'National Food Policies and Organisations in Ghana' in Thandika Mkandawire (ed) *The State and African Agriculture*. (London/Dakar: Zed/ CODESRIA 1987).
21. See Miracle, M.P. and Seidman, A., *State Farms in Ghana* Land Tenure Centre, Madison, Wisconsin 1968.
22. Kraus, J. 'The Political Economy of Agrarian Regression in Ghana' in Stephen Cummins, et. al. *Africa's Agrarian Crisis: The Roots of Famine*. (Boulder Colorado: Lynne Reineer publishers, 1986) p. 120.
23. Ibid P. 123.
24. Chambas, Mohammed 'The Politics of Agriculture and Rural Development in the Upper Region of Ghana: Implications of Technocratic Ideology and Non-Participatory Development' (Ph.D Thesis Cornell University, 1980.)
25. Kojo, Solomon. 'Financing the small Scale Farmer in Ghana.' (M.Sc. Thesis. University of Ghana, Legon 1979)
26. Ibid p.113
27. Bank of Ghana. *Annual Report for The Financial year Ended 30th June 1985*. P. 11.
28. The performance of the FDC has been reproduced in other organisations — like the Meat Marketing Board and the State Fishing corporation, which were established to intervene in the marketing and distribution of food in order to ensure reasonable price levels for urban consumers.
29. Jonah, Kwesi. The Politics of Economic Decolonisation: The Case of Ghana's Indigenisation Policy. (M.A. Thesis University of Ghana Legon, 1980.)
30. Ghana: *Five-Year Development Plan, 1975-80* (Accra. Ghana Publishing Corporation 1975) p.37.
31. For a study of the drought of that period and its impact see E. Ofori-Sarpong. 'The Impact of Drought in Ghana and Upper Volta, 1970-1977.' Climatology Research Paper No.1 Department of Geography University of Ghana. 1980.
32. For a discussion of this recurring problem of the harassment of women traders see Nyanteng, Kwame.' The Farmer/Trader Relationship: Is there Exploitation?' *The Ghanaian Farmer* Vol.18, No.1, October, 1978.
33. For an analysis of the politics of this period see Emmanuel Hansen. 'The State and Popular Struggles in Ghana, 1982-86' in Peter Anyang' Nyong'o, (ed.) *Popular Struggles for Democracy in Africa*. (London: UNU/Zed 1987) pp.170-208. See

also chapters 1 and 2 by Ninsin and Graham respectively in this volume.

34. Ghana. Ministry of Agriculture, *Annual Report, 1986* (Accra 1987) p.38.
35. Ibid P.39
36. *Land Title Registration Law* 1986 PNDCL 152.
37. Address delivered at the Annual Dinner of the Institute of Bankers, Accra, 21 December 1985.
38. World Bank. *Ghana: Towards Structural Adjustment* 1985 p.50.

9. POLICIES AND POLITICS OF EXPORT AGRICULTURE

E. Gyimah-Boadi

INTRODUCTION

Agriculture occupies a central place in the Ghanaian economy and in the whole scheme of national development. It accounts for roughly 57 per cent of the gross domestic product, close to 80 per cent of total exports and employs 55 per cent of the labour force. Indeed the drastic decline in agricultural production in the late 1970s and early 1980s (estimated at a rate of 0.3 per cent per annum in the 1970-80 period and 6.7 per cent and 1.5 per cent in the drought years of 1982 and 1983 respectively) was a major factor in the economic, social and political crises of the period. Therefore the expressed desire of the incumbent Provisional National Defence Council (PNDC) government to arrest and reverse the decline in agricultural production (as part of the economic recovery effort which is under way) is supremely justifiable. But the question is: What are the prospects for arresting and reversing this decline in agricultural production?

This paper discusses the issues posed by the above question. It situates the agricultural policies of post colonial governments in their political contexts and argues that the formulation and implementation of agricultural policy could be understood only in relation to the relentless pursuit of the interests of the social groups who dominate the various institutions of state. The focus is on export agriculture.

PROBLEMS IN GHANAIAN AGRICULTURE AND RESPONSES OF POST-COLONIAL REGIMES

The major problems facing Ghanaian agriculture at the dawn of 'self-rule' could be summarised as follows: monocrop dependency (on cocoa), low productivity in agriculture in general and food production in particular, stagnation and pest infection, farmer disatisfaction with the Cocoa Marketing Board and its control over the cocoa surplus, lack of credit and land tenure problems. Some of these problems came to a head in the World War II period and contributed significantly to the rural discontent[1] that provided further impetus to the anti-colonial movement.

Despite the resolve of post-colonial governments to deal with the above-mentioned problems through a programme of modernisation and diversification, the sector has remained manifestly unmodernised and undiversified. Successes such as the increases in cocoa production in the early 1960s, and in maize production in early 1970s have often been offset by overwhelming failures during subsequent years.

By the late 1970s and early 1980s, Ghana's agriculture bore all the symptoms of an extremely sick sector: namely, declining cocoa production; declining food production leading to a heavy dependence on food imports; severe bottlenecks in marketing with cocoa and foodstuffs reported to be locked up and rotting in the hinterland; etc. The section below looks at how successive governments have dealt with these agrarian problems.

The Convention Peoples Party (CPP) Period 1951-66

The agricultural policies of the CPP government went through two distinct phases:

1. the phase of revitalising the traditional small-holder and peasant based sector, and
2. the phase of large-scale mechanised public sector farming and centralised control over agricultural production and marketing.

Initially the government seemed to have recognised the dominance of the traditional, small-holder sector in Ghanaian agriculture, and accorded it some attention. The 1951 Development Plan, for example, showed that the government was determined to salvage the cocoa industry within seven years. Accordingly the government waged a massive campaign against the the troublesome swollen-shoot disease. It undertook the compulsory cutting-out of all infected trees. Personnel from the Ministry of Agriculture (MOA) went out to farms, examined cocoa trees and cut down those that were infected. Generous compensation was paid to farmers whose cocoa trees were so destroyed. Treated farms were periodically inspected and further cutting-out was undertaken where necessary. In 1957, this system was revised to grant extra compensation to farmers who exercised the option of voluntary cutting-out of trees that appeared to be infected. This programme was so successful that by 1961, the Chief Cocoa Officer of the MOA could report that the disease was well under control and only small losses should be expected if vigilance was maintained.

The CPP regime was also able to take rigorous measures to combat capsid seed infestation. From 1956 when the disease was discovered MOA personnel conducted intensive spraying of affected farms.[2] In 1959, the government started providing large subsidies on the price of sprayers and insecticides to farmers who did their own capsid seed spraying. Other forms of assistance given to the traditional small-holder farmer included demonstration and extension from the expanded chain of MOA agricultural stations and to some extent, from the newly established parastatal agricultural institutions. There were also experiments to introduce peasant farmers to bananas and oil palm production.

This emphasis on the small-holder sector changed under phase two the CPP government's agricultural policy which stressed state-sponsored, large-scale mechanised agriculture. To be sure, state-sponsored, large-scale mechanised farming had started earlier with the establishment of the Agricultural Development Corporation and the Gonja Development Company.[3] These institutuions were absorbed into the State Farms Corporation (SFC) which was established in January 1963. Other parastatal agricultural institutions created along with the SFC at the time included the para-military Workers' Brigade (WB), the United Ghana Farmers' Co-operative Council, whose co-operative wing organised co-operative farmers, and the Young Farmers' League which operated settlement farms for the youth.

The establishment of these institutions represented an attempt to shift Ghananian agriculture from a small-holder to a public and co-operative base.[4] These statist agricultural institutions were often large-scale, mechanised and involved extensive infrastructure and high overhead costs.

Accompanying this shift was a growing tendency to monopolise and centralise control over agricultural production and marketing. An example is the role performed by the United Ghana Farmers' Co-operative Council (UGFCC) which had operated as a government sponsored licensed buying agency (LBA) since the 1950s in competition with other LBAs (after the cocoa purchasing company became defunct). It was later appointed the sole LBA for the CMB.

The UGFCC was also charged with the responsibility of organising Ghanaian farmers and fishermen into co-operatives and of providing them with direct services. In addition, in 1965, the government established the Agricultural Produce Marketing Board (later called the Food Marketing Board) and Ghana Groceries Limited as the principal agencies for the marketing of agricultural produce. In this period too, the Timber Marketing Board was given monopoly over timber marketing. Thus by 1966, centralisation and monopoly control over the marketing of the country's principal agricultural products had been added to state-sponsored large-scale and mechanised agriculture as the key elements in the government's agricultural policy.

Albeit two interrelated political and economic factors appeared to have influenced these agricultural policies. These are:

(1) the imperative of political consolidation, and
(2) the imperative of capital accumulation.

Centralisation of, and monopoly over, agricultural production and marketing was a response to these imperatives. On the one hand, these controls provided a means to secure hegemony over the agricultural sector — in particular, the cocoa industry and to pre-empt political opposition from the rural areas in general, and from cocoa farmers in particular. Fears of the government for a rural-based political opposition were grounded in the 1954-1956 political developments when the challenge to the CPP and its political dominance centered around the price of cocoa and the increasing state appropriations of cocoa incomes, with the Ashanti Region as the centre of this opposition and the National Liberation Movement as its main instrument.[5]

The use of party wings such as the UGFCC in the distribution of vital agricultural inputs must have been very helpful to the process of political consolidation; because the CPP's victory over its regionalist opposition in the 1956 elections appears to have been possible with crucial assistance from the UGFCC.[6] The CPP was inclined to use its control over vital agricultural resources such as Gammalin 20 (the anti-capsid spray), portable spraying machines, cutlasses (the most important tool in peasant farming), tractor rentals, etc. to reward allies or punish its enemies.

The CPP's use of state control over input supply and distribution for political ends was not without precedent. In the 1950s the Cocoa Purchasing Company (CPC) that had been established to buy cocoa in competition with other LBAs and especially its Loan Agency (established to relieve farmer indebtedness) had been employed in this direction. The Commission set up to investigate the operations of the CPC concluded that the company's vehicles had been used by the CPP in its election campaign, and that it had also used its credit facility as a weapon to secure votes for the CPP. Thus party spokesmen knew what they were talking about when they gleefully described the CPC as 'the product of a master brain, Dr. Kwame Nkrumah' and 'the atomic bomb of the Conventional Peoples Party'.[7] Evidently, the CPP attached high value to the company's role as a powerful instrument in the local political struggles and so when it was liquidated, the government found it necessary to transfer its political functions to the UGFCC.

The desire to control farmers and mobilize the rural communities for political ends also played a role in the choice of statist agricultural strategies.[8] The state farms, for example, were key instruments of political mobilisation and patronage. For one thing they were sources of employment in an era of rising unemployment. Similarly, the Workers' Brigade was established specifically to absorb and mobilise unemployed ex-servicemen and school leavers; and the Young Farmers League was to establish 'socialist' schemes for the school leavers and the uneducated youth.[9] Working hand in hand with the ruling party, these state agricultural institutions were made to give priority to party activists in their hiring practices.[10] Under such circumstances, it is not surprising that the State Farms always kept a labour force that was twice as large as necessary.[11]

It must have been easier for the CPP to control public sector farming, but the continued dominance of the small-holder section in Ghanaian agriculture meant that the latter sector could not be left to itself. Therefore the CPP government enhanced the role of the UGFCC and its responsibility to 'keep the farmers informed of the government's good intentions and to support the government'.[12]

Since the 1920s Cocoa has been the main source of state revenue. The need therefore to strengthen the state's capacity to tax the agricultural (especially cocoa) surplus to finance government development plans was strong.[13] The centralisation and monopolisation of agricultural production and marketing was the outcome.[14]

The CMB and the UGFCC provided the nationalist government with a smooth and effective mechanism for extracting the economic surplus from the agricultural sector especially, the cocoa sector, for non-agricultural purposes. The CMB's farmer assistance programme and price stabilisation functions were de-emphasised while its ability to accumulate surplus for the state was greatly enhanced. In this scheme of surplus extraction, the UGFCC found its niche as the vehicle through which such appropriations were legitimised.[15]

The results of the CPP government's agricultural policies were generally disappointing. The promised modernisation and diversification did not materialise. By 1966, Ghanaian agriculture was already in deep trouble. The performance of public sector agricultural enterprises was generally dismal, while the small-holder agricultural sector had suffered considerable neglect. This was due in no small part to the fact that agriculture was generally underfunded, production and marketing over-centralised and inappropriate strategies — namely large-scale mechanised state farming as opposed to small-holder farming etc., had been adopted.[16]

POLICIES AND POLITICS UNDER POST-NKRUMAH REGIMES (1966-1971)

The agricultural policies of the 1966-1971 period followed two broad trends: under the National Liberation Council (NLC) government (1966-1969) and the Progress Party (PP) government (1969-71) the thrust of agricultural policy emphasised:

(1) disengagement of the state from production and marketing and
(2) encouragement of large-scale mechanised private farming by indigenous and foreign entrepreneurs.

NLC Policies

Under the NLC's economic stabilisation and liberalisation programme, some state farms were sold to private investors and others closed down. In addition, redundant workers on state farms were laid off. The system of cocoa marketing also saw some changes. The UGFCC was abolished and its assets and buying operations taken over by the purchasing division of the CMB. The CMB's Produce Buying Agency (PBA) now bought cocoa in competition with other LBAs. Under new regulations, Ghanaian private firms, co-operatives and individuals who would handle not less than 5000 tons of main crop cocoa were eligible for licensing to operate as buying agents of the CMB. Thus in 1967/1968, some organisations competed with the CMB's own PBA in buying cocoa.[17]

The NLC promised to repair the neglect suffered by the peasant farmers under the Nkrumah government. Towards this, various departments of the MOA that had been transferred to the CMB were restored to it, and its Cocoa Services Division collaborated with the CMB in the distribution of spraying machines and Gammalin 20 insecticides. The CMB was directed to undertake the rehabilitation of feeder roads in the cocoa producing areas and to give more scholarships to the children of farmers. Modest increases in the producer price of cocoa were also made.

However, it was to the so-called 'modern farmer' that the NLC directed its attention. The government-controlled media was used to conduct a back-to-the-land campaign, primarily aimed at the educated and professional class. It was this kind of farmer that the Agricultural Development Bank was primarily intended to serve. Additional packages of incentives, such as tax concessions and easy credits from the commercial bank were announced. These were to attract public servants and members of the professions who wanted to take to farming to do so.

Foreign investment in agriculture was also actively courted as a way of 'importing capital, technical expertise and superior management'.[18] Foreign management was brought in to run the sugar estates and mills, and the rubber estates were transferred to joint ownership with the Firestone Corporation of USA.

The effect of the NLC's agricultural policies were largely ineffective and negative. Retrenchment proved abortive as attempts to lay off redundant state farm employees and to make the state farms more profitable by charging market prices for their products met with protests from workers and consumers who had come to see the state enterprises as a source of service and employment. More significantly, nationalist sentiments imposed restrictions on the transfer of state enterprises to private (and particularly foreign) ownership or management.[19] For example the sale of the rubber estates to Firestone USA and use of foreign management consultants to manage sugar estates and mills were severely criticised by the Ghanaian Press and sections of the intelligentsia.

Given the preoccupation with economic stabilisation and retrenchment, the state farms that were allowed to remain were denied the resources necessary for the effective management of their assets. A vast amount of agricultural machinery was therefore allowed to disintegrate through lack of maintenance and protection.[20]

But the small-holder farmer did not fare any better as increases in the producer price for cocoa were only marginal and the restored MOA was not strong enough to halt stagnation and decline in this sector. Meanwhile, the NLC's haste to liberalise the cocoa trade, some weak and inefficient LBAs (who issued promissory notes in lieu of prompt payment of cocoa purchases) had entered the cocoa purchasing system, and by their fraudulent activities did considerable damage to the morale and confidence of peasant cocoa farmers.

The NLC's fiscal allocations seemed to favour the army and bureaucracy for whom new rounds of increases in salaries and perquisites were made. Indeed, while budgetary allocations for defence rose by 22 per cent from 1966-1967 to 1968-1969, those for agriculture fell by 27.2 per cent.[21]

On the whole the NLC government also failed to either diversify or modernise, or arrest the decline, in Ghanaian agriculture. Inherited problems in agriculture and newly created ones were simply passed on to the next government in August 1969 when the NLC handed over power to the PP government.

The Progress Party

The goals of agricultural development established by the PP government were a continuation of those of the previous regime; namely to rehabilite the cocoa industry, diversify the export sector and produce also for local industries as well as increase food production. Towards the attainment of these ends, the government adopted a two-pronged agricultural policy — with the focus on both the peasant and modern sectors.

Rural development was the chief means by which the peasant sector was to be developed. A comprehensive package of assistance to rural areas was formulated. It included the construction of feeder roads (abour 450 miles planned in 1970 alone); health posts and centres (12 were scheduled for completion in 1971); and the posting of medical personnel to rural areas, rural electrification and supply of good drinking water and improvement in rural housing through loans for building materials.[22]

In addition to infrastructural development, the government promised easy access to subsidised production inputs such as fertiliser and insecticides. Loans and cash advances were to be given through the newly revived Co-operatives, and NCedi1.5 million was allocated for that purpose in the 1970 budget. In addition, a World Bank-sponsored project was initiated to tackle the malaise in the cocoa industry through the 'scientific' rehabilitation of old cocoa farms. Under that project, farms were cleared, replanted with cocoa seedlings nursed by workers of the MOA and then handed back to their owners.[23]

The PP government also paid attention to large-scale mechanised agriculture as a means for modernising and diversifying agriculture. In this regard, it continued the NLC policy of encouraging the top public servants and members of the professional class, as well as foreigners to invest in agriculture. Special retirement benefits were provided for public servants who were planning to go into farming. (The 1970 budget established a 6 million cedis loan fund administered by the Agricultural Development Bank for this purpose). Tax holidays and import quotas were granted to Ghanaians and foreign companies investing in agriculture.

The government also entered into various agreements with foreign companies for agricultural ventures. For instance, the government entered into an agreement with the Standard Bank of West Africa for the establishment of commercial farms in the Atebubu area, and rice farms in the North. In June 1970, the government agreed to establish a Ghana Agricultural Development Company with four Italian firms to develop and manage poultry, livestock and quasi-public enterprises similar to the CPP government's Agricultural Development and State Farm Corporations. These were also large mechanised units and involved high overhead costs.

Though some modest successes were recorded, the fundamental problems of Ghanaian agriculture such as monocrop dependency, lack of modernisation and diversification remained. Additionally, some of the worst features of the internal cocoa trade — the issue of promissory chits to cocoa farmers in lieu of prompt payment — could not be curtailed.

Agriculture under the PP regime, as in the previous governments, was a victim of under-funding. When the rural development programme (on which the revitalisation of agriculture depended) ran aground, and many of its projects ground to a halt, the government could find a convenient excuse in the revenue crunch of 1971 which made government funds scarce. But it is also true that the windfall profits accruing from the boom in export price for cocoa in 1969 and 1970 was hardly invested in agriculture. Instead the government opened the way to a consumption spree under the 'Open General Licence' system of importation — which, among other things, saw a sharp rise in the registration of private cars.[24] Apparently, a popularly elected government with an eye on popular appeal and the next general elections found it too hard to resist the temptation to give the appearance of economic prosperity, even if the structural problems of the economy in general and agriculture in particular remained unresolved.

While it was easy to squander the benefits from the export price boom on imports to meet middle class consumption needs, it proved impossible, at least politically, to extract more revenue from the social groups that benefitted from the boom in order to finance development. Thus the austerity measures of 1971, including the taxes and other levies, which were instituted to raise development funds from non-traditional sources (e.g. the army, bureaucracy and the trade unions) proved politically suicidal for the regime: it created the political climate which made the coup of 13 January 1972 possible.[25]

If the PP regime's agricultural and rural development policies were marked by acts of omission (such as insufficient funding) there were negative acts of commission such as the decision to peg the producer price of cocoa at 8 cedis per 601b load at a time when farmers were aware that export prices had risen and that greater reserves had been accumulated by the CMB.[26] In the area of the internal cocoa trade too, the government's policy was equally self defeating. It resisted attempts by the Director of the CMB to weed out weak and inefficient LBAs (in order to eliminate a source of considerable farmer discontent). When the Director, Mr. U.K. Hackman, announced that five out of ten LBAs that applied for renewal of their licences would be turned down on grounds of poor record of performance, he was over-ruled and dismissed from his post with little ceremony.[27]

At the same time, the government endorsed a policy under which the LBAs were required to deliver cocoa to the CMB's central stores before they could be paid. In the event, weak LBAs could not make prompt payments to cocoa farmers and the notorious 'chit system' remained as a means of effecting payments for cocoa purchases.

Perhaps the greatest disruption in agriculture was caused by the government's controversial Aliens Compliance Order. On 19th November 1979, the government announced that it would enforce the law requiring the expulsion of aliens without valid residence permits. By June 1970, 213,750 aliens were officially known to have left the country. A large proportion of this number turned out to be migrants from neighbouring African countries who sustained Ghanaian agriculture — cocoa in particular — as farm labourers.[28] Their departure created a serious shortage of labour which produced a real crisis in cocoa agriculture.[29]

A plausible explanation for these self-defeating policies by a self proclaimed pro-agriculture and pro-rural development regime may be sought in the hold that the social groups who were based in the non-agricultural sectors of the economy — namely, the commercial and manufacturing sectors, had on the government. For example, certain individuals associated with the LBAs were also known to be financial backers of the ruling PP and some of their Secretary Receivers (depot clerks) occupied high positions in the local branches of the party. Therefore they were something of 'sacred cows' whose incompetent cocoa buying operations were covered by their seemingly strategic political positions.

Similarly the Aliens Compliance Order was enforced largely on behalf of the section of the Ghanaian business community who were engaged in commerce.[30] It was a fraction of this group of businessmen — mainly in the construction industry as contractors, whose rampant incompetence in executing construction programmes under the rural development programme contributed to the failure of the programme. The regime's promotion and subsidization of modern sector agriculture too appeared to have benefitted another fraction of this group — retired army officers and public servants. Once again the traditional small-holder farmer and rural dweller had lost in the struggle for attention and resource allocation to the 'modern' farmer and to non-agricultural interests.

National Redemption Council/Supreme Military Council Period (1972-1979)

The high cocoa output in 1972 (when the NRC regime came to power) could hardly obscure the mounting problems in Ghana's agriculture at the time. There was evidence that cocoa farmers were no longer maintaining their existing farms or establishing new ones, and in some extreme cases, cocoa farms went unharvested. The incidence of smuggling to neighbouring Côte d'Ivoire and Togo was on the increase; the internal marketing of cocoa experienced disruptions as financially weak LBA's issued more promissory notes to farmers in lieu of prompt payment; and the PP government's Aliens Compliance Order had triggered off an acute shortage of farm labour.[31]

The NRC/SMC adopted a wide range of measures to deal with the agricultural problems; but its initial efforts focused on reforming the internal marketing system of the cocoa industry. The 'chit system' was abolished and defaulting LBAs and their secretary receivers given severe punishment. Furthermore, weak LBAs were discouraged from participating in the cocoa trade through the imposition of a requirement that they paid a certain amount of money as security against possible default during their operations. The marketing co-operatives also saw major reforms.

Another plank in NRC/SMC agricultural policy was input subsidy. The government increased the subsidy on hand sprayers from 68.6 per cent in 1971 to 73 per cent in 1972 and that on insecticide from 20 per cent in 1971 to 79 per cent in 1973 and then to 89 per cent in 1975.[32] Labour costs was to be subsidised through a scheme in which the Cocoa Production Division (CPD) employed a group of 20 labourers in each of its 137 districts and hired this labour out to farmers at 2 cedis a day (with CPD providing food and transport).

The NRC/SMC moved to intervene more directly in agricultural production first by extending the Cocoa Rehabilitation Project (CRP) (started earlier in the Eastern Region under the PP government) to the Ashanti Region and second, by instructing the MOA and the CMB to establish cocoa and coffee plantations. Under the first scheme the CRP took over decaying farms for a period of two to three years for rehabilitation, and four years for replanting. During this period the management provided modern inputs such as cocoa hybrids, fertilizer, insecticides etc., in addition to labour. The farms were then handed back to the original owners who were expected to repay by instalment the total cost of rehabilitation.[33]

Bilateral and multilateral agencies were also enlisted to invest in agriculture either alone or in partnership with government or other public or private Ghanaian firms. Typical of such ventures was the Ghana Government World Bank Oil Palm Development Corporation's 22,000 acre oil palm plantation and its 'outgrower scheme' at Kwae in the Eastern Region.

Educated Ghanaians (e.g. civil servants, army officers and professionals) as well as businessmen and women were encouraged to go into commercial farming with tax and other concessions. For example, customs duties on agricultural machines and spare parts were waived; rent on farm land was reduced; the repatriation of profits on agricultural investments was guaranteed; profits earned in the first five years of operation were exempted from taxation; and minimum prices for some farm products which would be subsidised at government guaranteed bank loans were, above all, assured.[34]

Energetic efforts were put into countering smuggling of agricultural produce. Smuggling was redefined as an act of economic sabotage requiring decisive government action. Thus a prison sentence of, at least, 15 years was prescribed for those found guilty of smuggling. Additionally, the government initiated a propaganda campaign to educate farmers in the border regions, notably the Volta Region, about the pernicious effects of smuggling. Towards the end of 1977, it was announced that the war against smuggling would be taken to the farm level — where army and CMB personnel would check official cocoa sales against projected yields.

Despite these strenuous policy measures, the NRC/SMC's record in the agricultural sector did not yield appreciable results. Ghana's exports suffered a calamitous decline. Cocoa production fell from 422,000 metric tons in 1972-1973 to a low figure of 250,000 metric tons in 1978-1979. The country's share of world production declined from 29.3 per cent in 1972-1973 to 16.5 per cent in 1978-1979, thus moving Ghana from its traditional position as the leading producer and exporter of cocoa to third place — behind the Ivory Coast and Brazil.

With declining cocoa production Ghana could not take full advantage of the record-high export price of cocoa that prevailed during the period.[35] Above all, the country's dependence on cocoa in agricultural export increased despite the government's stated objective of diversifying her agricultural exports. The share of cocoa in total agricultural exports actually rose from 60 per cent in the early 1960s to 62.6 per cent in 1976 and 74.6 per cent in 1979.[36]

The reasons for the poor performance of the agricultural sector were complex and varied. But as was the case with previous regimes underfunding, misallocation of resources, political expediency, and corruption were significant causal .factors.

The initial progress that was made in streamlining the cocoa buying system was negated by an unprecedented degree of inefficiency, mismanagement, corruption, and distortions in the marketing system. Weak and inefficient LBAs returned and by 1979, about 15 of them owed huge sums of money to CMB. Embezzlement and misallocation of CMB funds became rampant. For example, CMB funds were used to pay bonuses and other allowances to CMB and government officials rather than support the cocoa industry. A category 'C' scholarship fund was established under which the Head of State, the Commissioner for Cocoa Affairs, Regional Commissioners, CMB officials and others could award scholarships to their favourites, relatives and friends.[37]

Furthermore, the level of inputs and other supporting services for the cocoa industry dropped sharply. For instance in 1975, there were sufficient sprayers for only 3 per cent of the entire cocoa area, while there was only enough insecticide for 9 per cent of it in 1976. By the same date, the seed multiplication programme was also on the verge of collapse.

Export agriculture suffered also because the terms of trade and barter were increasingly shifted against the rural and the small-holder producers who have traditionally constituted the backbone of that sector. The rural areas stagnated badly as rural development programmes were terminated or denied the resources necessary for their completion. Significantly, the Ministry of Rural Development was abolished and its functions placed under the Ministry of Labour, Social Welfare and Co-operatives. Fiscal allocations for rural development seemed to have been replaced by exhortations to rural dwellers to improve their lot through 'self-help' schemes.

At the same time, central government extraction of the agricultural surplus (through taxation of cocoa incomes) remained relentless. The periodic upward revisions in the producer price of cocoa remained insignificant in the face of rising inflation and high production costs. Thus for example, the producer price of cocoa (in real terms) went down from 151 cedis permetric ton in 1971-1972 to 90 cedis in 1975-76 and 52 cedi in 1977-1978.[38].

The agricultural sector as a whole was a victim of underfunding during this period also. Incremental growth in fiscal allocations were impressive only on paper. The period was characterised by rapidly rising inflation which eroded the value of the cedi. Indeed, budgetary priorities hardly provided convincing evidence of NRC/SMC's commission to agricultural development. For example, whereas the percentage of budgetary allocation to agriculture declined from 6 to 5 per cent between 1971-1972 and 1972-1974, that for defence rose from 8 to 9 per cent in the same period.[39] The military and police forces acquired much new hardware. For example, Italian Jet Fighters and German Fokker F-27 transport planes were delivered to the Air Force; the army received new trucks and flashy uniforms; and the police was showered with Nissan Patrol cars, BMW cars and motor-cycles, and armoured vehicles. Clearly, the restoration of 'officer amenities' showed that this military government was in to promote its own corporate interests.

Political expediency was evident in some of the measures and actions taken by the NRC/SMC government in respect of agriculture. For example the termination of rural development programmes was the inevitable outcome of the decision to reverse the PP austerity measures — measures intended, in part, to generate revenue from the urban salariat for rural development.

But the reversal of austerity had been crucial in securing public approval and legitimacy for the NRC regime in its early days. Army officials were 'retired' or 'honourably discharged' from the army and/or given special assignments with rehabilitation packages that included loans and other grants for commercial agriculture. Among the ranks of plantation owners and gentlemen farmers in the 1972-1979 period were men like Colonel (rtd.) G. Baidoo (ex NRC Regional Commissioner) and many other serving and retired army officers. It is likely that agricultural enterpreneurship helped to deflect the ambitions of officers who might have otherwise plotted a coup d'etat.

In other respects such credit facilities and subsidised inputs enabled individual large-scale farmers to reap abnormal profits. Other politically motivated measures included the appointment or secondment of top army and police officers to the leadership of newly created or existing agricultural institutions, for example Commander Addo to the Cocoa Marketing Board; Commander Boham to the State Fishing Corporation; Colonel Akwagyiram to the Ministry of Agriculture; Colonel Tetteh to the Meat Marketing Board; and so on.

The use of agricultural surpluses and other resources to promote political interests became even more blatant during the Union Government (Unigov) campaign and referandum. Evidence presented to the Archer Committee [40] revealed that the CMB had been extensively involved in the campaign. For instance, about 1 million cedis had been spent on drinks distributed to various chiefs in order to gain their support for the government; the CMB had entered into various illegal transactions in order to raise funds for the campaign; and 'donations' had been made to pro-Unigov organisations without the approval of the Board's directors. Thus even the meagre surplus that accrued to the state from rising export prices for cocoa did not benefit cocoa farmers or improve the agricultural sector in any meaningful way. Rather it was used to support political goals and to prop up the regime.

Peoples National Party Regime (1979-81)

The PNP regime came to office promising to make 'agriculture the bedrock of economic policy and to gear the budget, import policy, producer price policy, science and technology towards effecting a revolution in agriculture'.[41] But in its fifteen months of rule, the PNP regime was unable to offer much that was original or innovative towards the agricultural sector. It tried to revive the state farms and the cocoa rehabilitation schemes but wage disputes between the government and its agricultural workers crippled the programme even before they could get started.[42] The CMB headed by a PNP politician — Mr. Mumuni Bawumia, was charged with the responsibility for distributing the limited assistance to farmers and undertaking rural development programmes such as feeder road construction.

Even more significant is the fact that budgetary allocations to agriculture (some 48 million cedis in the 1979-80 Budget, which represented a 74 per cent increase over the previous year) was rather inadequate in view of the prevailing high rate of inflation (which averaged over 100 per cent in this period), and the severity of the agricultural crisis at this time. In any case, actual disbursement was bound to be much smaller as the economy was said to be 'bankrupt'. Therefore the regime resisted pressures to increase the producer price of cocoa so fiercely that when it finally relented (in November 1981) the new price of 360 cedis per 30 kilogram it decided to pay was considered too low and far below the 500 — 800 cedis that had been demanded by the producers. In effect, the PNP regime like others before it, also failed to provide adequate support for agriculture. Accordingly, farmer's dissillusionment persisted, and the production of cocoa and other export crops continued to decline.

THE PNDC AND AGRICULTURE (1981-1987)

The Provisional National Defence Council (PNDC) replaced the PNP government in a military coup on 31st December 1981. The measures taken by the PNDC to deal with the critical agricultural situation it inherited were initially of a short term nature. It mobilised University students and private resources to evacuate cocoa (and other agricultural produce) from the hinterland where they had been locked up because of the very bad state of the roads and railways and for lack of haulage trucks.

But the PNDC has since turned its attention to medium and long term policies. The most important one among them has been a steady increase in the producer price of cocoa and cash crops. The producer price of cocoa has gone up from 4,000 cedis per ton in 1981 to 12,000 cedis in 1983, 56,000 cedis 1985/86, and to 85,000 cedis in 1987.

To improve the efficiency of the Cocoa Board (formerly CMB) the PNDC has initiated a drastic program of restructuring, including a program of staff reduction which seeks to retrench about 27,000 workers from the Board within five years. The Board is also to be divested of some of its functions so that it can concentrate on its core functions of marketing, research and extension services. In connection with this, 52 cocoa plantations of the Board have been put up for sale. In addition, the distribution of the 'farmers package' of essential commodities (e.g. wax prints and cutlasses) has been transferred to the Ghana National Trading Company.

An innovative Akuafo cheque system has been introduced to reduce the incidence of cheating of cocoa farmers by unscrupulous cocoa purchasing clerks, and assure prompt payment to farmers of cocoa purchases. The Akuafo cheque system and the expended network of rural banks are expected to improve the credit situation for rural cultivators. It was designed to encourage thrift and savings habit among peasant farmers to his account. The farmer can start an account with the cheque issued to him/her for the value of the cocoa sold to the Cocoa Board. Or he/she can withdraw all or part of the money. After initial teething problems, such as lack of access to banking facilities, the system has now come to represent the new era of prompt payment for cocoa, coffee and sheanut farmers and an end to the notorious 'chit system'.

Macro-economic policies entailed in the PNDC's Economic Recovery and Structural Adjustment Programs such as the devaluation of the cedi from 1.75 to one US dollar in 1982 to roughly 182 cedis to the dollar in 1987, the 5 to 35 per cent retention of foreign exchange earnings by exporters of non-traditional items such as sheanuts, cola, pineapples and processed timber; the vigorous road and railway rehabilitation efforts etc. are considered to be highly favourable to the development of export agriculture.

In conformity with the regime's bias towards an open market economy a phased withdrawal of subsidies on insecticides, spraying machines, fertilizers and other vital agricultural inputs as well as reliance on private as opposed to public distribution mechanisms have been instituted.

However, as the agricultural policies of the PNDC unfold, it is clear that they share many similarities with past policies and that basic tensions remained unresolved. For example the general emphasies on tradeable commodities is exerting pressures against food production, the success in increasing cocoa production from about 150,000 tons in 1983 to 225,000 in 1987 has probably been a factor in the supply glut and accompanying drop in world market price; while the increase in timber exports from 14,800 cubic meters in 1984 to an estimated 42,155 cubic meters in 1987 has probably been at the expense of the counrty's ecological integrity.

Meanwhile storage and processing capacities remain insignificant with the result that post-harvest losses remain high, and value-added remains low. Rural development continues to be hampered by lack of funds; and funds for agricultural development remain problematic. For instance, of an estimated amount of $131.6 million needed for the cocoa rehabilitation program in the 1983-85 fiscal years only $16 million had been secured by the end of 1984; $80 million had been promised from bilateral and multilateral sources and the government was still searching for the rest. Attempts at mobilising revenue internally (through intensified tax collection, introduction of user fees for text books in secondary schools, withdrawal of subsidies on consumer items, labour retrenchment, etc.) remain extremely controversial, and politically explosive apart from the fact that they have not closed the budgetary gap. In fact they have caused considerable alienation of key support groups from the PNDC.

CONCLUSION

This review of agricultural policies and politics of post-colonial Ghanaian regimes reveals many continuities from one regime to the other. The Nkrumah government promised a decisive modernisation and diversification, but left behind a severely weakened agricultural sector; the NLC's attempt at liberalisation proved largely abortive; the PP's rural development program was frustrated by lack of funds; the NRC/SMC agricultural development program was bogged down in corruption and mismanagement; the PNP's 'new deal' was also mired in immobility, while the long-term prospects of the PNDC's policy of agricultural recovery remain highly uncertain.

In almost all these instances, with the possible exception of the PNDC, regimes have wavered between support for the peasant producer and large-scale mechanised agriculture. But invariably they have all been concerned with sustaining the basis for state revenue.

Despite this dependence on agriculture for state revenue all Ghanaian governments have under funded the agricultural sector in both relative and absolute terms. Development plans and budgets that promised to give priority to agriculture ended up by allocating only a miniscule percentage of funds to the sector. Priority has often gone to other sectors, notably industry as well as social and economic infrastructure. Funding for rural and agricultural development has often fallen casualty of the country's not in frequent revenue crunches. And government support, when available, has tended to go into large-scale mechanised — either private or public — farming.

As indicated above, the excessive extraction of the agricultural surplus has characterised state policies throughout the period; for the agricultural surplus has been the chief source of government revenue. But this surplus has been ploughed into non-agricultural sectors, notably industry, infrastructure, public administration and private consumption. The peasant producers have been deprived of rewards and vital support as non-agriculture, economic as well as political and bureaucratic interests remain entrenched in the key institutions of state. Imbued with the ideology of development as 'catching up with the West' post-colonial governments have pushed policies that would promote urban and industrial development. The legitimacy of the young state came to be tied to its ability to show the fruits of independence — measured in terms of the number of factories established, modern townships planned, social services and infrastructure developed, etc. The struggle to provide such evidence of progress became crucial to the process of consolidating the state and the power of regimes. This bias in development 'ideology' contributed to the neglect and underdevelopment of the rural and agricultural sectors.

Governments have been able to sustain this bias because of the exclusion of agricultural and rural interests from various government coalitions not even in the populist military government of the PNDC. Whether in cabinet circles or in the legislative and bureaucratic institutions the peasantry have not constituted a force that could compel governments to cater for their interests. Apart from the significant number of politicians, bureaucrats and professional people who derive their livelihood from agriculture, traditional rulers remain the only key group in the governing coalitions who have direct economic, social and political ties with the rural and agricultural sectors. However, traditional rulers have been too politically vulnerable, and have usually been manipulated by regimes for their own purposes. Accordingly they have not been effective in securing the interest of the rural producers. At best, they have sought to advance their own political and economic interests as a group. Thus, the representation of rural and agricultural interest is left, by default, to a ruling class whose sole interest in agriculture is to sustain production so that they could appropriate the agricultural surplus for their own economic purposes.

Seen in this light, the Ghanaian state faces an important and unresolved 'crisis of participation' — one which militates against the formulation and implementation of positive agricultural policies.

NOTES

1. See *The Report of the Commission of Enquiry into the Disturbances in the Gold Coast*, London 1948 (Chairman: A. Watson).
2. Killick, Tony, 'Cocoa' in Walter Birmingham et al (eds.), *A Study of Contemporary Ghana: The Economy of Ghana*, Vol.1 Northwestern University Press, Evanston 1961, pp. 441-445.
3. From the detached see M. Miracle and A. Seidman, *State Farms in Ghana*, Land Tenure Centre, University of Wisconsin, Madison 1968(a).
4. See M. Miracle and A. Seidman, *Agricultural Cooperatives and Quasi Cooperatives in Ghana 1951-65*, Land Tenure Centre, University of Wisconsin, Madison, 1968 and also E. Dadson 'Farm Size and the Modernisation of Agriculture in Ghana' in I.M. Ofori (ed.), *Factors of Agricultural Growth in West Africa*, ISSER, Legon 1973, pp. 193-202.
5. D. Austin, *Politics in Ghana*, 1946-60, Oxford University Press, London 1970, especially chapter 6 and also Bjorn Beckman, *Organising Cocoa Farmers*, Scandinavian Institute of African Studies, Uppsala 1976, pp. 59-77.
6. Austin, *op. cit.*
7. Austin, *op. cit.*, p. 173.
8. Beckman, *op.cit.*
9. Dadson, *op.cit.*
10. R. Bates, *Markets and States in Tropical Africa: The Political Basis of Agricultural Policies*, University of California Press, Berkeley 1981, p. 115.
11. Miracle and Seidman, (1968(b), *op.cit.*, pp. 45-46.
12 Beckman, *op.cit.*, p. 197.
13. Tony Killick, *Development Economics in Action*, Heinemann, London, 1978.
14. It is unlikely that Ghanaian farmers welcomed the imposition of excessive taxation contrary to claims by the UGFCC executive members; see J.E.A. Manu, 'Cocoa in the Ghanaian Economy' in R. Kotey et al (eds.), *Cocoa Production and Marketing*, ISSER, University of Ghana, 1974, p. 412.
15. Beckman, *op.cit.*
16. Miracle and Seidman, 1968, *op.cit.* and Dadson, *op.cit.*
17. R.A. Kotey and L.O. Gyekye, *Internal Marketing of Cocoa in Ghana*, Technical Publications Series, no.33, ISSER, Legon, 1974.
18. Dadson, *op.cit.*
19. B. Beckman, 'Ghana 1951-78: The Agrarian Basis of the Post colonial State' in Heyer et al (eds.), *Rural Development in Tropical Africa*, Macmillan Press, London, 1981, pp. 144-167.
20. Beckman, *ibid.*
21. See *Two Year Development Plan*, Ministry of Finance, Accra 1967.
22. See T.K. Buxton and D.M. Dunham, 'Some Aspects of Regional Planning and Rural Development Policy in Ghana in *Development and Change*, Vol. II, no.3, 1970-71, pp. 11-29.
23. Beckman, *op.cit.*
24. Killick, *op.cit.*, p. 308.
25. See D. Goldsworthy, 'Ghana's Second Republic: A post mortem' *in African Affairs*,

LXXII, 1973, pp. 8-25, also V.P. Bennet 'Malcontents in Uniform: The Non-Politicians Takeover', *Africa Report*, Vol. 17, no.4, April 1972, pp. 19-22.

26. According to some estimates, at 8 cedis per 601b bag, the price of cocoa in 1969 was actually lower than its price 10 years earlier. See *West Africa*, September 27, 1969, p.1073.
27. See West Africa, October 15, 1969, p.1286. It appeared that some LBAs were also financial backers of the PP or occupied high positions in the party's local branches.
28. M. Peil, 'Expulsion of West African Aliens', *Journal of Modern African Studies*, Vol.9, no.2, August 1971, pp. 205-230, also *West Africa*, issues of November/December 1969.
29. J. Adomako-Sarfoh, 'The Effects of the Expulsion of Migrant Workers on Ghana's Economy' in Samir Amin (ed.), *Modern Migrations in West Africa*, International African Institute, London, 1974, pp. 138-155.
30. J. Esseks, 'Government and Indigenous Private Enterprise in Ghana', *Journal of Modern African Studies*, Vol.9, no.1, May 1971, pp. 11-30.
31. This section relies heavily on Panel Nugent, *Rural Producers and the State in Ghana, 1972-1979*, MA Thesis, School of Oriental and African Studies, University of London, 1985.
32. See V.K. Nyanteng, *The Declining Chana Cocoa Industry: An Analysis of Some Fundamental Problems*, ISSER, University of Ghana, 1980.
33. V.K. Nyanteng, Cocoa Sector Rehabilitation: The Eastern Region Cocoa Project, 1971-1976.
34. See A. Shepherd, 'Agrarian Change in Northern Ghana', in Heyer et al (eds.), *op.cit.*, pp. 169-191.
35. R. Pace, 'Neo-Colonialism and Ghana's Economic Decline: A Critical Reassessment', *Canadian Journal of African Studies*, Vol.18, no.1, 1984, pp. 163-174.
36. See J. Henderick and J.J. Sterkenburg, 'Agricultural Policy and Production in Africa: The Aims, Methods and the Means', *Journal of Modern African Studies*, Vol.21, no.1, 1983, pp. 163-194.
37. For details of irregularities and mismanagement in the cocoa trade in this period. See *The Report of the Committee for the Investigation of CMB Affairs*, (Chairman, Justice Archer) Government Printer, Accra 1978.
38. See Robert Franco, 'The Optimal Producer Price of Cocoa in Ghana', *Journal of Development Economics*, Vol.8, 1981, pp. 77-92.
39. D. Rothchild, 'Military Regime Performance: An Appraisal of the Ghana Experience, 1972-78 *Comparative Politics* Vol.12 no.4, Jult 1980, pp. 459-479.
40. Archer Report, *op.cit.*
41. See the Manifesto of the *Peoples National Party*, Accra, 1979.
42. *West Africa*, August 11, 1980, p.1256 and November 16, p.2744.

10. PROBLEMS OF THE HEALTH CARE DELIVERY SYSTEM

Kodjo Senah

INTRODUCTION

This paper attempts an examination of the problems that have attended the post-colonial effort to provide adequate health care for the people of Ghana. The searchlight is mainly on the public or state sector of the health delivery system. In examining the problem of the post-colonial health system, the focus will be on health financing and health coverage: two central issues with immense social, political and economic implications for the development of the health industry in this country.

The arguments in this essay are based on the view that the task of providing an efficient, adequate and accessible health system is part of the general effort since independence to realise and maintain a healthy society. Like any aspect of the national development task, the provision of adequate health care is a task which invariably involves the collective effort of both the government and the governed. The problem, especially in the post-colonial era, is that the quantum of input expected from each party — the government and the governed — towards the realization of this objective, has always been in dispute. Briefly then, in looking at Ghana's public health system, this paper addresses itself holistically to the problem of social development and specifically to the political, economic and social forces that have influenced current policies and the structure of the public health system.

The task of nation-building has perhaps been more problematic in the post-colonial era. In Ghana, as in almost all newly independent nations, the entire burden of initiative into hitherto unexplored fields of economic, social, cultural and almost all other spheres of development, is thrown on the state. Private initiative even when present must be buoyed up by government financing and support largely because of the pressing need to accomplish so much in a relatively short time.

The medical field is no exception. The government has to take the initiative and maintain a lead on private enterprise or standards fall and the health of the nation is endangered. Thus in the midst of political instability, balance of payment crisis, and mass poverty, advances in the health care delivery system have assumed an instrumental value in the developmental process. Also the productivity of labour depends in part on the state of the nation's health. An efficient health care delivery system therefore has tremendous economic value, and plays a crucial role in the developmental processes of a nation.[1]

As the largest provider of health services, successive governments have, and continue to experience, great difficulties in meeting the large capital component needed by the health sector. Consequently, there has been much reliance on external sources. And yet the country's achievements in the field of health since independence are incomparable to that obtained under colonial rule. For example, there are now two medical schools which turn out between 80 and 90 doctors annually, one state-owned pharmaceutical factory and a training school for pharmacists. None of these existed at Independence. In terms of public health facilities, as at 1981, there were about 71 health centres and 230 rural health posts as against 10 and 9 respectively at independence; and currently, there are 6 public nursing training institutions and 7 public midwifery training schools in the country. At independence, there was only one public nursing training college.

Also a primary health care programme is being implemented. As will be discussed in greater detail later, this programme emphasises preventive or promotive medicine and community involvement in health matters, and is gradually making health care more accessible to the people. The cumulative effect of all these advances on the general quality of health has been considerable. In the 1960s life expectancy at birth was estimated at 49 years for males and 52 years for females. By 1983, these figures had risen considerably to 57 years and 61 years for males and females, respectively.[2]

However, inspite of these impressive achievements, the health care service remains a problem to both the government and the people. Governments are unsure of the acceptable ideological underpinnings of health policy as the provision of public health services remain an intolerable burden on the exchequer while it is, at the same time,limited to a few Ghanaians, notably those in the urban centres and large towns. Although it is accepted that given our socio-demographic characteristics and inadequate national resources, it is the preventive, socio-economic and educational aspects of the health care systems that are most needed, the health system, especially in terms of financing, is still over-weighted in favour of its colonially inherited capital-intensive programme.

Besides many other aspects, children especially die of preventable diseases. It is estimated that 9 per cent of all deaths or about 16,000 deaths per year are attributable to malaria. This sickness also accounts for 30 per cent of out patient visits and 9 per cent of hospital admissions while 5 per cent of all deaths are attributed to measles.[3] With infant mortality rate at 107 per 1000 live births[4] the infectious diseases of most concern with regard to life and health of mothers and children are malaria, measles, pertussis, gastroenteritis, respiratory infection, helminths, poliomyelitis, tuberculosis, schistosomiasis, guinea worm, tetanus and skin infections.

Given the enormity of the health problem, government cannot depend solely on external aid. Efforts must be made to mobilize internal resources, including human ones, to assist in the task of improving the health status of the people. But this has not been easy. An appreciation of the current problems relating to public health financing and coverage would require an insight into the modus operandi of colonial public health service. As Berger[5] has rightly argued, this appreciation is necessary because there is nothing that is happening today which is free of ties with the past. This is more so in the case of the modern health service which came to this country as part of the baggage of colonialism.

THE COLONIAL HEALTH SERVICE

Colonialism, according to Nkrumah[6], is the policy by which the colonial power binds her colonies to herself by political ties to her own economic advantage. The nature of this relationship depends on the opportunities offered by the resources of the colony, and on the power to exploit these resources by the colonial power. The history and development of bio-medicine in this country can therefore be explained, in part, by the nature of the political and economic relationship that prevailed between this country and Great Britain.

The development of a colonial health service may be seen in three major phases. The first phase which marked the early beginnings of the service probably dates from 1471 when the first European explorers landed on the coast to about 1844, when the British signed a peace pact with some coastal chiefs. This period also marked the peak of European mercantilism and the concomitant scramble for colonial possessions. This period was at the same time significant in European history for its advances in medical knowledge: Louis Pasteur's 'germ theory' or 'contagionism' had revolutionised medical thinking. This theory perceived the germ as the cause of pathogenic conditions. In the therapy management process therefore, the individual was atomised and cured. Coinciding as it did with the age of capitalism, this theory ensured that health problems would be individualised.

The main aim of the medical service in this phase was to safeguard the health of European residents through prompt diagnosis and treatment, and through their physical separation from the local population. As Simpson observed:

> The policy has been to provide a European quarter in order that the risk of malaria infection from the insanitary conditions of native houses and from infected natives may be reduced.[7]

The Bond of 1844 ensured relative peace and security in the region and this promoted intense European economic and missionary activities in the area. However, it soon dawned on the British colonial administration that the health of the European could not be guaranteed unless some effort was made to attend to the health needs of the local population also. The second phase of the medical service was thus born.

In this phase, therefore, few Africans in the colonial administration were given medical coverage. A few towns, especially those with a sizeable European population or those of political significance, were provided with piped water and a few other sanitary facilities. The first hospital was built in 1868 at Cape Coast (then the colonial capital town) as a result of a report on the health situation in the colony written in 1867 by Thomas Jones, the colonial surgeon at the time. Subsequently, general hospitals, specialised hospitals and rural dispensaries were built. The Gold Coast Medical Department was established in this phase.

The new medical orientation did not have an easy beginning: the traditional medical system loomed large. The colonial administration devised a method to neutralize the influence of healers and thereby promote the popularity of the new medical system. Anti-malaria tablets were sent to all health centres and postal agencies to be sold cheaply to the local population and to be distributed free of charge to Europeans. In 1878, legislation was passed to liquidate traditional medicine. Official documents described traditional healers as 'insincere jujumen living on the neurosis of the illiterate folks'. This was followed by a campaign of 'enlightenment' to persuade urban dwellers, the educated and opinion leaders to shun traditional healers. Persons who worked in the colonial bureaucracy were expected to seek medical aid from the health service; and only colonial medical officers were authorised to issue certificates of disability. Missionaries also participated actively in this campaign.

The last phase (1901-1957) may be described as the period of consolidation and expansion of the colonial health service. Following the defeat of Asante in 1901 and the acquisition of the Northern Territories efforts were made to cover the entire colony with health facilities, The 1920s especially saw the development of basic infrastructural facilities — roads, harbour, rail network, markets, piped water, decent housing, schools and health centres — across the length and breath of the colony. Under Governor Gordon Guggisberg, the highest point in colonial public health delivery was reached with the building of Korle-Bu Hospital in 1923. This hospital was meant for use by Africans and also for research into tropical diseases.

Although the task of providing health care was shared also by missionary bodies, mining companies and a few private individuals, the greater share of the responsibility fell on the colonial administration. To reduce the financial burden of providing this service, civil servants paid dispensary fees ranging between 6d and 5s but were entitled to free medical attention. All others, except paupers, paid professional fees in government hospitals. This was in addition to hospitalisation fee, theatre fee, dispensary fee and cost of drugs and x-rays.[8] Given the general poverty of the local population and the size and number of fees charged, many did not avail themselves of the facility. Tables 1 and 2 below show the extent of health coverage and range of professional fees paid in government hospitals.

TABLE 1: DISTRIBUTION OF NEW PATIENTS TREATED IN GOVERNMENT HOSPITALS (1920-1930)

YEAR	TOTAL TREATED	% OF TOTAL POPULATION
1920	58,385	2.3
1921	57,263	2.2
1922(1st Quarter)	20,231	
1922-3	70,821	2.7
1923-4	77,224	2.9
1924-5	81,957	3.0
1925-6	97,443	3.5
1926-7	104,811	3.7
1927-8	132,446	4.5
1928-9	214,605	7.5
1929-30	248,325	8.2

Source: Patterson, D.K. *Health in Colonial Ghana: Disease, Medicine and Socio-Economic Change* (1900-1955). (Waltham, Mass Crossroads Press 1981), p.113.

Although users of health facilities made some financial contribution towards the cost of health care, this was not enough. Between 1922

TABLE 2: PROFESSIONAL FEES PAID IN COLONIAL HOSPITALS

Type of Consultation	Charges
1. Brief out-patient visit to Medical Officer	2s -5s
2. First Out-patient visit to Physician-Specialist	£2. 2s
3. First visit to Surgical Specialist	£2. 2s
4. Major surgical or Gynaecological operation	8 to 25 guineas[1]
5. Emergency Caesarian section	8 to 25 guineas
6. Any consultation or Operation for paupers	Free

Source: Konotey-Ahulu Committee Report, (Accra: Government Printer. 1970)
Notes 1: One guinea = 1.1 shilling

and 1932, for instance, not less than an average of 10 per cent of total government expenditure went into public health financing.[9] Governor Guggisberg underscored this at the formal opening of the Korle-Bu Hospital.[10]

The colonial medical service was largely curative. But the 'Sanitary Movement' in Britain and the sudden outbreak of the bubonic plague in 1908 drew attention to the need for preventive medicine; and in 1909 a 'Sanitary Branch' was set up as part of the Medical Department. This Branch was charged with the responsibility for 'the prevention or removal of the causes of conditions leading to the presence or propagation of diseases amongst the general population'[11].

This vague responsibility involved the Sanitary Branch in a number of unglamorous tasks such as nuisance abatement, clearing of drains, latrines and dustbins, vaccination; inspecting of markets, slaughter houses, restaurants, and perhaps the most vexatious of all, mosquito control. Unfortunately, the philosophy of the Sanitary Branch which located diseases in the social and physical environment of the people was not very popular with the colonial administration. Ostensibly, its activities tended not only to be financially burdensome but also to favour the local population. Thus following a drastic cut in health expenditure between 1931 and 1932, the Sanitary Branch was reduced to a skeletal urban service; and it remained in that situation long after independence.

Following the attainment of internal self-rule in 1951, the Ministry of Health was created and a commission was appointed to look into the colony's health system. In its far-reaching recommendations, the commission demanded, among other things, that all public hospitals and health centres be placed under the control of the new ministry; that hospital fees be abolished; and that urban and district councils be made responsible for sanitation. These recommendations had a significant influence on the health policies of the nationalist government after independence.

However, by independence, the colonial health system had developed certain features. Some of those features which were inherited by post-colonial governments, include:

a) a strong curative and urban bias.
b) a centralised medical administration with the least concern for the rural communities;
c) central government as the largest provider of health services; and
d) the subordination of traditional healing systems to biomedicine.
e) a north-south disparity in the provision of health care services and facilities with the southern-half of the country as the greater beneficiary.

FINANCING POST-COLONIAL PUBLIC HEALTH

At independence, Ghanaians yearned for the dawn of a millenium. Each town or village wanted an electricity supply, roads, decent housing, piped water, schools, health services and more. The challenge posed by the social problems and demands that faced the new government was serious enough to make Nkrumah declare soon after independence:

> We shall measure our progress by the improvement in the health of our people ... The welfare of our people is our chief pride and it is by this that my Government will ask to be judged.[12]

In an apparent effort to grapple with the immense social and economic problems, the Nkrumah government launched a Ten-Year Development Plan in 1951. This plan proposed an expenditure of £120 million of which social services (education, health, housing and social welfare) were to take up about 33 per cent.[13] Between 1959 and 1961 also other development plans were launched. Expansion in the facilities of the social services was emphasised in all these plans. Table 3 shows the degree of expansion in health care facilities.

Efforts to bring social services closer to the people did not stop at the expansion of physical facilities. The cost to users of health facilities was also drastically reduced; it was made free in some cases. Toward the realization of this goal the government withdrew the

TABLE 3: POST COLONIAL EXPANSION IN HEALTH FACILITIES (1957-63)

FACILITY	1957	1958	1959	1960	1961	1962	1963
1. Health centres (a)	10	12	16	22	27	33	41
2. Health Personnel (b)							
— Doctors	330	342	346	586	726	879	904
— Dentists	18	14	17	17	22	29	36
— Midwives	616	691	789	900	1008	1104	1235
— Nurses	800	986	1627	1848	2023	2191	2366
— Pharmacists	312	311	326	298	329	342	355

Source: (a) *The Health Services in Ghana*, MOH 1967
(b) Statistical Year Book, C.B.S. Accra, 1963.

privilege of private practice from its medical officers and dentists in September, 1958.[14] And on 9th October, 1961, private professional fees being charged by government doctors, dentists and specialists, were abolished. They were paid an annual allowance in lieu of private practice.[15]

In May 1962, a further concession was granted to the populace: (a) children of 16 years or less were to be treated free of charge except when treated in superior hospitals; (b) government employees, employees of government corporations; members of the armed forces, workers brigaders and the teaching service were to be treated free of charge at out-patient clinics; (c) for the rest of the population, a fee of 5s was to be charged for first attendance and 2s 6d for subsequent attendance; and (d) mission hospitals (whose fees were high) were to be reimbursed by the Ministry of Health for treating the categories of people mentioned above. Thus for the first time Ghanaians were to pay a token fee for out-patient treatment. In addition, government employees who hitherto had paid a fee for out-patient treatment were to be treated entirely free of charge.[16] Table 4 provides a good picture of the symbolic amounts Ghanaians were asked to pay for the improved medical services that the CPP government was providing.

The government's health expansion programme did not favour urban centres and large towns only. Provision was also made for the rural areas. Thus between 1960 and 1966, 35 rural health centres and 9 rural health posts were established.[17] The latter were manned by a health post superintendent, community health nurse and a medical auxillary staff. They treated minor cases and referred more serious ones to the district or regional hospitals.

In concert with Nkrumah's determination to promote the 'African Personality' — the quest for an authentic African way of life, in 1963,

TABLE 4: NEW HOSPITAL CHARGES (1962 to 1971) OUT-PATIENT MEDICAL ATTENTION AND TREATMENT

CATEGORY	CHARGE
1. Children (Ghanaian and non-Ghanaians)	Free
2. Civil Servants	Free
3. Ghanaian non-civil servants	Free
4. Non-Ghanaians	Free
IN-PATIENT MEDICAL ATTENTION AND TREATMENT	
1. CIVIL SERVANTS	
Basic Salary	Per Diem
Over Nc 1840.00	80p
N 1442.00 — 1,840.00	75p
N 902.00 — 1,440.00	60p
N 566.00 — 900.00	40p
N 418.00 — 564.00	25p
N 310.00 — 416.00	15p
N 144.00 — 308.00	10p
Less than N 144.00	03p
2. Personnel of the Police Force, Customs and Preventive Service, Forest Guards and Cattle Patrol.	03p
3. All others including aliens	10p (ordinary ward) 1.05 (special ward)
4. Cost of drugs to all	25p — 30p

Source: Konotey-Ahulu Committee Report (Accra: Government Printer 1970).

he initiated steps 'to study and organise traditional healers to form an association for the advancement of their art and techniques in the delivery of health care'.[18] This led to the formation of the Ghana Psychic and Traditional Healers Association in that year.

Although socially, politically and economically, the expansion and provision of free social services such as health was necessary and justifiable, it nonetheless placed a heavy burden on the economy. Available statistics on central government expenditure for 1963/64 show that of the estimated expenditure of £G.144 million, about 31 per cent was earmarked for social services. This was at a time when Ghana's main foreign exchange earner, cocoa, had suffered a massive price decline on the world market. Thus, even though Ghana's cocoa production doubled by over 200 per cent from 1956 to 1964/65, this could fetch the country an increase in revenue of just 7.7 per cent.[19]

The resultant financial strain on the central government budget led to the imposition of restrictions on imports and foreign exchange allocation. A capital-intensive service such as health delivery immediately felt the impact of the new restrictions as new equipment and other essential medical supplies could not be procured; nor could faulty ones be repaired. Deterioration in the public health system and discontentment among health personnel were logical consequences. Ghanaian doctors — an elite group who had considered themselves as the proud inheritors of the colonial medical system, were the most critical and the most aggrieved, especially when their persistent efforts to turn the health sector into a private industry had been frustrated by the Nkrumah government. Their feeling was contained in the report of the Easmon Committee set up by the National Liberation Council (NLC) in 1968. The report observed:

> Recently, an over-ambitious expansion of the health services through the provision of health facilities was undertaken without the planned training and recruitment of staff to cope with it. This coupled with national propaganda, promising the provision of free health services for all has led to a stagnation and deterioration of the service. Frequent changes of leadership, the withdrawal of authority from professional leaders and the over-injection of politics into health matters have all helped to produce a state of affairs in which empty credos replaced proper formulation and implementation of well-considered policies in their accepted order of priorities.[20]

The NLC, the military junta which overthrew the Nkrumah government in 1966, was pro-West. And in its bid to court western financial assistance, it started to reverse the Nkrumah government policy of involving the state deeply in a wide range of social and economic tasks.[21] The appointment of the Easmon Committee was part of this anti-Nkrumah policy. In its report to government, the Committee recommended, among others, that hospital fees should be raised and their collection strictly enforced.[22]

In line with its policy of divesting the state of some of its social responsibilities, the NLC on the 6th February 1968 introduced a statutory dispensing fee of 30np (new pesewas) in addition to the token hospital charges already in existence. The public outcry against this directive was enough to have destabilized the government and the directive was quickly withdrawn. However, on the 20th January, 1969, this directive was gazetted as NLC Decree 360 to be effective from 1st October, 1969 when the NLC would have safely handed over power to the newly elected civilian government of Dr. Kofi Busia.

Again another round of public outcry led to the suspension of the decree.

When the Busia administration took office, it also set up the Konotey-Ahulu Committee to investigate all matters relating to hospital fees. On that sensitive subject the Committee observed:

> Considering the cost to the Government that these drugs dispensed free must bring, we recommend that for the generality of patients including Civil Servants, out-patient care and treatment (including ante-natal care) should no longer be free, and that something be paid towards the cost of drugs dispensed in Government hospitals and clinics.[23]

An Act of Parliament[24] was passed by which charges were instituted for various services and other categories of persons-like aliens and members of the diplomatic corps who hitherto had not been required to pay for health services at government hopitals. However, in a subsequent legislative instrument[25] which detailed who was to pay for what services, attendance at rural health centres and posts was made free. Also patients referred from urban health centres, district hospitals or general practitioners to regional or central hospitals were to pay 1.00 cedis for first attendance and 50p for subsequent attendance. However, private patients were to pay 10.00 cedis per attendance. Charges for in-patient services were also raised.

It is worthy to note that the Busia government had a clear rural bias. In the first place it enjoyed little political support especially in Accra, the capital city; and secondly it had campaigned to redress the urban-rural imbalance. Thus it was the only administration which developed and pursued vigorously a clearly articulated policy on rural development. In its 27 months in office, it formulated a National Population Policy (making Ghana the first to do this in Africa), built 12 rural health posts, constructed several miles of feeder roads and expanded rural electrification and piped water supply all in an attempt to improve the quality of rural life.[26]

The National Redemption Council/Supreme Military Council junta which seized power from the Busia administration did nothing with respect to hospital fees. It was however, able to make generous budgetary allocations to the health sector, due to sudden improvements in the economy during the early years of that government. Beyond this, the situation remained unchanged even under the civilian administration of Dr. Limann which took over from the Armed Forces Revolutionary Council (AFRC) government. As a government which claimed to be very sympathetic to the ideals of Kwame Nkrumah, the least it could perhaps do was to maintain the status quo with regard to the health financing of public health delivery system in the country. After 27 months in office however, it was overthrown.

The Provisional National Defence Council (PNDC) seized power from the Limann government in December 1981, when the nation was experiencing a very serious economic crisis. The per capita G.N.P. had fallen from 620 cedis in 1974 ($1 = 1.15 cedis) to 447 cedis in 1981 ($1 = 2.75 cedis). Real wages had declined by 80 per cent and total volume of import, by 50 per cent. By 1981, about a third of the nation's earnings was being spent on crude oil; and inflation was running at 116.5 per cent. This situation reached a head in 1983 when cocoa production dropped to as low as 40 per cent of the 1960 production level while capacity utilization in the manufacturing sector was only 20 per cent.[27] To compound the problem of an ailing economy, a long drought had set in causing wide-spread bush fires and food shortages.

For the health sector, the picture was even more gloomy: inadequate financial resources had badly affected the supply of drugs and other medical supplies. In 1983, the introduction of surcharges on the delivery of imported drugs and hospital equipment worsened the situation as firms which normally imported drugs on behalf of the Ministry of Health found it difficult raising the required amount of money to establish letters of credit. In some public health centres, so critical was the situation that patients had to provide not only their beddings, drugs and food requirements, but also stationery for their medical records. The exodus of professionals from every sector of the economy affected the health sector also.

The PNDC was expected to act quickly to save the public health system from imminent collapse, more so when on assumption of office it had accused the ousted civilian government of Dr. Limann of among other things, turning the hospitals into 'transit camps to our graves'. As part of the efforts to salvage the health services, the PNDC raised fees for all kinds of hospital services.[28] For instance, out-patient consultation which had been free in certain areas attracted a flat rate of 5 cedis per visit. For the first time also non-Ghanains were discriminated against in the payment of hospital fees; they were required to pay anything ranging between 100 and 120 per cent of what Ghanaians were to pay. The argument for those increases was that the state could no longer bear the full cost of health delivery services.

Even with these increases, it was clear to government that something more drastic had to be done in view of the fact that per capita expenditure on health had fallen with rapid population growth and the persistent request for better health care services. Thus following the PNDC's Economic Recovery Programme (1984-1986) and the concomitant structural adjustment of the economy, new and higher hospital fees were again introduced on the 15th July, 1985. Table 5(a-c) show the comparative increases in hospital fees between 1971 and 1985.

HOSPITAL FEES: 1971, 1983 AND 1985
(OUT-PATIENT SERVICES ONLY — in cedis)

TABLE 5(a) — 1971

Institution/Service	Amount Payable
Rural Health Centre	Free
Rural Health Post	Free
District Hospital/Urban Health Centre	0.20
Regional/Central Hospitals	
(referred cases)	1 for 1st visit
	0.50 subsequent visit
(Private cases)	10.00

TABLE 5(b) — 1983

1. General out-patient attendance:	Adult:	5.00
	Children:	2.50
Non-Ghanaians:	Adult:	20.00
	Children:	10.00
2. Specialist out-patient clinic:	1st visit	25.00
	: subsequent visits	5.00
Non-Ghanaians:	1st visit	50.00
	: subsequent visits	10.00

TABLE 5(c) — 1985

1. Teaching Hospitals	Adults	Children	Non-Ghanaians
a. Specialist Consultation:			
(1st visits)	200.00	100.00	400.00
Follow-up visits	50.00	25.00	100.00
b. General Consultation	75.00	40.00	200.00
2. Regional Hospitals	75.00	40.00	100.00
3. District Hospitals	50.00	30.00	80.00
4. Urban Health Centres	50.00	30.00	80.00
5. Rural Health Centres/Posts	30.00	20.00	80.00

Sources: (a) Hospital Fees Regulation 1971, Legislative Instrument 706, Government Printer.
(b) Hospital Fees Regulation, 1983, Legislative Instrument 1277, Government Printer.
(c) Hospital Fees Regulation, 1985, Legislative Instrument 1313, Government Printer.

The public outcry that followed the introduction of higher hospital fees in 1985 was not unexpected. Ghanaians, since 1962 had been used to paying next to nothing for health services. The government, however, stuck to its position, more so when it had no electoral politics to contend with. In an ex-post facto rationalization, the Secretary for Finance and Economic Planning observed:

> If we continue to saddle the Government budget indefinitely with high cost for social services without a programme for generating revenues to sustain these costs into the future, we will simply initiate a self-destructive course.[29]

The need to generate revenue to meet costs of social services might be attributed to the economic conditions of the time. It is equally true however, that since independence, health revenues have always formed a very insignificant fraction of health expenditure. Table 6 shows the expenditure-revenue pattern between 1970 and 1975.

TABLE 6: HEALTH EXPENDITURE AND REVENUE 1970-1975 (in cedis)

Financial Year	Govt. Health Expenditure	Total Health Revenue	% of Expendit.
			%
1970/71	34,504,500	707,569	2.05
1971/72	34,025,700	714,181	2.10
1972/73	41,965,200	1,214,386	2.89
1973/74	71,223,400	1,574,560	2.21
1774/75	103,269,400	2,582,929	2.50

Source: Brooks, R.G.: *Ghana's Health Expenditures 1966-1980: A Commentary*, Glasgow, University of Strathclyde, 1981. p.31 and 43.

The argument about the need to generate revenue can therefore not be credible. What appears plausible is the government's decision to 'sell' at their market price all social services which the state had hitherto subsidized. On these grounds the PNDC government seems to be continuing from where the NLC-Busia governments stopped.

Meanwhile, figures released periodically by the Ministry of Health show impressive financial returns. For instance, it is reported that in 1986, the Ministry of Health bagged a total of 496.1 million cedis in hospital fees.[30] Significantly, no national effort has been made to ascertain the effect of fee-payment on the utilization of health services by the rural folk. According to official sources, however, a comprehensive health insurance scheme would ultimately be put in place to give health coverage to about 80 per cent of the population. How this programme can effectively operate, given the socio-demographic characteristics of the population, is yet to be determined.

Clearly, public health financing has been very problematic given its political, economic and social implications. It seems, however, that the present policy on health financing has not been designed with much consideration for its impact on the behaviour and health of service users. The rationale for the policy appears to be based more on economic and professional expediency than anything else. Health professionals (with vested interests in hospital-and curative-based health care system) have argued rather forcefully that an efficient health care system must be grounded on adequate financial resources derived from those who use it. Thus as observed by the Konotey-Ahulu Committee Report, there can be no health service without fees. This view has been further supported by Badoe[31] and Nyame[32], both medical officers. Indeed, as Nyame argued rather humorously, but seriously, 'The disease the health service in Ghana is suffering from is a serious case of 'apecuniosis' (lack of money). Only Ghanaians, from their own wallets can cure it'.

In our social circumstances, however, a policy of hospital fee payment (such as the present one) which affects not only those who can afford it but also the poor, aged and infants-both urban and rural dwellers, is not only oppressive but ultimately more expensive in its long term physical, social, economic and political implications. The grinding pauperism, particularly of rural existence, created by colonialism and nurtured by the post-colonial states' elite and urban biased health policies does not recommend such policy options.

Indeed as Kunnes[33] has observed, the payment of hospital fees is not only a health hazard but also a psychological barrier to health care. Hospital fees are, he argues, a roadblock to good health and makes a mockery of health care as a right, rather than a privilege: it makes the service increasingly a luxury to the majority who are also the poorest. In our circumstances the rural poor are the most vulnerable.

Free health care, especially to the rural poor is possible when among others, effective management and supervisory techniques are employed in the administration of public hospitals. Efficient management is an important device in the exercise of minimising cost. Unfortunately, in Ghana as Addo[34] has observed, the practice is to put senior medical officers in charge of administration even when these are not trained in hospital management; and no effort is made to train them. The consequences are obvious and costly.

Indeed as the Konotey-Ahulu Committee Report revealed, in 1967,

Korle-Bu Teaching Hospital alone lost 9,380 linen items through managerial lapses. The linen items ranged from bedsheets, blankets, doctor's coats to hand towels. Besides, an appreciable number of refrigerators, table fans, air conditioners and furniture could not be accounted for. At the national level, the financial loss to the state if a proper inventory of stock is taken, could be substantial. As this Committee admitted, 'If the colossal wastage that goes on in Government Hospitals is not stopped, no amount of hospital fees can prevent a deterioration of the state of chronic poverty of the Ministry of Health...'[35]

THE PROBLEMS OF POST-COLONIAL HEALTH COVERAGE

The discussion on the problems of health financing has so far identified one serious handicap of the post-colonial health system. The colonial health system was necessarily curative and urban-centred. For political, social and economic reasons, post colonial governments found themselves following the same health policies even though a greater effort was made to provide the rural areas with some health facilities. Thus today, in the face of heavy post-colonial medical expansion, medical facilities for the urban centres in contrast with rural facilities continue to grow and improve in quantity and quality. Also as in the colonial era, the South continues to enjoy more and better health facilities than the North (i.e. Northern, Upper East and Upper West regions).

Commenting on the rural-urban disparity, the Easmon Committee Report notes that the rural areas have been neglected and that the preventive emphasis of health has not been taken seriously. It argues that in preventive medicine, Ghana is thought to be worse off than during the colonial period and that one adult in every three, besides an appallingly high number of children, normally die from preventable conditions.[36] Sai in a similar vein observed that the number and distribution of hospitals and clinics were such that 'they cannot offer any kind of service to more than at most 20 per cent of the population.'[37] In 1978, Ewusi also estimated that Greater Accra, with about 9.4 per cent of the total population, had 47 per cent of total government doctors, 34 per cent of hospital beds and 12.2 per cent of all hospitals in the country. Further more, all the nine regional capitals (counting upper East and Upper West regions as one) with only 15 per cent of the total population of the country had 55.4 per cent of all hospitals in Ghana and 51.2 per cent of all hospital beds.[38]

The allocation of resources in terms of money, personnel and health facilities was also characterised by inequity. The disparity in resource allocation has been forcefully stated by Ofosu-Amaah: in the 1974/75 financial year, over a third of the health budget went to Korle-Bu Teaching Hospital and the Greater Accra Region alone.[39]

In comparative terms, the disparity in the provision of health facilities and personnel is even more skewed when the Northern and Southern parts of the country are considered. It may be argued that since the South has a relatively bigger population (79 per cent) than the North (21 per cent), the provision of health facilities must reflect this population differential. The reality of the situation, however, is that as in colonial times, the post-colonial distribution of health facilities — and indeed, of any social facility — has never at any time reflected the actual population differential.

For instance, in the distribution of medical officers, the South has 526 (93 per cent) of such personnel while the North has only 40 (15 per cent). With respect to health institutions, the South has 451 (84 per cent) while the whole North has only 87 (16 per cent). Of equal significance is the population — hospital bed ratio for the North and the South. While the North has a ratio of 1,293:1, the South has 847:1. Tables 7, 8 and 9 below show in more concrete terms, the disparities in the distribution of regional health facilities.

TABLES 7: DISTRIBUTION OF DOCTORS IN THE PUBLIC HEALTH SECTOR

COMMUNITY	TOTAL NUMBER OF DOCTORS	% TOTAL
Accra	322	46.8
Communities with population of about 20,000	242	35.2
Communities with population below 20,000	124	18.0
TOTAL	688	100.0

Source: *Ghana, Five-Year Development Plan 1975/76—1979/80* Part II, (Accra, Ghana Publishing Corporation, 1977).

THE NEW ORIENTATION

In the 1970s it became clear to health policy makers that something radical had to be done; for not much impact had been made on the health of the people despite the huge financial outlays since the 1960s.

TABLE 8: DISTRIBUTION OF PUBLIC DOCTORS AND DENTISTS BY REGION (AS AT 31st DECEMBER, 1973)

REGION	NUMBER	%
Greater Accra	267	47.2
Western	58	10.3
Central	30	5.3
Eastern	37	6.5
Volta	32	5.7
Ashanti	80	14.1
Brong-Ahafo	22	3.9
Northern	24	4.2
Upper	16	2.8

Source: Brown, C.K. 'Strategies for rural development in Ghana' in *Universitas* (Legon) Vol. 4 No. 1, 1974 p.111.

TABLE 9: REGIONAL DISTRIBUTION OF HOSPITAL BEDS (1985)

REGIONS	Total Pop. (1000)	Total Hosp. Beds	1 Bed/Pop.
Gt. Accra	1.504	3.020	1/ 498
Volta	1.273	1.653	1/ 770
Eastern	1.765	1.579	1/1118
Central	1.201	1.912	1/ 628
Western	1.216	1.004	1/1211
Ashanti	2.196	2.151	1/1021
Brong Ahafo	1.268	981	1/1292
Northern	1.224	877	1/1396
Upper East	812	498	1/1630
Upper West	460	555	1/ 829
TOTAL =	12.919	14.230	1/ 908

Source: Health Statistics Unit, Ministry of Health, Accra

The thinking was that since the rural areas, especially, experienced the highest mortality, morbidity and fertility rates, an integrated approach to rural health problems would be most appropriate.

In 1970 the Danfa Comprehensive Rural Health and Family Planning Project took off with the important aim of developing an effective, high quality and affordable primary health care in the rural areas. As a joint-project between the Ghana Medical School and the School of Public Health, University of California, Los Angeles, it was essentially demonstration, teaching, and research oriented. Then in 1974, perhaps in an attempt to exploit the medicinal potentials of the country's flora and also tap the knowledge of traditional healers, a Centre for Scientific Research into Plant Medicine was established at Mampong.

In 1976, however, the first most significant step towards primary health care was taken when the Ministry of Health, with assistance from WHO established the Brong-Ahafo Rural Integrated Development Project at Kintampo for the training of middle-level personnel for the proposed Primary Health Care (PHC) programme. The project was also aimed at determining in a practical way, the social processes that would help to institutionalise the participation of traditional healers in a health care programme.

Following the successes and failures of this project, the government in 1977 accepted a proposal to adopt a Primary Health Care (PHC) programme which would attempt to treat or prevent the vast majority of the causes of morbidity and mortality. The goal was to extend health care coverage to 80 per cent of the population. It is clear, however, that the current impetus which the PNDC is giving the programme stems from the WHO Alma-Ata conference declaration of 'health for all by the year 2000'.

After about a decade of the PHC programme in this country, the question is often asked: How successful has it been? And where are we? Answers to these questions are difficult to find especially in the absence of reliable statistics and monitoring systems. However, as Adjei and others have found from their limited study, only moderate gains have been made.[40] The Director of Medical Services also upheld this view when he observed that 'progress of the PHC has been very slow.'[41]

In terms of progress, Adjei et al observed that 64 per cent of the population had access to health care services in the form of a health post, or clinic within one hour travel time. According to the report, this percentage is about twice the figure in 1977. In the area of immunization also, public education has resulted in a massive increase in coverage while for measles in particular immunization has increased by 60 per cent over the record for the two previous years. The report noted also that in terms of pregnancy management, about 92 per cent of mothers had been examined at least once by trained medical personnel during pregnancy. However, between 50 and 70 per cent of deliveries took place at home with over half of such deliveries done by traditional birth attendants (TBA). The success story ends here.

The PHC programme is fraught with all kinds of problems resulting, in the main, from its organizational structure. The PHC is structured on three levels: (a) the community level or level 'A'; (b) the health institution level or level 'B'; and (c) the district level.

The Community level involves three types of community health workers — traditional birth attendants, village family health workers and the village development worker. These are selected and are supposed to be compensated by the community. Their training is done by the Ministry of Health. It is anticipated that there will be one such team within a catchment area of 12 square kilometres and that there will be 300 or more in each district. The main functions of this health team include preventive and promotive services, simple curative measures, pregnancy management, environmental protection and mobilization for health-related community projects.

The health institution level is the first referral point for community health workers in level 'A'. A health team at this level is made up of (a) a medical assistant; (b) a community health nurse/midwife; (c) a health inspection assistant and (d) a senior field technician for communicable disease control. These officers undergo retraining to equip them to supervise activities at the village level. They are to undertake all routine immunization and care for patients at level 'A'. It is hoped that there will be at least one level 'B' health institution within an area of 8 kilometres radius.

The last level, the district level, is expected to serve a population of between 150,000 and 200,000. This level is supposed to manage the entire system. A District Health Management Team (DHMT) is made up of the following: (a) a district medical officer; (b) a district public health nurse; (c) the district technical officer for communicable disease control; (d) senior medical officer responsible for the district hospital and (e) a district health inspector. This team is expected to work in conjunction with the district council to facilitate an integrated approach to community development. It is responsible for the planning, implementation and evaluation of health services for the entire district.

To make the PHC programme more effective, the PNDC government in 1984 set up a high level National Primary Health Care Committee made up of 17 governmental and non-governmental organizations all of which are involved in health-related activities. This committee has selected five main health areas for maximum promotion. These areas are:

(a) Expanded programme on immunization
(b) Control of diarrhoeal diseases
(c) Health education
(d) Environmental sanitation; and
(e) Growth monitoring.

One of the difficulties with the administrative structure of the PHC programme is that whilst the structural organization of the programme is clearly defined from the district down to the community level, the structural linkage from the district to the national headquarters is ill-defined. The result is that the districts find themselves without any support from the top.

To add to this difficulty, the National Primary Health Care Committee has not been very active; it has met only twice since its inception in 1984. This administrative problem is further compounded by inadequate technical support. The staffing projections which were made are yet to be realised and most of the districts find themselves without district medical officers, a situation worsened by the fact that none of the positions in the DHMT is an established one. Therefore, the DHMTs find themselves saddled with great responsibilities but without any authority whatsoever. The programme faces also a good deal of difficulties with logistics. Financially, the districts lack autonomy and since no direct budgetary allocations are made to the PHC, health personnel's allegiance to their divisions still persists, a situation which further weakens the basis of commitment to the programme.

These administrative difficulties have implications for programme implementation also. The expectation was that programmes would be developed with the orientation and retraining of the personnel in the system. However, after the initial training, subsequent retraining could not be undertaken because of unanticipated high cost of such exercises. The result is that the teams are left without any programme to follow. And since they have not been trained to develop programmes to meet health needs, they are left to continue operating as before.

At the grass-roots level also there are many problems, some unknown to policy makers. In a recent nation-wide study[42] to evaluate the activities of retrained TBAs and their trainees the lack of transport facilities to enable effective supervision of TBAs was found to be very pronounced. Thus with the consequent break in communication, some TBAs — and most are illiterate — have forgotten what they had learned and are back to their previous methods. Besides, because TBAs are often old men and women there is a high rate of attrition as some of them soon die or retire after retraining. For instance, of the 60 or more TBAs trained under the Danfa Project, only about 20 are still in active service.

For the TBAs however, the most problematic areas of concern are the procurement of equipment, remuneration and community support. It is clear from the study that in different areas, the TBA kit, the focal point in TBA training is either given out free of charge or sold to graduates at the end of the training session. Besides, the contents differ from place to place. In the Danfa area, for instance, a kit normally contained the following:

(a) a brush for washing hands;
(b) several sterile cord packs, each containing: 2 gauze dressings, 4 cotton swabs, 4 pieces of string, a new razor blade and a safety pin wrapped in paper, autoclaved and placed in a plastic envelope;
(c) a bottle of gentian violet in alcohol for use on cord dressing;
(d) two small plastic bowls for cord care;
(e) family planning items: one can of contraceptive foam, one packet of contraceptive pills, one IUD and one packet of condoms for demonstration purposes.

In addition to these, each TBA is expected to provide 2 clean towels, a plastic sheet, a cake of soap and a bandage.[43]

The major problem with the kit is that, however it is acquired, its contents cannot be easily replaced. In the Danfa area where some of these contents are supposed to be supplied free of charge, this has not been possible due to the Ministry's own financial difficulties or to transportation problems or to both. Also, TBAs are not expected to charge fees for their services, their expanded roles consequent upon their retraining notwithstanding. As in the traditional system, they are still expected to receive gifts in cash or in kind for their services. Under these circumstances, the TBAs are finding it very difficult to replenish their kits. To resolve this problem, some of them have began to charge fees fixed by their own associations while some have either abandoned the practice or have reverted to the old system of delivery where not many expensive items are required.

The PHC programme is expected to benefit from active community support and involvement. At the community level, the community is supposed to select recognised TBAs and other village health workers for retraining. The community is required also to help those selected by ensuring that they are paid after their training. The study has shown clearly that most communities have not fulfilled the latter part of the bargain. It appears that communities are finding it difficult to accept the fact that a retrained TBA must now work full time and be paid by them when previously, she combined delivery services with her other ocupation, most invariably farming.

The apathy of the community has other implications. Since ill health is essentially the result of man and environment interaction, an interventionist approach to adjust or reshape the values and attitudes of the society becomes a priority. However, this community intervention by way of mobilizing community resources to effect a sanitated environment has received very little support. In this day and age, it is not unexpected that quite often, requests from chiefs and people invariably include a clinic. A village clinic is a status symbol for that community; it is psychologically attractive and it commands a modicum of village esprit de corps. But it does not usually go with changes in sanitary habits and social values and attitudes.

Perhaps out of political expediency, governments have also been responding to these requests by building more clinics and thereby emphasising the curative aspect of health care at the cost of the preventive.

In a recent reaction to this phenomenom, the Director of Medical Services is quoted to have observed that the building of clinics and training of community health attendants 'are all scratches of the tip of the iceberg of the package deal of the PHC', adding that 'these are all glamorous aspects of the PHC which is quite wrong'.[44] As he rightly pointed out, for the PHC to exert the desired impact it was meant to achieve, there must be good drinking water, clean environment, control of all communicable diseases, proper care of the pregnant mother through delivery, growth and development of the new-born, health education, safe disposal of waste and good nutrition.

It is obvious that this task is beyond the capability of the Government alone, given the state of the nation's financial position, and the geographical spread of the population. However, the policy of asking rural folks to provide for most of their needs is likely to depress their material conditions even further. At the moment a rural community is expected to finance the provision of its own school building, boreholes, electrification, a clinic building, market, toilets, and even roads while the central government provides most of these amenities for the urban population.

Although government often lends a helping hand, it is clear that a village without an adequate resource base to initiate such programmes is doomed to stagnation. The local councils cannot be counted upon either because most of them suffer from a combination of political, economic and social problems which render them highly ineffective in the task of community development. The health of the rural poor continues to suffer as a result of this. As Adjei et al. have observed, 11 per cent of rural and peri-urban children are seriously malnourished while kwashiokor is still as rampant as it was 50 years ago.[45]

CONCLUSION

Ghana's developmental problems, like those of any third world nation, are complex: they span the economic, educational and health sectors. It appears, however, that all these problems have a common denominator in the politics of society. The policy at independence to adopt and literally apotheosise western models in our desire to be counted among the comity of 'civilized' nations, accounts for the present inequalities. Although long ago, the basic premise of western health service models have been challenged by thinkers like Ivan Illich,[46] the inappropriateness of this model of health service is only now being appreciated.

It is clear, however, that the political will to provide a health system which reaches most Ghanaians is lacking. Indeed, many class and vested interests operate to make this impossible. And as it is common knowledge, a ruling class whatever its orientation rules first and foremost for its own benefit and only incidentally for that of others. The determination of health policies seems to have been affected by prevailing elite and ruling class interests.

To solve our health problems there is the need for a serious search for an answer to the fundamental question: What kind of health system do we need? The shortcomings of post-colonial health policies indicate a strong bias for a socialized medical system in which government is expected to make equal health care services available to all. However, as experiences from China, Nicaragua, Tanzania and Cuba, have shown effort at equalized and socialized health care is not possible without the involvement of the entire population in the process of decision-making as part of national political effort for effective and radical social transformation. In these countries, the process of democratization of the political system has raised serious questions relating to the appropriateness of the economic, technical and social bases of the health care system.

The early years of the present revolution would have provided the best opportunity for such social transformation as communities for once directed their own destinies through the 'People's Defence Committee', the revolutionary organs which were to ensure that grass-root democratisation would be achieved. But with the present routinization of charisma, the opportunity seems lost. Viewed from this perspective, our public health care system will remain expensive and restricted to a few until an appropriate political framework has been established. If a healthy populace is the bedrock upon which rests a functional body-politic, then adequate health care for all Ghanaians must be seen as a right, not a privilege.

NOTES

1. Myrdal, G. Asian Drama: *An Inquiry into the Poverty of Nations*. Vol III Pantheon Press, N.Y., 1968.
2. *The World Bank World Development Report 1885* (The World Bank) New York

Oxford University Press, 1985.

3. *Danfa Project Final Report*, Accra. University of Ghana Medical School and U.C.L.A. School of Public Health, 1979.
4. *World Population Data Sheet*. Washington Population Reference Bureau Inc., U.S.A. 1986.
5. Berger, P. — *Invitation to Sociology*. Harmondsworth, Penguin Books Ltd., 1963.
6. Nkrumah, Kwame — *Towards Colonial Freedom*. Kingswood, Surrey: The Windmill Press Ltd., 1962.
7. Simpson, W.J. — *Sanitary Matters In Various West African Colonies and the Outbreak of Plague in the Gold Coast*. Crown Agent, 1909 pp.13.
8. *Report of the Committee Appointed to Investigate Hospital Fees* (Hereafter referred to as The Konotey-Ahulu Committee Report) (Accra, Government Printer, 1970).
9. Patterson, D.K. — *Health in Colonial Ghana: Disease, Medicinal and Socio-Economic Change* (1900-1956) Waltham, Mass.: Crossroads Press. 1981, p.112.
10. *Korle-Bu Hospital 1923-73*, (Accra Advent Publishing House, Accra 1973), p.37.
11. *Gold Coast (Ghana),Organization and Activities of the Public Health Service of the Gold Coast*, (Accra: Government Printer, 1926.
12. *Axioms of Kwame Nkrumah* (London, Panaf Books Ltd., 1969), p.51.
13. Dowse, R.E. — *Modernization in Ghana and the USSR* (London, Routledge and Kegan Paul.1969), p.38.
14. *The Konotey-Ahulu Committee Report*, 1970, p.12...
15. Ibid.
16. Ibid.
17. Ghana, *Ministry of Health Report*, (Accra Government Printer, 1967) p.16...
18. Dapaah, M. 'Traditional Healing', *Ghana Journal of Science*, 21, 1968. pp.16-21.
19. Birmingham, W, Neustadt, 1I and Omaboe,: E.N. *A Study of Contemporary Ghana*. Vol.1 The Economy of Ghana (London George Allen and Unwin Ltd., 1966), p.27.
20. *Report of the Committee Appointed to Investigate the Health Needs of Ghana* 1969 (Accra: Government Printer, 1969) p.1 (Hereafter referred to as The Easmon Committee Report).
21. For further details see Killick, T.: *Development Economics in Action*. (London, Heinemann, 1978).
22. *The Easmon Committee Report*, p.81.
23. *The Konotey-Ahulu Committee Report*.
24. Hospital Fees Act, 1971, (ACT 387).
25. Hospital Fees Regulations, 1971. Legislative Instrument 706.
26. For further details see Gyimah-Boadi, E., 1987: 'The State and Agriculture Policy in Ghana', (In this collection).
27. Economic Commission for Africa. *Survey of Economic and Social Conditions in Africa 1983-1984*. (Addis Ababa,) UNECA, April, 1985 p. 34.
28. Refer to the Hospital Fee Regulations, 1983: Legislative Instrument 1277.
29. *Business Weekly*, (Accra), February 23rd to 1st March 1987.
30. *People's Daily Graphic* (Accra) 14th May, 1987 See also the issue of June 20th 1986.
31. Badoe, E.A.: 'We can stop the decline of our health service', in *Daily Graphic*. February 23rd 1980 pp.8-9.
32. Nyame, K.: 'Medical services: To pay or not to pay' in *Daily Graphic* February 28 1980 p.5.
33. Kunnes, R.: *Your Money or Your Life: Prescription for the Market Place*. (N.Y. Dodd, Mead and Co., 1972) See also Jajoo, U.N.: Gupta, O.P. and Jain A.P. 'Health System — Rural Health Services, Towards a new strategy' *World Health*

Forum, Geneva. Vol.6 No.2 150-153, 1985 and de Ferranti, D.: 'Paying for health services in developing countries: A call for realism,' Ibid p.95-105.

34. Addo, E.A.: '*The Pattern of Management in Government Hospitals: A study of the medical administrator pattern of management in selected government hospitals.* 'Unpublished Legon: School of Administration, University of Ghana. 1973.
35. *The Konotey-Ahulu Committee Report*, p.60.
36. *The Easmon Committee Report*, p.2...
37. Cited in Patterson, D.K., p.180.
38. Ewusi, K.: *Planning for the Neglected Rural Poor in Ghana*. (Accra:New Time Corporation, 1978).
39. Ofosu-Amaah, S.: 'Reflections on the Health Budget' *Ghana Medical Journal*, Vol 14 No. 3 September, 1975.
40. Adjei, S.; Osei, W.; Sampson, W.; Adamafio, A. 'P.H.C. Review'. (An unpublished report).Accra, WHO/UNICEF PROJECT, 1984.
41. *People's Daily Graphic* 24th October, 1984 p. 8.
42. Twumasi, P.A. '*Traditional Birth Attendant Review Programme in Ghana*'. Unpublished study commissioned by Ministry of Health, (Accra, 1987).
43. '*A Programme Manual for Traditional Birth Attendants*'. Danfa Project, Accra. 1977.
44. *People's Daily Graphic*, 24th October, 1984, p.8.
45. Adjei, S. et Al., 1984, op.cit.
46. Illich, Ivan. Medical Nemesis: *The Expropriation of Health*. (London: Calder & Boyars. 1975).

INDEX

A

Abbot case 41
Abeka, S. 79
Accelerated Plan for Education 79
Accra 64, 83
  City Council 88
  District Council of Labour 64
  markets in 82
  -Tema area, workers in 45, 48, 52
accumulation
  national 37-8
  private 20
Acheampong, I.K. 17, 26-7, 105, 147-50, 205, 210-11, 213-4, 215-6
  see also National Redemption Council
Adamafio, T. 78
Addo, H. 149
Addo, J.S. 217-8
Adjei, S. 260, 261, 264-5
AFRC see Armed Forces Revolutionary Council
African Youth Command 81-2
Agricultural Development Bank (ADB) 173, 174, 206-7, 208, 228, 229
Agricultural Policy, Medium Term 214-6
Agriculture, Ministry of
  and cocoa production 223-4, 227, 228, 232
  and rural development 229
agriculture/agricultural 75
  centralisation of 224, 225-6
  collectives 205-6, 229
  credits 174, 206-7, 229, 237
  crisis in 186, 187-90, 223, 226
  Development Corporation 224
  export 222-40
  labour 18-19
  loans 173, 174
  machinery 205-6, 215-6, 224
  marketing 208-9, 225, 226
  modernisation of 168
  multinational involvement 189, 210-12
  prices 208-10, 218-19
  problems and responses 222-27
  Special Scheme for Participation in 174, 210-11, 212, 215-6
  strikes 25
  support for 172, 173
  lack of 180
  surpluses 235, 240
  see also food
Agyeman-Rawlings, N.K. 87
Ahmad, N. 119
aid
  agricultural 224
  food 186, 187
  to rural areas 229
Akatapore, A. 57
Akuafo cheque system 237
Akuffo, Gen. 105, 107, 126, 128
  see also Supreme Military Council
Akwagyiram, Col 235
Algeria 147
Alhassa Committee 175-6
Aliens Compliance Order 231, 232

All Women's Association of
Ghana (AWAG) 84, 87-8
Allied Foods Limited 31-2, 34, 52, 55-60
Amarteifio, E. 78
Amin, Idi 147
Ankrah, J.A. 149, 156
Annan, D.F. 153
Archer Committee 235
armed forces 7, 67
Armed Forces Revolutionary Council (AFRC) 9, 29, 31, 48
and health care 252-3
and IMF 106-8
Asamoah, O, 156-7
Ashanti 18
goldfields 25-6
health provision 259-60
markets in 82
Asofaa 83
Assembly of Women, Ghana 80
Assene Household Enamelware Ltd 37, 67-70
Atim, C. 50, 51

B

Ba, Ousmane 142
Badoe, E.A. 256
Baidoo, G. 235
balance of payments 185
and IMF 97, 98
Banking Act (1970) 132
banks/banking 206-7, 208, 228, 229, 230
credit 125
development 130-1, 173, 174
intervention in 6
loans and advances 128-30
loss of confidence in 125-6
pre-independence 120-3
reforms 132-3
rural 207-8
Bawumia, M. 236
Bentsi-Enchill, K. 170
Berger, P. 244
Bernanke, B. 129
birth attendants, traditional 260-1, 262-4, 264-5
Blay Commission 169
Block Farming System 215-6
Boafo-Arthur. Kwame 11, 137-62
Bogner, J. 195
Boham, Commander 235
Boigny, Houphouet 142
Bolgatanga 82
Botchwey, K. 153
Brazil 233
bride price 76
Britain 156
Brong Ahafo
health provision 258-60
Rural Integrated Development Project 258-60
Busia, K. A. 144-5
see also Progress Party
Business and Professional Women's Association 81

C

Cabral, A. 1, 2
Cadbury-Schweppes International 55, 58
Canada 156
capital
and labour relations 15-39
scarcity of 15
capitalism
growth of private 21
state 19-20
Cargo Handling Company 50, 64
Central Region, health provision 259-60
Chambas, M. 205
chiefs and land 167-8, 171, 175-6, 177
China 152, 156, 157
health care 265

'chit system' 167
Civil Servants Association 48
strike 27-8
Civil Service Act (1960) 22
clinic, village 263-5
see also health care; rural
co-operative farms 229
cocoa industry 74
'chit system' 167
export prices 230
internal marketing 232, 234
intervention in 5
labour shortage 231
and land 167
production 152, 189, 191, 225, 226, 237
Rehabilitation Project 232
revenue 250-1
workers in 22-3
womens protest 77
Cocoa Marketing Board 5, 22-3, 214-5, 223, 226, 231, 234, 235
coffee plantation 174
and PNP regime 236
Produce Buying Agency 227
Cocoa Purchasing Company (CPC) 206-7, 225
coffee plantations 174
colonial/colonialism 76
health service 244-8
inheritance 1, 5, 16
overthrow of 43
Commercial Bank, Ghana (GCB) 173
Commey, L. 88
Committees for the Defence of the Revolution 21, 34-6, 67, 85
communal lands see stool lands
community health workers 260-2
see also health care; rural
conflict and land 179
Constitution, Independence 4
Constitutional Commission 16, 172
and land 176
construction industry 18
Convention People's Party (CPP) 15, 17, 19, 41, 43
and agriculture 223-27
policy 199-200
and control of labour 21-4, 25
development strategies 4, 5, 96-7
and IMF 97-100
and land 166-71, 174-5, 178
overthrow of 6
and state enterprises 20
Côte d'Ivoire 142, 143, 210-11, 232, 233
cotton production 54
Crabbe, Azu 172
credit
bank 125
agricultural 174, 206-7, 229, 237
Credit Commodity Scheme 206-7, 208
crisis
economic 44, 184-5, 253
health care 253, 257
social 9
see also under agriculture/agricultural
Crisp, J. 45
crops 206-7
export 212-13, 216-17
performance of major 217-18
see also agriculture/agricultural; food
Cuba 87, 152, 156
health care 265
Cudjoe, H. 77, 78
customary land law see land law

D

Dadson, J.A. 194, 195
dam projects 188
Danfa Comprehensive Rural Health and

Family Planning Project 258-60, 262-3
debt, Third World 140
defence budget 235
defence committees see National Defence
Workers Defence
demonstrations 64
see also Pioneer Food Cannery
devaluation 237
development
banks 130-1, 173, 174
plans 223
and agriculture 239
Five Year 193
Seven Year 6, 22-3, 80
problems 2-3
solutions 3-12
strategies 3-4 5, 96-7
indigenisation 4, 8-9, 17, 27
statist 4, 7
ultra-liberal 4, 7
Development Corporations, Regional 204
discrimination against women 80, 81
diseases 244, 245, 264-5
Doku, S. 77, 78, 79
drought 186, 188, 212-13, 218-19, 253
Dunkwa miners 37
Duval 140
Dzatsui, A. 78

E

Easmon Committee 251, 257
East, M. 154
Eastern Region, health care 258-60
economic/economy
crisis 6, 9, 12, 22, 27, 44, 253
foreign control of 6, 8, 16-17, 169
and labour relations 31
post-colonial scene 117-18
and state intervention 38-9
Economic Recovery Programmes (ERP) 17, 47, 84, 214-5
banking reforms 132-3
education 190, 248
Education Act (1961) 79
Egypt 142
electricity industry 18
strike 28
Employers Association, Ghana (GEA) 55
employment 44-5
Ennin, A. 84
enterprises
Development Decree 28
industrial 20
state 20
Europe see Western Europe
Ewusi, K. 194, 257
exports
agriculture 222-40
earnings 4

F

Factories, Shops and Offices Act (1970) 68
family planning 258-60, 262-3
famine 186, 191
Fanon, F. 1
Farm Service Centres 216-17
Farmers Co-operative Council, (UGFCC) 22, 23, 199, 201, 224, 225, 226
farms/farming
capitalist 172-80
co-operative 229
large scale 168
and ruling classes 166-72
see also agriculture/agricultural
Federation of Ghanaian Women (FEGAWO) 73
Financial Institutions, Association of 49
financial sector 134
indicators 121, 135

intermediation and economic development 116-35
banking pre-independence 120-3
loss of confidence in banks 125-6
role of intermediaries 118-20
intervention in 6
food
agriculture
public expenditure on 202
and the state 184-219
Distribution Corporation (FDC) 201, 208-9, 210
imports 172, 187, 195
market prices of 194
Marketing Board 225
policies 197-203
colonial background 197-99
under First Republic 199-200
under Second Republic 200-3
production 186, 189-219
and development 190-2
schemes 203-6
security 192
shortages 156, 186-7, 191, 192-7, 253
foreign policy 137-59
determinants of 138-41
economic 149-51
of NLC 141-3
non alignment 154-8
NRC 147-9
PNDC 151-4
and Progress Party 143-7
towards South Africa 144-7, 150
Freeman 140

G
Ga Mantse 78
German Democratic Republic 157
Ghana Groceries Ltd. 225
Ghana National Trading Company 80, 237
gold miner strikes 26
Gonja Development Company 224
Graham, Yao 11, 18, 32, 43-72
Gramsci 17
Greater Accra Region 18
health provision 257, 258, 258-60
Green Revolution 212-13
Group Loans Scheme 206-7
Guggisberg, G. 246-7
Guinea 142
Gyimah-Boadi, E. 222-40

H
Hackman, U.K. 231
Hansen, Emmanuel 11, 110, 184-220
Harley, J.W.K. 156
Harvard Advisory Group 201
health care 190, 242-65
colonial 244-8
crisis 253, 257
distribution of provision 257-8, 258-60
education 243-4, 261, 264-5
expansion of 248-9
expenditure on 248, 250, 251, 253-4, 255
fees for 246-7, 249, 251, 253-5, 256
financing 244, 247, 255-6
post colonial 248-57
new orientation 259-64
personnel 243, 249, 251, 258
post colonial 257-9
preventative 243-4, 247, 257
primary 243, 259-60
private 249, 251
training facilities 243
Hopkins, A.G. 121
hospitals 243, 245, 246, 247
fees 253-5, 256
housing 248
human rights, UN Declaration 191

I
Illich, I. 264

immunization 261-2
imperialism 17
import-substitution industrial programme 18
imports 5, 230
  duties 96
  food 172, 187, 195
  licences 56, 58, 96
independence 43
  Constitution 4
India 212-13
Indians in Ghana 144
indigenisation development strategy 4, 8-9, 17, 27
industrial
  accidents 68
  and Commercial Workers Union 49, 56, 57, 60, 69
  Development Corporation (IDC) 19
  industrial enterprises
  growth of 20
  relations 43-4
  Acts 22, 27, 45-6, 70, 71
industrialisation-by-invitation 3, 4
Industries, Association of (AGI) 55
infant mortality rate 244
inflation 7, 27, 28, 44, 194, 236, 253
Interim Management Committees 49, 52
Interim National Co-ordinating Committee of PDCs 51
International Federation of Women Lawyers (FIDA) 81
International Monetary Fund 24, 26, 36, 37, 39, 47, 58, 60
  and AFRC 106-8
  co-operation with 94-114
  and CPP 97-100
  and food policies 217-18
  liberalization policy 127
  and PNDC 110-13, 114
  and PNP 109-10
  recommendations 97-9
  Structural Adjustment Programmes 110, 112
investment
  and agriculture 214-5, 228, 229
  Centre 20
  foreign 19, 23
  Policy Decree 28
  private 21
  and savings 127-8
Issifu, A.M. 49

J
Jonah, Kwesi 11, 94-115, 158, 211-12
Jones, T. 245
Juapong Textiles Limited 32
June Four Movement 81, 83

K
Kapwepwe, S. 142
Karikara, K.A. 146
Katsviku, I. 109
Kenya 142, 210-11
Kissinger, H. 138
Konotey-Ahulu Committee 252, 256
Korle-Bu hospital 246, 247, 257, 258
Kraus, J. 44, 45
Kumasi 32, 37
Kumfu, G. 69
Kunnes, R. 256
kwashiokor 264

L
labour 44-5
  agricultural 18-19, 189, 205, 212-13, 217-18, 228
  and capital 15-39
  character of 18-19
  cocoa 231
  Department 51, 52
  District Councils of 32, 51

laws 45
manufacturing industry 18
organisations 74
relations 21-4, 25, 29, 67-70
confrontation 24-7, 28-39
rights 75
strength of 27-30
women 75-6
see also working class
Labour and Social Welfare, Ministry of 52, 55, 56, 57-60, 66
and Assene 68
Labour Unions, Association of (ALU) 32
land 165-82
chiefs and 167-8, 171, 175-6, 177
law 165
radicals and 166-71
rents 168, 169
tenure systems 165-6, 167-72, 175
and conflict 179-80
Land Registry Act (1962) 178, 179
Lawyers, Association of Democratic (GADL) 69
Lebanese in Ghana 144
Lewis, A.W. 4, 5, 19
Libby, R.L. 150
Liberia 142
Libya 147
licensed buying agencies 224
life expectancy 243
Liman, J.J. 43
Limann, H. 43, 94, 106, 109, 213-4, 252-3
see also People's National Party
loans
agricultural 173, 174
bank 128-30
see also agriculture/agricultural credit
Local Defence Committees 48

M

Macnamara, R. 184
Madina 83
maize 211-12, 216-7, 218
Manganese Corporation, National 28
Mankoadze Group 66
Manu, T. 89
manufacturing labour force 18
Maritime and Dockworkers Union 63-4
market women 82-3, 88
marriage laws 93
Martei, M. 79
Mate-Kole, N.A. 172
Meat Marketing Board 208-9, 235
medical teams 260-1
see also health care; rural
medicine, traditional 245, 248, 250, 259, 260
see also health care
Mills Odoi Report 23
mining industry 18, 177-8
Ministry of Health 247, 253
and fees 255
and PHC 260
see also health care
missionaries and health care 246
Mobisquads 217-18
mortality rates 244, 257, 259
Mozambique 191

N

National Council of Women and Development (NCWD) 81
National Defence Committee (NDC)
and Allied Foods 55, 56
and GTP 53
and Pioneer Food Cannery 65-7
National Liberation Council (NLC) 7, 17, 20, 26, 36

agricultural policy 200-3, 210-11, 227-9, 238
foreign policy 141-3
and health care 251-2
and IMF 100-1
and labour relations 21, 25
National Liberation Movement 225
National Mobilisation Committee 217-18
National Reconstruction Corps 205
National Redemption Council (NRC) 7, 17, 81, 203
and African policy 147-9
and agriculture 232-36, 238
Operation Feed Yourself 203, 211-12
and health care 252
and IMF 102-5
nationalist movement 2, 4
neo-colonialist labour relations 67-70
New Democratic Movement 64, 81, 83
Nicaragua, health care 265
Nigeria 142
expulsion from 217-8
Nikoi, A. 109
Ninsin, Kwame A. 1-42, 165-83
Nkrumah, Ama 109
Nkrumah, Kwame 1, 41, 99-101
on agriculture 199, 206-7, 213-14, 226
on colonialism 244
contribution to Africa 142
foreign policy 137-8, 140, 142
towards South Africa 144-5
on freedom 147
government see Convention Peoples Party
on health 248, 250-1, 253
and IMF 105
non alignment 155-6
Revolutionary Guards 81
on state capital 203
on women 77, 79
NLC see National Liberation Council
Nnoboa system 205-6
non alignment 154-8, 155-6
North Korea 152, 157
Northern Region, health provision 259
NRC see National Redemption Council
Nwaogugu, A.C. 141
Nyakotey, E.L. 109
Nyame, K. 256
Nyongo, P.A. 34, 185

O

Obuasi gold mines 26
Ocran, R. 63, 66
OECD resources, access to 47, 60
Ofusu-Amaah, S. 258
Oil Palm Development Corporation 233
oil palm projects 174, 177
oil refinery (GHAIP) 66
Ollenu 170
Operation Feed Yourself 8, 173, 203, 205-6, 211-12
Organization of African Unity 142
Owusu, V. 144-5

P

Pasteur, L. 244
Patterson, D.K. 246
Peil, M. 19
People's Courts 33
People's Defence Committees (PDCs) 50-1, 265
People's Movement for Freedom and Justice (PMFJ) 29
People's National Party (PNP) 9, 10, 19
and agriculture 236, 238
and IMF 109-10
and labour relations 21

overthrow of 43, 48
petty-bourgeoisie 2, 6, 7, 20
and land 166, 170, 171-2
Pioneer Food Cannery 32, 34, 62-7
solidarity fund 64
PNDC see Provisional National Defence
PNP see Peoples National Party
police action 67
policy
food 197-203
labour 25
monetary 7
social 36
political
corruption 169
interests and surpluses 235, 240
organisations 30
women 73-90
power 76
population 184
growth and health care 253
National Policy 252
populism 39
poverty 3, 12, 243
PP see Progress Party
prices, agricultural 208-10, 218-19
Primary Health Care programme 259-63
see also health care; rural
Progress Party (PP) 7, 17, 25, 26
agricultural policy 200-3, 227, 229-32
foreign policy 143-7
towards South Africa 144-7
and health care 252
and IMF 101-2
Provisional National Defence Council (PNDC) 19, 43, 47, 49, 62
and agriculture 213-19, 222, 236-38
and Allied foods 58-9
banking policy 132-3
economic policy 61
and ERP programmes 237
and timber and mining 177-8
and health care 253-5
financing 254
primary 260-1
and IMF 110-13, 114
and labour 21, 30, 32, 33, 35, 37
and land 178-80
and WDCs 50-1, 65, 66-7
and women 89
women's issues 73
and working class struggle 44, 52
Psychic and Traditional Healers Association 250
public expenditure 97
on agriculture 202
Public Utility Workers' Union 48

Q
Quaison-Sackey, A. 142
Quaye, L. 77

R
Raw materials 166, 173
agricultural 177, 180
Rawlings, J.J. 43, 48, 49, 50, 57, 94, 151, 153, 196, 213-14
resources for health care 257-8
Revolutionary Guards 81
rice 211-13, 216-17, 218
capitalist farming 172, 173
Rosenau, J.N. 138
rubber estates 28, 228
ruling classes 16, 17, 30
rural areas
development 229, 230, 234, 235, 238-39
health care 249-50, 252, 259-60
distribution of provision 257, 258

and fees 255, 256

S

Sai 257
Sanitary Branch of Medical Dept 247
savings and investment 127-8
Sawyerr, A. 45
Seddoh, E.T.K. 142
Sekondi-Takoradi region 64
  workers in 18, 45, 48
Self-Sufficiency, Festival of Food 8
Senah, Kodjo 12, 242-67
Simpson, W.J. 245
slogans, government 8
SMC see Supreme Military Council
Smith, Ian 143, 156
smuggling 232, 233
social
  conditions 1-2, 3, 74-5
  crises 9
  policies 36
  reform 80
  services 36, 248-9, 250, 255
  values 16
  welfare 1, 2, 248-9
  see also health care
Social Democratic Front 46
Somalia 142
South Africa 150
  foreign policy towards 144-7, 150
  and PP foreign policy 144-7
South Korea 157
Soviet Union 87, 152, 156
Soviet Women's Committee 84
Sowa, Nii Kwaku 116-36
Standard Bank of West Africa 230
standards of living 7, 74
state
  capitalism 19-20
  weakness of 27-30
state farms 175, 201, 226, 228, 230
  Corporation 199, 224
State Fishing Corporation 208-9, 235
statist development strategy 4, 7
stock market 131-2
stool lands 165-6, 167-8, 175-6
  government control of 168, 170, 178
  moderates and 171-2
strike action 23-4, 26, 28-30, 46
  agriculture 25
  general 43, 44
Structural Adjustment Programmes 34, 36, 37, 95, 110, 112
Sudan 191
sugar estates 228
Sullivan, M.P. 138
Supreme Military Council (SMC) 7-9, 17,19
  and agriculture 173, 177, 210-11, 232-36, 238
  Operation Feed Yourself 203
  and health care 252
  and IMF 105-6, 107
  and labour relations 21, 29
  and land 175, 176, 178
  policies of 31
surpluses, agricultural 235, 246
Syrians in Ghana 144

T

Takoradi, markets in 82
Tamale, markets in 82
Tano Irrigation Project 173
Tanzania 142
  health care 265
Tarkwa 64
  gold mines 26
Teachers, National Association of 48
Tema 32
Ten-Year Development Plan 248

Tetteh, Col 235
Textile Printing Company, Ghana (GTP) 32, 52-5
31st December Women's Organisation 84, 85-7, 88-9, 90
Thomas, Clive 24, 39
timber 169, 177
  Marketing Board 169, 225
title to land see land, tenure
Togo 142, 232
trade, foreign 97
  and state control 96
trade unions 43, 44, 46, 47-9, 56, 57, 60, 63-4
  Congress 22, 26, 32, 35-6, 37, 48, 49, 81, 82
  Ordinance 45
  and WDCs 50-1
  see also Workers Defence Committees
Tsikata, Edzodzinam 12, 73-93

U
Uganda 147
ultra-liberal development strategy 4, 7
unemployment 226
  and state farms 175
Unions, Association of Local 49, 70
United Africa company (UAC) 54
United Kingdom see Britain
United Nations
  Declaration of Human Rights 191
  Development Decades 116
United States 156
Upper East and West Regions, health care 257, 259
Upper Region Agricultural Development Programme 173, 174, 204-5

V
'Verandah Boys' 4
Volta Aluminium Company 52, 108
Volta region
  health provision 259
  Regional Agricultural Development (VORADEP) 205
  River Project 97
  River Authority 179

W
wages 44, 196
  control 25, 26, 35
  decline in real 253
welfare see social
West Germany 156, 157
Western Europe 96
  banking interests 167
  credit from 99
Western Region 18
  health provision 259
Woddis, J. 43-4
women
  Association of Ghana, All (AWAG) 84, 87-8
  apolitical phase (1966-81) 80-1
  in post-colonial period 74-7
  Federation of Ghanaian Women (FEGAWO) 83-5, 87
  Ghana Federation of 78, 81
  League 77-8
  market 82-3, 88
  National Council of Ghana Women (NCGW) 79, 88, 89, 90, 92
  organisations (CPP) period 77-80
  political organisations 73-90
  professional groups 81
  resurgence of political organisation (1982-7) 81-8
  status of 76-7
Work and Happiness, Programme for 6, 80
Workers Brigade 199, 201, 224, 226
Workers Defence Committees

(WDCs) 31, 49-51, 64, 82
activists 61
of Allied Foods 56, 57
of GTP 53
Workers Solidarity Council 48, 49
working class
composition of 45
rights of 47
struggles 43-4, 46-52, 67-71
by women 77
demobilising 60-7
first phase 51-60
working conditions see Pioneer Food;
working class
World Bank 24, 26, 36, 37, 39, 58, 61, 95
and agriculture 217-18, 219
ERP of 152
Structural Adjustment Programmes 95
World Health Organisation 259, 260

Y

Yakasi, A.T. 144
Yeeye 77
Young, C. 154
Young Farmers League 199, 201, 224, 226

Z

Zaire 147
Zambia 142, 147
Zimbabwe 156
ZONTA Club 81

www.ingramcontent.com/pod-product-compliance
Lightning Source LLC
LaVergne TN
LVHW101443200926
848483LV00001B/32